THE
BOOTLEGGER'S
LEGACY

The Bootlegger's Legacy
Ted Clifton
ISBN 978-1-927967-53-9

Published by PurpleSage Books, LLC
www.TedClifton.com

Produced by IndieBookLauncher.com
www.IndieBookLauncher.com
Editing: Nassau Hedron
Cover Design: Saul Bottcher
Interior Design and Typesetting: Saul Bottcher

The body text of this book is set in Adobe Caslon. Chapter headings are set in Holden by Alterdeco Inc.

Also Available
Ebook edition, ISBN 978-1-927967-55-3

PROLOGUE

Oklahoma City, Oklahoma, 1952

Deep Deuce was swinging tonight. The Billy Parker Band was hitting every note. The sound was magnetic, attracting dancers young and old. Blacks and whites alike were enjoying great rhythms from one of the best big bands of the time.

John Giovanni didn't come for the music, though—he had never been accused of being cultured. He was in town to meet one of his customers. He hated all of his goddamn customers, but what the hell—if he killed them all he wouldn't have any business. Giovanni was originally from Brooklyn, but he had moved to Dallas at the urging of his uncle. Uncle Tony had made it clear that Giovanni should move, or Tony would cut his throat. The threat was accompanied by an easy-to-understand gesture. Giovanni had slept with Uncle Tony's ugly daughter, and Uncle Tony was pissed. She was only fourteen.

Giovanni realized his options were limited, so he moved. He started selling illegal liquor to the shitkickers who lived in the backward world of Texas. God did he ever hate Texas.

Tonight, Giovanni was in Oklahoma City, another useless shithole. The only people who could tell the difference between Texas and Oklahoma were the assholes who lived there, and to them the distinctions were enormous.

To Giovanni the only good thing about this ugly part of the country was they still had prohibition—at least Oklahoma did, and parts of Texas. That's why Giovanni was here: to feed the beast all the illegal hooch it wanted.

Giovanni had dreamed about being alive in the twenties and thirties, raising hell like Capone. Man, what a wonderful time to have been alive. So, when Uncle Tony said to get lost fast before he sliced Giovanni up really bad, Giovanni did a little research and discovered gangster nirvana in the southwest.

Using all of his well-honed skills, which mostly had to do with killing anyone who got in his way, he became the major wholesaler of liquor in the region in just a few years. If Uncle Tony hadn't hated his guts, he would have been proud.

Why he was meeting this creep in the black section of town, he had no idea. Giovanni wasn't particularly prejudiced—he just mostly hated everybody who wasn't Italian, so color didn't really matter. As a matter of fact, being up to 1950 standards of racial harmony, his favorite whore was black. Her name was Lacy, and Giovanni liked screwing her almost as much as he liked killing fuckin' Texans. She was with him tonight, along with three bodyguards and his dumber-than-dirt cousin, Marco.

"Marco what the hell kinda music are they playing?"

"That's jazz Johnny. Really cool jazz."

"What the fuck do you know about jazz? What the fuck do you know about anything?"

"Hey, why do you talk to me like that? I'm your goddamned cousin—you shouldn't talk to me like that."

"How about I just blow your fucking brains out, right here in this stupid jazz hip-hop joint, how would that be, shithead?"

Marco was never sure how far Johnny might go. He had seen him do some pretty horrible things.

"Okay, okay, sorry Johnny. It's just sometimes you make me feel like I'm stupid or something."

"Well, yeah. Maybe I'll be nicer. How's that? Maybe you should take Lacy out to the car and get a little—how would that be Marco?"

This caused Lacy to give Johnny a *never-turn-your-back-on-me-asshole* look. One way or another Johnny wasn't likely to make old age.

"Why are we here Johnny?"

"I'm expanding. Dumb shitkicker who runs the largest Oklahoma bootleg operation is going to retire. We've been selling him some of his booze for a while, but now he's decided to buy from those Mexican fuckheads out of Juarez. Can't have that, so he's going bye-bye."

"You going to kill him?" Marco seemed nervous. You never knew with Johnny. He might do it right here, right now.

"Don't worry baby Marco, it won't be tonight. But once everything gets transferred over to me, he'll be dead. I'll be the booze king of fuckin' Oklahoma."

PART ONE:
1987

CHAPTER 1

Oklahoma City, Oklahoma—February 1987

Depression seemed like an old friend. There was comfort in being able to describe, with medical precision, the reason you weren't successful, weren't particularly happy, were overweight—you get the picture.

Joe Meadows was a CPA who had experienced only minor success as an accountant and hated every aspect of his tedious life. His wife Liz was mostly pleasant, although she was preoccupied with her own activities. These centered around their two teen children, who seemed totally absorbed in their own realities, and her church, The Church of Christ. Joe often thought that it was possible that his family wasn't fully aware of his existence in the sense that he wasn't a distinct individual to them. He was the family provider, but there was little doubt that they didn't give a shit about Joe the person.

Joe's appearance was mostly unremarkable. Some people said he was handsome, with his longish, dark hair. He was just under six feet—never said five eleven. He used to have sparkling eyes that seemed full of mischief, but the years of tedium and boredom—and a little too much drinking—had toned the gleam down some. His best quality still remained: an engaging smile.

It was February 1987. Joe lived in Oklahoma City with a bunch of cowboy rednecks who enjoyed beer, big-

9

breasted women, guns, and pickups—not necessarily in that order. Everything about Joe's life felt foreign to him, like he was visiting from another planet. Where he was supposed to be in this world, he didn't know, but it sure wasn't where he was right now.

By the standards of the American dream, Joe was doing just fine. He had a nice-looking wife and two beautiful kids, he was a professional with his own business, and he had a house, two cars, and probably a dog somewhere—what the hell was the matter with him? He wasn't sure. It just seemed like there should be something more to life. What that something was, he didn't know. Nor was he making any effort to find out. He showed up for his life each day and clocked in, and he anticipated that nothing would change.

Monday morning, and Joe was headed to a client's office to discuss the company's financial condition. The client was Mike Allen, owner of Allen's Hardware. Mike's business had lost a bundle the previous year and he wanted Joe to tell him why. Joe knew why: Mike was an idiot—or at least acted like an idiot.

Mike was either drunk, or getting ready to get drunk, and almost certainly chasing a woman who wasn't his wife, leaving very little time to focus on the hardware business. And he had been Joe's best friend since grade school.

They became best friends in Mrs. Smith's second grade class at East Side Elementary. They had formed a bond on the playground to improve their defenses against the girls—especially one girl. A second-grade boy's worst nightmare is the inevitable bully girl on the playground.

It's one thing to be beat up by some boy—but by a girl? That's just terrible. Jane Waters was their nemesis. She was meaner and tougher than most of the boys in the school. Rumor had it that she had been held back in second grade—twice.

Jane had been tormenting the boys for months. Recess had become hell. Much of it consisted of threats, but the boys had seen her in action. She had pummeled Ray M so bad he had to go to the nurse's office. He was out of school for three days. Jane was gone for a few days, too—to everyone's relief.

The only way to improve their position was to form an alliance. Once the boys made their bond, cementing the deal with a ritual handshake and spit, they stood up to her in a frightening display of little boy courage. She left them alone from that day on, and Mike and Joe had been best friends ever since.

Joe parked in front of the hardware store and sat in the car for a while, not wanting to tell Mike how bad things really were. The store had belonged to Mike's father for more than twenty years and was something of a town institution. The original owner, before Mike's dad bought it, opened in the current location sometime in the 1930s. But times change, and a new Walmart down the street had cut the store's business in half overnight. Mike's dad had died about ten years ago, so at least he hadn't had to see what had happened to the "best little hardware store in OKC." As the store declined, Mike's drinking increased. There was probably little Mike could do to help his business, but what he was doing was the opposite of helping.

Joe entered the store and was once again struck by the feeling it had to be hundreds of years old. Everything about the place seemed to be from another era. Even the old cash register was more antique than functional. The store was crammed full of a variety of merchandise, some of which hadn't been moved in years. On the other hand, if you needed a part for a thirty-year-old washing machine they just might have it. There was comfort in being inside the store—like it was a wonderful part of your past you had forgotten.

"Joe, come on back and give me the good news." Mike was standing in the doorway of his small office and didn't look so good. His eyes were bloodshot, and he hadn't shaved. He had a strange look about him these days, like he wasn't quite real. There were times it seemed like Mike was an actor in a movie, playing himself. Never a real sharp dresser, now he looked like he should be sitting on the sidewalk outside the store with a bottle in a paper bag rather than occupying the owner's office.

Mike had inherited a strong physique. Standing at least six feet two, he was often mistaken for an ex-football player, though he had never been good at sports. Wearing his hair cut short gave a no-nonsense quality to his de-meanor. Developing a small stomach was about the only change to Mike's physique since high school.

Joe went into the office and took a chair at Mike's desk. He began, "The loss last year was a lot more than you can stand. You have no cash, you're past due with your suppli-ers, you owe back payroll taxes to the IRS, and the bank note is four months past due. Mike, you're broke. I'd be surprised if the bank doesn't call your loan and put you out of business." So much for small talk.

Mike just stared off into space. After a short while he turned to Joe, "What can I do?"

"You're going to need to get some cash—I would say somewhere around $25,000—in order to keep things from imploding. You don't have much time. The most important thing is to stop the losses—you can't keep digging a hole and filling it with borrowed money."

Mike looked dejected. He was quiet. It was evident that this was hard for him to take. His expression reflected something worse than just disappointment.

"My gut tells me you need to shut the business down. Use the $25,000 to buy some time to get a plan in place. I don't think you can sell the store. So, more than likely, your only option will be bankruptcy and liquidation." Joe was Mr. Doomsayer today.

Mike erupted. "What kind of fuckin' friend are you? Is that the best you can do?"

"Look, if it was up to me I'd wave a magic goddamned wand and make everything perfect—but I don't have a wand and, if I did, I'd use it on my own fucked up life." Joe and Mike shared some stress issues.

"Mike, you can just walk away and lose everything, or you can try to get some cash and have an orderly closing— maybe save your house and some of your other assets. But I think the store is gone. The climate for your type of business has just changed too much. There are plans for a Home Depot only ten minutes from here—what would that do to your business? You need to try to protect as much of what you have as you can and then get on with something else."

"Something else? Listen to you—you know there's nothing else for me. I've worked in this stupid business since I busted out of college. I don't know anything else. Maybe I could get a job at Walmart and slowly starve to death. Samantha—I'm sure she'll understand. We'll just have to downsize and learn to like living in a mobile home. None of her snotty friends will even notice we're suddenly white trash."

Samantha Allen, Mike's wife, had been his high school sweetheart. She was the prom queen, football queen, homecoming queen—pretty much queen of everything. And she was gorgeous. Mike had always felt lucky that she was his wife, but he was also intimidated by her beauty. He had developed serious insecurities about himself because he hadn't lived up to her standards.

The room was quiet. Joe felt bad for his friend and at the same time thought he had done very little to prevent the mess he was in. Mike had always lived way beyond his means. If he had a good year and made $50,000, he would spend $70,000—mostly on things he could live without. Mike's wife seemed to think that they actually had money, and she lived just that way.

"Mike, I can loan you maybe $5,000 or so. I'm only going to do that if you can come up with more, so you can have a chance to work out a plan that will let you get out of this business without a complete collapse."

"I don't want you loaning me money. Why make you more miserable just to give me a few more hours before I go down the tubes? I need a way to make some big bucks, and fast—not just keep borrowing and struggling from one month to the next. I need a plan."

Joe agreed: Mike needed a plan. They made a plan to meet for a drink around four that afternoon at Triples, a local bar and restaurant down the street from the hardware store. That wasn't really a plan at all—it was more like an old bad habit that should be broken—but it was the best they had right now.

Driving back to his office, Joe began to think about how Mike could make some quick money. They were both forty-four—the perfect age for nothing. If you were going to be one of the successful people you read about, it would have already happened. Now there wasn't much to do except wait for some sort of miracle or death. Joe knew his fate. Working late, drinking too much, and wondering what might have been. The problem Joe had was that even if he was able to start over, he wasn't sure what he would do differently. He had no vision of what an ideal life would look like, although he was pretty sure lots of money would help. He just wasn't very interested in much of anything.

Joe knew that Mike thought he had hit his peak when he married Samantha. She was the most beautiful girl in their senior high school class—Mike had hit the jackpot. But it seemed to Joe that Mike had never really been happy after they were married. He had won the prize, now what did he do? After all, there was something very contradictory about the fact that he worked in his father's hardware store and was married to the most beautiful woman in the world. It felt unreal, and Mike seemed almost to be waiting for her to leave him—or maybe his behavior was a way to get her to leave. The pressure of his marriage seemed to be all in his head, but it was as real as could be to Mike.

Although they lived beyond their means, Mike and Sam still lived a modest lifestyle. They didn't have a mansion or drive fancy cars. They lived a few blocks from the hardware store, on Hudson just off Eighth. Their house was older, in a nice neighborhood. Mike had always planned on fixing it up more than he had. Someday he would get around to that—well, maybe. Their whole life had a demoralized quality to it that made itself felt in every one of their interactions. Everything was stretched very thin. They were waiting on something, but they didn't know what.

CHAPTER 2

Oklahoma City, Oklahoma

At 4:15, Joe walked into the darkened confines of Triples looking for Mike. He was over in a corner booth, obviously already headed toward drunk, sipping his usual scotch and water. Joe slid in and waved a finger at the bartender, who immediately begin fixing a gin and tonic—his usual.

"How long have you been here?" Joe wasn't sure he would stay if Mike was already beyond discussing anything.

"Just a little while. I have had only a couple of drinks—so don't get all high and mighty on me!" Mike made an ugly face as he said his piece. Under more normal circumstances, Joe would have left to avoid the conflict headed his way. He had seen Mike like this before. But today he felt he needed to help Mike the best he could.

The bartender brought his drink, and Joe sat back and sipped without comment. In a little while the tension seemed to let up some. Mike was still sulking, but he was doing it with a more pleasant expression on his face.

Joe had given thought to Mike's financial problems. Without some surprise he didn't think there was much hope. Mike was like a lot of people, including Joe—he had borrowed as much as he could in order to live the life he wanted to live, right now—to hell with the future. Credit cards had been a way to live beyond their means and enjoy the good life. Everyone did it—why not him?

Joe had counseled Mike several times about the debt and the declining revenues of his business—even when he felt like a hypocrite doing it. Mike would just shrug his shoulders and say, "Everything'll be better next month." It never was.

"Let's get to it, okay?" Joe prodded Mike. "Do you have any assets you can sell?"

"Everything is hocked to the max. Even if I could sell something, it'd just go to pay off debt—there wouldn't be any cash." While not a surprising answer, at least Mike seemed lucid and over the anger Joe had encountered when he first arrived.

"How about Samantha. Does she have any assets or family money she could get?"

"Well, even if she did, I wouldn't ask. I'm sure she's already planning her life after we're done. My guess is that she's hidden a tidy sum somewhere that I can't reach so once everything starts to collapse, she'll have a nest egg to use when she starts over without me. I know she got some money from her brother's estate after he died—she never told me how much, although I'd guess it was considerable."

"Well shit, what kind of deal is that? She's your wife. That's as much your money as hers, and you need it—now!" Joe was stunned that Sam would have her own funds and not be helping deal with the family's financial woes. She and Joe had never gotten along, so it was easy for Joe to think ill of the bitch.

"Maybe legally, but I'm not going to pursue it. I just don't want to talk about that—it's not going to happen."

Mike was beginning to lose interest in the conversation. You can only talk so much about your failures. Eventually it becomes pointless.

"There is something that could be—oh never mind, that's crazy." Mike seemed to be drifting again.

"Crazy? This whole conversation is crazy. Listen, Mike, I know we're different. I'm not much of a risk taker, but crazy is the mess you're in right now. You have big financial problems, and we're in an expensive bar sucking down costly drinks. Is that crazy? If you have any ideas, even crazy ones, now's the time to hear about them."

"Okay, okay stay calm. This is a strange area for me. You know my father kind of lost his mind before he died. My mother stayed with him until the last few months. When she couldn't take it anymore she asked me to help her with him. During his last years he and I had become a little closer, although he was always distant with me. Or maybe I was a little bit distant with him, I don't know. Anyway, she asked me to help."

"I looked around for a place he could be moved to. There just wasn't much that was very pleasant. Then there was an incident with him and my mother and I started to worry about her safety. So, I decided he had to be moved to a nursing home. Putting him in that nursing home was the hardest thing I'd ever done. It felt like I betrayed him. Because of that I didn't want to be around him, and when I was, he seemed to just talk nonsense."

Joe knew some of this about Mike's dad. He had heard from other people that Mike's whole family was just a little weird. Mike's dad, Patrick Allen, had been something of a legend in the 40s and 50s, when he had been the biggest bootlegger in Oklahoma. Joe had always thought the stories were exaggerated, because the man he had known was a grandfatherly, easy-to-be-around kind of guy. He was much older than Mike's mom, although he was always energetic, very outgoing and friendly.

"Come on Mike, what's the crazy part?"

Mike looked worried, then finally spit it out. "My dad kept telling me he had buried millions from his bootlegging days, but that he couldn't remember where."

"Millions—as in dollars?"

"I guess. Much of this I think was just him losing his mind toward the end. I mean, I knew the stories, that he'd been a big-time bootlegger in the past. I thought they just amounted to him arranging a few bottles of something for his neighbors. I asked my mother, and she said he never was into selling whisky. That was just a bunch of rumors made up by people who were jealous of my dad's success selling insurance and buying his own hardware business. Anyway, I never knew what was true."

Mike decided to order another drink, so to be polite Joe joined in. Millions buried in Mike's backyard—that would go a long way toward solving Mike's problems. And, of course, he would give some to his best friend since the second grade. Why not relax and see where this was headed?

The bartender brought their drinks over and asked them to clear the tab since he was going off shift. Joe flopped out his American Express card and gave it to the bartender, mentally noting that this was a business expense since Mike was a client. Of course, Mike hadn't paid him in about six months—maybe with his dad's millions, things would look better.

"I know you're thinking this is nuts, but the strange thing is that after he died, I received a package from a lawyer in Dallas with a letter from my dad and a key." Mike took a drink and eyed Joe to see if he was snickering or actually listening.

"Go on—tell me what was in the letter." Mike had his attention.

"Some of the letter made sense and some didn't. I have it out in the car in my briefcase—wait just a minute and I'll go get it."

While Mike went to his car, Joe decided to take a bathroom break and use the payphone to call Liz.

"What the hell are you doing out drinking with Mike? Didn't you just tell me he was broke and would probably be going out of business? No doubt you'll be picking up the tab. Sometimes I wonder about you Joe. It's like you're smart and stupid at the same time. I don't want to hear any made-up stories about why this is important—if you want to go waste your money drinking and carousing with your lowlife friends, you go right ahead. I'm sick and tired of it—unless you want to consider living alone with no family, maybe you ought to give ol' Mike a hearty goodbye and get your ass home. This is just about the last—"

Click. Calling home may have been a mistake. She hadn't even given him a chance to explain how important this was to Mike. But of course, she thought Mike was scum, so she didn't really care. Hanging up on her was going to create a serious problem. Her threat to divorce him had been going on since about the six-month anniversary of their marriage. Well, he would deal with her later. The first trick was to avoid her until morning, so he would stay out late, sneak in, and sleep on the sofa in his home office. He kind of liked it there anyway.

Mike returned and slid into the booth. He handed Joe the letter.

Dear Son,

I know we've had some rocky times, all my fault and I'm sorry. This letter is to let you know that I loved you and you have always meant the world to me. Maybe I didn't show it the way I should have. It was just easier for me to let your mother handle everything. I was too old to be your typical dad— more like your granddad—but you gave me great joy and made a lot of the things I had done in my life seem okay.

Since you're reading this, my time will have come to an end. Don't overly grieve. I had a good life and have no regrets.

With this letter you will receive a key. I cannot tell you what this key is for or I will risk other people discovering my secret. I know you may think that I've lost my mind and that this letter is nonsense, but trust me, this is important. I know you know I was a bootlegger before I retired and started running the store. Well, son, I was a very successful bootlegger. I stockpiled a shitload of cash. It is waiting for you. You'll think this is the madness of an old man, but let me assure you, it's true.

I couldn't just give you the money without creating problems. If you can discover how to find the cash, you'll have demonstrated that you're clever enough to figure out how to use the money without causing problems.

You may or may not want to pursue this. If you do and you're successful there will be a big reward. If you decide that this is too crazy and you're not interested in my farfetched stories, I understand. Just do what you think is best. I only want you to be happy and have a good life.

I think you are a lot smarter than I ever was, so I'm sure you can figure out what this is about.

Dad

P.S. Don't talk to your mother about this. She'll just tell you that I always had a screw loose—and she's right. And remember your path to financial independence goes through Deep Deuce at the St. Francis.

Mike gave Joe the key.

Joe sat quietly for a while. He wasn't sure what to make of any of this. If Mike's dad had millions to give his son, why make it so difficult? *Dear Son, here is the secret number to a Swiss bank account that has millions for you. Thanks, your Dad.* But this seemed almost crazy—just like Mike had said.

"How in the hell can you find out what this key is for? Didn't he tell you any more toward the end?"

"Well, that's what I mean. He did tell me more, but it never made any sense. After I got the letter, I was curious.

I don't know. It just went into the back of my brain as some nutty thing my dad did at the end. I wanted to forget the whole thing."

"Let's start over. He told you he had buried millions, right?"

"That's what he said, but Joe, he was out of his mind—it was just nonsense."

"Did you contact the attorney in Dallas?"

"Nope—didn't do anything except run the store into the ground and drink a lot."

"Did he give you any hints where it might be buried?"

"Joe, listen to you. You're starting to believe. It was all nonsense. My father lost his mind before he died. He was just making up stuff. Complete and absolute bullshit."

"Stop feeling sorry for yourself—I think this is worth exploring further. After all, you may not believe it, but my dad told me that your dad was once one of the wealthiest men in the city. I always thought he was just joking. Maybe he wasn't."

"Yeah, I heard some of those stories. They never made sense. He was old from my first memories. There was no way his being a bootlegger made sense to me. And we lived okay, but we were sure as hell not rich. Why would we live the way we did if he had millions? He worked his butt off every day in that hardware store, waiting on grumpy old farts who needed a bolt. Why in the hell would you do that if you had millions?"

"Well, yeah, that's a fair question. One that I don't have an answer for. I know it doesn't make much sense—but there's something so odd about all of this. So odd that I'm not sure someone would make it up. I think we need to see if we can determine what this key is for. What does this mean about Deep Deuce at the St. Francis? Does that make any sense to you?"

"Well, I'm not sure. Although I seem to remember that the black area just east of downtown was called Deep Deuce. Least I think it was, not real sure. I think my dad had even mentioned that area many, many years ago as a part of town that had lots of nightclubs with live music way back when. He said he had gone there a couple of times. But St. Francis doesn't mean anything to me."

Joe thought about what that might mean. Was Mike's dad trying to give his son millions of dollars after he died by sending him a strange letter and key? This didn't seem to fit the picture he had of Mike's dad. The guy sold nuts, screws, and shovels for goodness sake.

"Regarding the key, the guy who supplies our key-making kiosk would probably know how to figure that out—if there's any way to actually do that. Could be this is just an old key he left me for no reason at all except he'd lost his mind." Mike's mood was getting worse. If they were going to decide anything tonight, it would have to be pretty soon, before Mike slipped into a deep depression.

Joe responded, "Okay, you're right—this is probably just some kind of strange joke, and your father was lost in a different world toward the end. We just have to make the effort and see if this is nonsense or not. When can we contact your guy about the key?"

"I'll go call him right now and see if he can meet us in the morning."

Mike returned quickly after making his call. "He said no problem, he'll be there tomorrow morning at ten. Will that work for you?"

"Sure, I'll see you at your store. I think I'll hang out here for a while. Better if I can sneak in later without having a battle with Liz tonight. She's no doubt beyond pissed since I hung up on her earlier right in the middle of her 'Joe's a shithead' speech. See you tomorrow."

Joe sat in the booth alone and gave some thought to his life. He remembered his school days with Mike, when everything had seemed possible. They had always thought they were going to be something—something special. But it didn't happen that way. Joe had periods of success. He didn't want to be an accountant, but when he passed his test and got his CPA license, he felt successful. It was just that the work didn't suit him—he wanted to be creative, build things, not track other people's success by crunching numbers.

He and Mike had stayed close after school, and that was an important part of Joe's life. Mike considered him the smart one, and Joe liked that. Joe thought Mike was more daring than he was—often that wasn't a good thing for Mike, leading him to make risky decisions. After his father died and Mike took over the business, Joe thought that the change would be good for Mike, but now he wasn't so sure. Failing at running your dad's hardware store was a heavy burden, one that Mike wasn't handling well.

Joe wondered what things would be like for them in ten years. He guessed he'd still be doing taxes and hat-ing it, and Liz would still be yelling at him, or worse yet, ignoring him—basically the same as now. For Mike, he didn't know what was going to happen—it worried Joe.

CHAPTER 3

Oklahoma City, Oklahoma

Liz had had it with Joe. He was a drunk and he was a terrible husband and father. She had worked every day at making their marriage a success. She was exhausted from the effort. How many years can you be married to someone who seems to always be in a fog?

When they were first married, Liz had real hope. She thought Joe could be a success. He worked hard and, except for his drunken nights out with his useless buddy Mike, he was a good provider. Liz had used every alluring skill she had to get Joe to propose to her—but once he did, she immediately stored her charms away for some future use. Liz had never really enjoyed sex, and Joe's constant need repulsed her. After years of her coolness he began to leave her alone—of course by then they had two children.

While sex wasn't vital to her life, her children were. Somewhere in the recesses of her brain it was as if the children had nothing to do with Joe, as if they had been conceived and born only of her. With the kids her life took on a new meaning, and Joe started to blend into the background.

Like most people in Oklahoma, Liz was a Christian. Her beliefs, based on the Bible as the literal word of God, grew as her children grew. She took them to church at least twice a week, often more. They participated in extended Bible school in the summer and attended summer camps devoted to their faith. She knew it was vital that the sinful ways of their father be cleansed from her children.

Liz's first impulse to divorce Joe probably came within a year of their marriage. But the birth of the children and Joe's ability to provide financial comfort were barriers to her ever taking action. While she had never asked for a divorce, sometime in the early years of their marriage she effectively divorced herself from Joe. He was necessary for her to have a means to support herself and her children, so she stayed. She knew that without her constant nagging for him to apply himself he would more than likely fall into an alcoholic stupor and become an even more useless drunk. She had to stay to make sure that didn't happen.

There was a constant pressure on Liz to steer her children in the right direction and to keep Joe working and earning money. She never relaxed, knowing that without her unwavering dedication to making sure that everything was done in the way she prescribed, it would all fall apart. She also knew that no one appreciated the sacrifices she had made for her family. She was alone, but she wasn't about to be stopped.

Liz sometimes dreamed about what her life could have been if only she had married someone she could have loved. She hadn't had that luxury, though. Her family was poor. Her father had been a drunken bully who beat her mother, until one day he left and never returned. Her mother was broken-hearted when the bastard left. To this day Liz couldn't understand why her mother was so devastated. After her husband left, her mother became the family drunk—and ignored her kids. Liz had hated her family and spent part of each day planning how to escape.

As a teenager, Liz was attractive. She knew she was no beauty queen but with a little make-up and some borrowed clothes she could be very appealing. She wasn't particularly good at school and knew her best hope for getting away from her mother and their mind-numbing poverty was to marry. The goal every day in high school was to find a husband. Liz's best friend was Judy. Liz suspected that Judy had been having sex since the eighth grade, and she was the class expert on attracting a man. Judy told stories to Liz and her friends that had made Liz blush and hide her face. Liz listened to Judy and was soon walking and talking differently. They had spent hours working on how Liz could use her eyes to flirt. Liz thought much of this was silly, but before she knew it boys were noticing her. Her first reaction was disgust at the fact that these guys could be so easily manipulated. Judy declared gender victory.

After a period of practice, Liz focused all her new skills on a single target: Joe Meadows. She chose Joe based on a very non-scientific method involving his looks, the fact that he seemed to have some money, a car, and that he was in her homeroom. Joe was obviously smart and made reasonable grades in school. She knew he was on a pre-college path and had heard he was expected to graduate a semester early and enroll in the local college. This, she felt, made Joe a good prospect to succeed at whatever he decided to do and be able to provide for his family. Plus, in an it-really-doesn't-matter way, she kind of liked him.

Once Liz set her sights on Joe, he had little chance. He

wasn't very experienced, and she was able to control him easily throughout their senior year. Once Mike, his idiot best pal, got engaged, it was inevitable Joe would want to marry Liz. But Joe's parents stepped in and insisted on a delay until Joe finished college. This was not to Liz's liking, although she mostly lived with Joe his last two years in college.

After Joe graduated, they were married. Joe was offered a great job right out of school at the local box manufacturing plant. He was an assistant controller. Liz thought that sounded important. She had never really cared what Joe did, as long as he was making money—and leaving her alone. It had been easy to turn Joe's sex drive on—it turned out to be a little harder to turn it off.

Joe spent a lot of time at work. He also spent many evenings out drinking with his work buddies. Liz thought that was fine, as long as he gave her his paycheck every two weeks. Joe was quickly promoted into more responsibility and money. After a short while they had plenty of money. Liz was very happy.

Once Joe passed the CPA exam, he started talking about opening his own accounting practice. Liz wasn't supportive. She just wanted Joe to continue to make money and not risk anything. Joe didn't listen. But it worked out. Joe knew a lot of people, some of whom he met drinking and hanging out at bars. His business grew quickly, and he was a success.

While Joe was growing the business, Liz was having children. The world according to Liz couldn't have been better—of course, Joe wasn't a factor in that world, except to provide money.

Liz had sacrificed so much to make everything better for everyone. She knew they didn't appreciate what she had done, but it didn't matter. She had kept her family together all of these years, and one day her children would thank her for it.

Liz prayed every day for the strength to continue to make the world a better place for her children and herself. She knew that the day was coming when she would leave Joe. He just didn't have the same moral standards as Liz and her children. In some ways she regretted ever marrying Joe, but she had done what she had to do—there hadn't been a choice. She knew she would leave Joe, but it would have to wait until she had more financial security.

Joe's accounting practice was growing every day. One day soon she would get a divorce and get half of all of the assets, including the business. She dreamed about that prospect: half of the money and no Joe.

The other aspect of her life that was important to Liz was associating with important people. Of course, they were also rich—that's why they were important. This had begun at church. She had organized several charity events that had been attended by the high society of the community, and she quickly became enamored. Coming from dirt poor people, she had never dreamed of hobnobbing with the elite, but here she was sipping wine with the upper echelon of society. She was hooked. It was like a drug. She wanted to attend every event and couldn't get enough. Of course, Joe wouldn't go. "Who gives a shit about the high and mighty?" he would say rudely. It made her realize how much she had grown, while Joe had not.

Liz attended one society event after another—Joe never went. Liz spent money like it was free—Joe worked until he went to drink, never doubting that he was digging a hole with his credit card that he could never fill. It couldn't go on much longer—but it continued without changing. One of these days it would have to.

CHAPTER 4

Las Cruces, New Mexico—March 1987

Ray Pacheco had been the Dona Ana County sheriff for over nineteen years. A good life. He had always taken pride in his job and his department. Ray didn't just give lip service to his role serving and protecting his community—he lived it. These were his neighbors and his neighbors' kids, no matter how bad or rotten they sometimes were.

Law enforcement was Ray's life. He had lost his wife to cancer more than five years before, and his only son had moved to Boston to take a job with a top-notch law firm. Ray was proud of his son, but he also agonized over a deep resentment he felt toward him for moving so far away.

Ray was originally from Macon, Georgia. That was where he met and married his wife. His first years in law enforcement were in Macon. He also spent a short time with the Jacksonville, Florida, police force before he answered an ad in a law enforcement magazine for a chief deputy sheriff in Las Cruces, New Mexico. Ray and his wife debated the craziness of moving to New Mexico— the distance, the difference in cultures, all the various risks. They were excited about the opportunity for Ray to advance in his career, but also concerned about moving so far away to such an unknown place.

Even when the Dona Ana sheriff's office offered Ray the job, the mixed feelings remained. After heart-searching discussions, their decision was made. They took the plunge, and they fell in love with Las Cruces and Dona Ana County. Ray's wife became active in civic matters almost at once and began to feel connected. She made Las Cruces seem like home to Ray.

He did well in the department. He and the sheriff made a good team—the sheriff was very political, while Ray knew law enforcement—so the sheriff could spend time at meetings and political events, which he enjoyed, while Ray ran the department, where he excelled. Ray formed some great relationships with the deputies, and they learned to trust him. He always backed his men, and he became a resource for everyone in the department on the best way to handle any matter.

The job of sheriff opened up rather suddenly when the old sheriff was seriously injured in an auto accident. Unable to perform his duties, the sheriff resigned. The county commissioners scheduled a special election. Many people encouraged Ray to run, and he decided to give it a shot. His biggest hurdle was that he was totally non-political. He answered every question as truthfully as he could, and if he didn't know the answer he said so.

Ray's last name was Hispanic—Ray was not. He had never paid much attention to his Spanish heritage when he lived in Georgia. He had never much cared what tribe people belonged to—he treated everyone more or less the same. The old Sheriff had made a mistake when he hired Ray, sight unseen, based on his Hispanic last name, although it had worked out well for everyone.

There was a three-person race for the sheriff's job and

both the other candidates were Hispanic, one from the department and the other a car salesman with local political connections. They attacked Ray for being white and an out-of-stater. The white part was never said outright, but often implied. The other candidates captured the majority of votes, but Ray got the most votes of any individual candidate. There was no process in place for a runoff—Ray was sheriff.

His first year was a little rough. Ray tried the best he could to be a little more political, or at least diplomatic, but on occasion he still ruffled some feathers. Soon, though, it became obvious to anyone who was paying attention that there had been an overall improvement in the department. After that, he was entrenched in the job. His ability to successfully run a sheriff's department and fairly represent everyone's interests overrode his sometimes less-than-politically-correct, direct manner. He won the next race in a landslide.

Ray was generally described as burly, about six feet one and just a little on the heavy side. He had recently grown a mustache, which gave him an old west cowboy appearance. He dressed in his sheriff's uniform every day, except Sundays and the one other day he took off each week, which rotated. On those days he was most comfortable in jeans, an old work shirt, and a cowboy hat.

Nothing felt the same to Ray after his wife died. She had kept him connected to the world outside of the sheriff's department. Her death and his son's move across the country to Boston caused him to withdraw from most civilian activities. The department became his family and law enforcement his life. The county was his sole focus. He made it his goal to know everyone by name, and to make sure they knew him.

Still, the last few years had presented some problems. The new deputies he was hiring seemed different. Where Ray saw neighbors and friends, most of the new people saw threats and danger. The world was changing, and Ray wasn't sure he liked what he saw.

Dona Ana County covered an area about the size of some states back east, with a population of a little over 150,000 that was concentrated in Las Cruces. With a major college located in town—New Mexico State—there were another 25,000 or so visiting students. Like most of New Mexico, most of the population was Hispanic and proud of it. Green chilies and Mexican food were the cuisine of choice—the hotter the better. Most people described this part of the country as unique, picturesque, and extremely friendly. To Ray it was home and very comfortable.

Ray had been re-elected sheriff about two years before to a three-year term. At sixty-four, he had decided this would be his last term. He still hadn't given much thought to what he might do when he retired—he made up his mind to retire the previous year during a very difficult time dealing with the county commissioners over changes they wanted made to the department. Every commissioner except one, in Ray's opinion, was a complete asshole. A couple of the new commissioners were in their thirties and acted like they knew everything there was about running a sheriff's department. It was during this period of confrontation, while dealing with complete morons, that Ray decided it was time to step down. He loved his job. The politics were something he couldn't handle anymore.

The biggest jerk on the county commission was Bill Emerson, the son of the richest man in town, Jim Emerson, bank president and owner of about one third of all Las Cruces real estate. Not only was Bill a complete know-it-all, his dad was the biggest piece of shit Ray had ever had to deal with. He would not miss any of the dealings he had to endure with the Emerson family.

Today Ray was headed toward downtown Las Cruces for a Kiwanis club executive committee meeting being held in the board of directors' conference room at Citizens Bank. The Bank owned by Jim Emerson. Civic activities like this, which came with the job, were the least enjoyable part of Ray's duties.

The Citizens Bank was located in one of the oldest buildings in Las Cruces, dating from the late 1800s. The stories about the building included years as a brothel, several murders, and almost eighty years as a bank. The beginnings of the bank were rumored to be rooted in substantial deposits from some rather unsavory citizens of Mexico. Ray was of the opinion that the building itself had much more character than its owner.

The ornate conference room had the distinct atmosphere of a different time. Ray could imagine sitting in this room seventy years before discussing the major events of 1915. The room still had a certain flair about it that gave any gathering a grand feel. The attention to detail that showed through in every aspect of the bank building, and the conference room, in particular, was something from a different time. The level of craftsmanship in the construction was breathtaking.

Ray sat back and tuned out a discussion about the Kiwanis club's plans for the annual Spring Arts Festival. From his perspective this meant overtime for his deputies, dealing with crowds, and a very popular beer tent that had grown over the years to cover almost a whole city block.

"Hey, Ray, looking forward to retirement? Going fishing every day. Boy that sure is what I'd do. Hear the fishing is really good right now at Elephant Butte. Maybe you should move up to Truth or Consequences and enjoy the good life." This burst of wisdom was directed at Ray by Max Johnson. Max owned several car washes in town and seemed to mostly do very little except empty the coin machines a couple of times a day. He was also very active in the county Republican Party. Ray had never really figured out where Max had come up with the money to build those car washes. Rumor had it that someone in his family had died and left him some substantial cash, but Max had never confirmed that as far as Ray knew.

"Yeah, maybe that is what I should do alright, Max. The biggest problem is that I always hated fishing. But living on the lake up at T or C might be just the way to go when I retire. Don't you have a cabin or something in that area, Max?"

"My family used to—dad sold that a long time ago. We used to use it some after he sold it, because the guy who bought it was never there. My dad had a deal where he could use it if he looked after it. But after my dad died, we lost contact with the guy—I think he lived in Oklahoma somewhere." What the hell was he doing chattering on like this to the sheriff? Shut the fuck up you moron. Max's eye started to twitch. Hell, it didn't matter, the stupid sheriff was never going to go up there anyway. "Gotta run. I can hear those quarters calling me now. See ya later, Ray."

Ray always figured Max was not the sharpest knife in the drawer, although he had done okay for himself. He had a lot more money than Ray, that was for sure. He gave some thought to what Max had said. Living at the lake in an old run-down cabin actually sounded just fine to Ray. His needs were mostly on the Spartan side of things. Moving an hour away from Las Cruces and out of Dona Ana County might also simplify his remaining years.

Later that same day Ray dropped by Owen's Realty to see his old buddy, Chuck, who had been selling real estate in New Mexico for as long as Ray could remember. He had made a fortune doing very little except acting as Jim Emerson's realtor. Ray always thought the real talent Chuck had was sucking up to Jim to maintain those commissions over the years. All in all, Ray thought Chuck was an alright guy.

"Afternoon Chuck, what the hell's going on?"

"How the hell would I know Ray? All I do is sit at this desk and talk on the phone. There are days when the whole town could sink into a black pit and if it didn't affect my office or the phone lines, I wouldn't even know. If it wasn't such easy money, I'd give it up."

"Well, you could always become mayor and go around kissing ass for nothing. At least you're paid well."

"Not sure I like that kissing ass remark—but shit, you're

right. If you're going to have to be nice to all of these ass-holes, might as well make some bucks, right? What brings you to my playpen? Somebody accuse me of a crime?"

"Not yet. I'm sure you know this is my last year as Sheriff, and I don't really have a good idea of what I'm going to do next. A couple of things have come up and I wanted to run some stuff by you."

"I say use your authority and steal as much money as you can in the next few months, then head off to a Mexican beach with the prettiest, youngest senorita you can find—how's that for advice?"

"Sounds like that might fit someone else's fantasy. My situation is a little less exciting. You know I have that big old house out by Hatch, and I was wondering what you thought I could get for it? Also, I had a chat with Max at the Kiwanis meeting this morning and he suggested I should look at maybe buying something on the lake up in T or C—what do you think?"

"Okay, I'll keep the senorita fantasy to myself. As far as your house in Hatch, I'd have to do some research. That area has some appeal with the newcomers moving into Dona Ana. Let me run some numbers and then I can give you a good idea what you could get and how long it'd take. There are lots of cabins in T or C for sale, some dirt cheap and some very expensive. Did you have a price range?"

"Once I see what I can get for the old homestead I can make a better estimate of what I'd want to spend. Max mentioned something about an old cabin his dad used to own. Said he'd sold it to some guy in Oklahoma years ago—maybe fifteen or more years back. Said they were allowed to use it to compensate his dad for some upkeep he did, but then once his dad died they lost contact with the Oklahoma guy. Maybe you could do some research and see if that might be something I'd be interested in?"

"Sounds like it could be a dump by now. Let me check the records, see what Max's dad used to own up there, and then track down the current owner. Give me a couple days, and I'll see what I can do."

"Okay. Thanks, Chuck."

CHAPTER 5

Oklahoma City, Oklahoma

Waking up on the small sofa in his home office was less than comfortable. Joe's head hurt and he was cold. On the other hand, there was one real benefit—he hadn't had to deal with Liz. He heard her and the kids in the kitchen while he remained in the office, hoping she wouldn't come in and start one of her lectures about his shortcomings. After a while he heard the garage door open and close. Feeling a little guilty about hiding out until they left, he also felt a sense of relief that he didn't have to start his day off with more confrontation. He headed toward the kitchen, looking for coffee and aspirin.

Joe called in to the office and told Lucille, his office manager, that he was meeting with Mike again this morning and would be in the office about noon. Lucille didn't say anything. "Hello, did you hear what I said, Lucille?"

"I heard you, Mr. Meadows. You'll be in about noon."

"Thanks, Lucille."

What a pain in the butt she was. Joe had thought about firing her hundreds of times, but she was just too good at what she did to let her go. She was the best bookkeeper and organizer Joe had ever seen. But in her world, there were the good guys and the bad guys. The good guys went to church, didn't drink, didn't dance, didn't cuss, didn't . . . well, just about everything they didn't do, including and especially, anything to do with sex. How children came about in Lucille's world, he wasn't sure. Joe and most of his clients were the bad guys in her Bible Belt concept of reality. So, Joe just put up with her thinly veiled disapproval—one more person damning him to hell probably didn't make a whole lot of difference.

After a little coffee and some toast, with the aspirin starting to kick in, Joe was beginning to feel more human. His depression wouldn't leave him alone though. Some days were worse than others. Just for a while this morning he had felt like he couldn't go on anymore. But the feeling passed. He knew he wasn't suicidal, although if he had told someone about his feelings they might have thought that was exactly what he was. He didn't want to be dead, what he really wanted was to be someone else. With a coffee go-cup in hand, he headed out to see Mike and maybe find out about the mystery key.

"This is for a bank lock box." Mike's key guy, Fred, looked even worse than Joe felt. *My gracious, this guy looks like he slept in a dumpster.* But Mike seemed to think he knew what he was talking about and they sure didn't know anyone else who might be a key expert.

"These guys have a unique design. They have special security measures to make it difficult to duplicate the keys, and if they're not inserted along with the bank's key, they can break off in the lock. I used to work on these for some banks in town—well, before my little slip."

Joe had heard that Fred's "little slip" involved theft, followed by four years in prison. Good thing he hadn't had a big slip.

"Can you tell what bank this key came from?" Mike looked like he was starting to believe the key was some kind of magic wand. Joe thought it was just a little key to a bank lock box issued by one of, say, five thousand banks. *I suppose narrowing it down to banks is progress, but how can we figure out which bank?*

"Not really. On the front you can see the lock box number: 487. And on the back, there are letters stamped right into the metal, CB. Maybe that's the initials of the bank—like Commerce Bank, City Bank, Citizens Bank, Colorado Bank, Connecticut Bank. Or maybe Central Bank—no way of knowing. Could be those are the initials of the manufacturer of the lock boxes—Columbus Boxes, California Beaches—anything. Sorry, Mike. I'd like to help you more, but I have no idea how you'd narrow it down."

Joe spoke up, "Well, since this was your dad's key, I think we can assume it was an Oklahoma bank, and maybe even an Oklahoma City bank. We have a Commerce Bank in the city, a Cattleman's Bank, a Central Bank, and a Citizens Bank. That's four banks—not hard to go by each one and see if this is their key."

"Well hell, Joe—you make it sound easy. At least it's something to do. If it works, great—if not, we just give up since we could have hundreds, if not thousands, of banks after the short list is exhausted. It makes sense that dad would use a local bank, so let's get going."

Mike was looking more like a believer today. Maybe he had dreamed about the millions and how they could make all, or almost all, of his problems go away.

"Mike, you know I want to help, but I've got a ton of things that I need to do today. How about you visit the banks and see if you can learn anything. If I can help after that, you give me a call." Mike didn't look happy that his playmate couldn't play anymore, but he cheered up quickly and agreed that he would go see the banks that day and the next, then give Joe a call to let him know what happened.

"Hey Joe, not much luck in my bank visits."

"What did you find out?"

"It's a pain in the butt to drive all over town in this heat and humidity and with the crazy Oklahoma drivers."

"Anything about the banks?" There were times Mike made conversation difficult.

"Yeah. Well I visited all four banks. Essentially, got the same answer everywhere. Not their key. They said as far as they knew no one in this area ever had CB on their keys. Their keys always had the bank's full name stamped on the back because there were other banks in their market with the initials CB. One guy suggested that I look at banks in smaller markets where the CB would be unique to one bank in that town. Mostly this has been a waste of my valuable time. Oh wait, my time is not worth crap, so no harm."

"Shit, what now?" Joe wasn't sure they would ever find out about the key.

"Well, that isn't all I learned. They told me even if it had been their key, I'd have to have a bunch of legal shit before they'd allow me to access the box. One guy said that alone could take months. Plus, if the box rental hasn't been paid after a certain period of time then the bank can open the box and, if there's anything of value, they turn it over to the state."

Mike went on, "So, if they'd opened the box and found a bunch of cash, they would have given it to the state. Who, I imagine, would contact the police or the IRS or somebody who would have come snooping around to try to find my dad and arrest him, or tax him, or something. That never happened. I think this whole thing is a waste of time—nothing more than dad losing his mind and giving me an old key he probably found somewhere."

"Yeah, well it does kind of sound like a pipe dream. You need money and suddenly the strange things your dad did at the end of his life start to sound less strange, maybe a solution to your money problems. I think we're just fooling ourselves into believing something magical is going to happen that will fix the world—but we both know it's not."

"How about I meet you at Triples?"

When in doubt, drink.

They met at Triples, but rather than talk about the world's problems—including Mike's impending financial woes—they discussed football at great length, with special emphasis on the OU Sooners and how they were expected to fare the following year. Kind of hard to live in Oklahoma and not be an OU fan. Discussing sports at length can be a balm to a wounded male ego. *Might be a complete failure in life, but I sure as hell know a lot of useless information about sports teams and their players.* It's amazing the depth of knowledge a beer-guzzling lowlife might have about some long-ago college football game or long-dead baseball hero.

Months passed, not much happened. Joe was preoccupied with tax season and kept his head down and concentrated on work. Liz and the kids went about their business without much interest in what he was doing or not doing as long as the bills were paid and the credit cards worked. Joe gave some thought to seeing a doctor about his depression, but the idea of being put on some kind of happy pill for the rest of his life was—well, depressing. Instead, he decided to continue occasionally self-medicating with a little gin and hope for the best.

Joe talked to Mike almost every week, helping him gather information about his finances. The bank had been more understanding than Joe had predicted and hadn't foreclosed or forced much of any action on Mike's part. The store was generating enough cash to spread around among the parties and keep anyone from taking any immediate action. Mike knew this couldn't go on forever, but he had little motivation to force anyone to do anything. He would follow the Joe mental health plan—he would occasionally self-medicate with a little scotch and hope for the best.

Neither of them forgot about the letter, or the key, or what Mike's dad had said—they just had no idea how to proceed. They discussed the possibility of finding someone else to look at the key, but it seemed like a waste of time. Mike's father's ramblings seemed increasingly likely to be meaningless the more they thought about them. Without some further hint, their search for the buried millions would stop before it really began.

Maybe it was for the best. They both needed to face the reality of their day-to-day circumstances and deal with them. Dreaming about millions would only delay the inevitable pain of facing life and its various problems. So long to get-rich-quick fantasies.

CHAPTER 6

Las Cruces, New Mexico—April 1987

"**Ray, this is Chuck**—give me a call when you get this message. Think I have the name of the owner of that cabin up in T or C you asked me to check into a couple of months ago. Sorry it took so long but looks like I have a lead now and I was wondering if you wanted me to pursue it. Talk to you later."

Ray was not really sure what he thought of Chuck. The man was annoying, but also oddly likable. Chuck had gotten back to him very quickly on an estimated value on his house—no doubt because there was a real chance of a fee on that deal. Ray still couldn't make up his mind if he wanted to move, or not. The old place sure held a lot of memories, but it was about five times the amount of space he needed. A small, simple cabin would be something he could take care of by himself for many years without having to deal with housekeepers or pay a bunch of people good money to keep the place in reasonable condition. It made sense to move into something smaller and to get away from all of the nosy gossip that went on in Dona Ana County.

"Chuck, this is Ray. What do you have for me?"

"Glad you called back, Ray. You've been giving some thought to listing your house—now's a good time as we move into spring."

God, you could not have a normal conversation with this guy. He was always in salesman mode. "Well, I'm still thinking about it. What did you learn about that cabin Max's dad used to own?"

"Yeah, sure. But, remember, don't wait until you're ready to move to put your house on the market. More than likely it'll take a few months to find a buyer. So as soon as you're sure, we need to get a listing signed."

In an ideal world Ray would just hang up on this annoying little pest and go take a nap. "You bet, Chuck. As soon as I decide, I'll give you a call. How about the cabin?"

"Well, I was able to get the records by searching for Max's dad's name, so I found the details of the sale. You may not remember this, but Max's dad was Bud Johnson—he was something of a mystery man."

"What do you mean mystery man?"

"Well, this is old gossip, mostly from my grandfather. He thought Bud was a crook. He was long gone before you became sheriff. I think he died in the sixties—not real sure, but I think that's right. Anyway, my granddad said all of Bud's money was from illegal liquor. Mostly he was talking about the late 1920s and early 1930s, when there was prohibition. My granddad said that Bud was a big shot in this area and also had a bunch of holdings in El Paso. He said the rumor was that he was connected with some of the wealthiest Mexican families in Juarez. How much of this is true is kind of beyond me. Seems like there are a lot of unsavory stories about a lot of our best citizens. But who am I to gossip, right?"

The wiseass answer would have been *you're the biggest*

gossip in town—that's who you are. But this was interesting stuff—why not let him continue? "Wow, that's interesting Chuck. So, when did Bud sell the cabin, and who did he sell it to?"

"The records indicate he sold it in 1953. That means this cabin could be nothing, just a pile of trash by now. Even if Bud or someone was taking care of it into the sixties, that's still a long time to just sit up there abandoned. It's kind of an intriguing story, but I really don't think you want to retire and spend your last remaining years restoring an old broken-down cabin, do you?"

"You're probably right, Chuck. Did you get an address? Maybe, just as a lark, I'll run up there this weekend and see if anything still exists."

"Sure, 405 North Deer Trail. This is in fact a Hot Springs address, before they changed the name to Truth or Consequences. I have no idea if that street—or trail, or dirt road, or whatever—still exists. But let me know if you find anything."

"Thanks, Chuck, will do." Ray hung up and debated whether this meant anything to him or not. But the weekend was looking to be unusually warm, and this would be a good excuse to get out and spend some time doing something other than dealing with one bureaucratic screwup after another at the department. It occurred to Ray that Chuck hadn't told him who Max's father had sold the property to. He debated calling Chuck back, but the thought of listening to him drone on some more persuaded him to leave it until later. It might not matter—there was probably nothing left of the cabin to buy.

The Saturday morning was as promised: sunny skies and warm temperatures. Spring had arrived in the high desert. Ray had only lived in this part of the country for about twenty years, but he learned to love the desert and mountains as much as if he had been raised here. The trip to T or C was an easy drive of about fifty minutes. It was early morning when Ray reached the town and he decided to stop at the Lone Post Café, which many locals considered one of the best breakfast places in New Mexico.

Ray was in his civvies, so he didn't expect anyone to bother him. He settled into one of the well-worn wooden booths and ordered coffee and a breakfast burrito with lots of green chili. The smell of the place alone was worth the visit. He had grabbed an El Paso paper from one of the boxes outside and settled in to wait for his breakfast.

"I'll be damned, is that Ray Pacheco? How the hell are you, Ray? Kind of a long way to come for breakfast."

What luck. Staring down a long cigar was none other than Hector Hermes, the sheriff for Sierra County. Not one of Ray's best buds, Hector complained to anybody who would listen that his county got the short end of state and federal money because they weren't considered as important as Dona Ana.

"Hey, Hector. How're things going?"

"As well as can be expected, I guess. What're you doing in my neck of the woods on such a beautiful Saturday morning?"

Ray understood that Hector's friendly act was just that—the man wanted to know what the hell he was doing in his private domain. Ray decided the best approach with this guy was to be honest. What he was doing up here had nothing to do with their less-than-friendly competition. Plus, maybe this jerk didn't know he was retiring—that ought to make him happy.

"Well, Hector I've decided to retire at the end of my term. So, been thinking maybe I would move into your county and become an old fogey livin' in a remote cabin, just enjoying my remaining years." Ray was starting to annoy himself.

"Retiring—no I hadn't heard."

"Well, it's not a secret—not anymore. I just recently decided. Could be you'll want to run for the opening."

"Golly, I don't know. Wow, this really is sudden."

"By the way, maybe you can help me with an address. I was looking for an old cabin that was owned by a Las Cruces resident a long time ago. His son mentioned it to me, and I thought I would check it out in case it fits my needs. The address is—let me see—four zero five North Deer Trail. Know where that is?"

"Hmmm . . . North Deer Trail. Sounds familiar, but I'm not sure. Let me run out to the car and radio the station and have them look it up for you. Just take a second."

Before Ray could say anything, Hector had gone out to his car and was on the radio. Ray hadn't been sure how he was going to proceed once he got here, so running into Hector had turned out to be a good piece of luck, at least once the man had gotten past his initial suspiciousness.

While Hector was gone, the waitress brought Ray's breakfast. The burritos were large enough to feed a family of four, but Ray was willing to give it his best shot. Spicy and delicious. He was about halfway through when Hector came back in.

"You going to need any help with that, Ray?"

"Just might, but I'm going to give it a good college try. What'd you learn?"

"Kind of strange, we don't have a North Deer Trail anywhere in the county. You know a lot of those older names were in areas that no longer have any residents, usually due to fire or flooding. So the names just get dropped. Sorry for your wasted trip Ray. I'm sure you can contact a realtor up here or in Cruces—there are a lot of cabins for sale around the lake. Good to see you, though."

Hector left. Something about their exchange struck Ray as odd. Hector had seemed nervous and eager to leave. Maybe it was just his imagination. But now how was he going to find the address if the county had no record of it?

Ray decided the best solution was the one he often used in Las Cruces, the public library. He was a frequent visitor to the library to research anything that had happened years before or to locate information about something that was going on in the area. He found the main library just a few blocks from the restaurant. He had visited the T or C library once before when he was assisting with a federal operation at Elephant Butte Lake.

"Hello, I was wondering if you could help me find an old address from back when the town was Hot Springs."

"Sure, no problem." The woman behind the counter could have posed for a Norman Rockwell painting of a small-town librarian. She guided Ray toward the back of the library and began pulling down books of maps. She quickly went through them and gave Ray instructions on how to use the map book to search for the address he needed. After she thought he had a good idea of what to do, she went back to her post at the front desk.

Ray spent considerable time going through the books, looking for the right year and then searching for the street name. Eventually he found the street on the map. He took the book up to the librarian and asked if he could get a copy of the map.

"Sure, I can do that right now. It'll just take me a minute." She was gone for just a few moments, then came back with a copy and gave it to Ray. She told him that she was fairly familiar with the area since she'd lived around the lake her entire life.

"This was an area that had a massive wildfire and most of the high-dollar cabins up there burned to the ground, although a few survived. After the fire there was a huge rainstorm and it washed out almost all the roads in the area. Once that happened it was mostly just abandoned." She was pretty sure that the county didn't maintain any roads up there since there was nobody living in the area. "If you go up there, you need to be careful—it can be a dangerous area."

Ray wasn't really sure he wanted to venture off into an unknown area. The wise thing to do would be to just forget it and go back home. Although after that mega-calorie breakfast a little walking might be just the thing he needed. And it was still a beautiful early spring morning.

"Well, thanks for your help and the map. I was looking for an old cabin that probably isn't there anyway—but still it's a beautiful day for a hike—so I guess I'll go have a look. Thanks again."

It took Ray almost an hour to find the spot the librarian had pointed out on the map. While the area wasn't deep wilderness, the roads turned out to be horrible. This alone caused him concern about moving into the area. Maybe Sierra County wasn't getting its share of state money after all, or if it was it sure wasn't being spent on road maintenance. He rocked along in his old four-wheel drive Jeep for a very uncomfortable mile or two, then decided to stop, get out, and explore a little.

The area felt much more remote than the distance from town could justify. It was for sure there wasn't much up here. Ray hadn't seen any houses or cabins for at least a half hour. There were no other cars on the in-need-of-repair road. And while there was a comfort in being away from people, there was also an unease in being away from people. He would have been embarrassed if someone had seen his jumpiness, but it didn't matter—there was no one around. He reached into his glove box, removed his service revolver, and stuck it in his belt. Alone or not, it made him feel better.

Off to one side, about fifty feet from where Ray had parked, there was a gate with some kind of sign. He hiked over in that direction. There was no path, and the gate looked out of place as a result. When he got closer, he could see that on the other side of the gate was a very primitive road. The sign on the gate wasn't much help: *Keep Out.* The whole area seemed to be fenced off. The fence wasn't high, and it wasn't very strong—obviously just a boundary, not a serious attempt to keep anyone out.

Ray wasn't sure of his legal ground but given what the librarian had said there was every indication that it had been abandoned—he could at least make an argument that he was allowed to enter. Besides, he had mentioned it to the local sheriff. Hector hadn't dissuaded him, and openly talking to the sheriff like that was evidence that Ray wasn't being surreptitious. All in all, that was enough of a rationalization for Ray.

Quickly hopping over the fence, he began walking up the makeshift road. The terrain was rough, and there was ample evidence of water damage over the years. If Ray was serious about buying something up here that he would actually live in, there would have to be some fairly major improvements to allow him reasonable access. Once again it crossed his mind that this was something of a wild goose chase and probably a waste of time. But as soon as the thought occurred to him, he realized that this was pretty much all he had to do today: waste time. He relaxed and started to enjoy the hike and the day.

About a quarter of a mile from the gate, Ray could see some kind of structure off the road a hundred yards or so. There didn't seem to be a driveway or any kind of path toward the structure, although there might be something on the other side of the cabin or whatever it was. The more Ray looked, the more it seemed like some kind of outbuilding, maybe used for storage. He decided to stay on the road, which curved, to see if it maybe went around to the other side of the building. Anyway, he felt better staying on the road than blazing his own trail through the trees.

Ray remained on the road. It did slowly curl around to the other side of the outbuilding, and once he got clear of that he could see a pretty good-sized cabin further along. Sticking with the road, he soon came upon a small road or driveway that looked like it led to the cabin. There was no gate and no indication of the address or who might own the cabin. He started up the driveway.

After a walk that probably seemed longer than it really was, Ray reached the cabin. While it was obviously very old and in need of some repairs, it was, at least from the outside, in surprisingly good shape. It was a large structure made of logs. The rustic nature of the original construction had allowed the building to maintain its condition, even though it looked like it had been many years since anyone had been here. He climbed the few steps up to the large wraparound porch. On his right, he saw numbers on the cabin: 405. The five was dangling and looked like it would fall at any moment, but there it was, proof that this was the old cabin once owned by Max's dad. He felt like he had just discovered a lost land or something.

Ray stood back and examined the outside of the cabin. It was an impressive structure—two-story, with an elegant design. The quality was obvious, even after being neglected all of this time. He was impressed.

He walked the length of the porch trying to look in through the windows, but they were all boarded up from the inside. The last person to leave this place wasn't expecting to come back any time soon. Although he still felt like he was likely wasting his time, he was also intrigued by the mystery of the place. Not sure what he wanted to do next, he made some detailed notes and a new map of the location of the road, gate, and cabin.

The time slipped by and it was now almost noon. Ray had spent several hours poking around and making his notes and diagram. Deciding that his next priority of the day was a nap, he settled on heading home. Walking back down the road everything was quiet, but he had an eerie feeling that he was being watched. He made up his mind that it was just the result of being out in a remote place and brushed it off. Normally when his instincts raised a red flag he heeded them, but who would be watching him up here?

He headed back home. The trip had been uneventful, and once home he enjoyed a long nap—a habit that had been his Saturday afternoon secret for some years now. He awoke at the sound of his phone. Slightly embarrassed that someone had caught him napping, he took his time picking up so he wouldn't sound sleepy when he answered.

"Ray Pacheco, is that you?"

Ray hadn't even said hello before the person started talking. "Yeah, this is Ray Pacheco. Who is this?"

"Pacheco, nobody wants you sticking your fucking nose in Sierra County business—if you're smart you'll find another place to retire. It could be real dangerous, got it asshole?"

"Max, is that you?"

Click.

What the hell was that about? Ray was used to some strange calls but seldom at home. His number was unlisted. Of course, other law enforcement people and agencies had it, so maybe it was more available than he realized, but why tell him to stay out of Sierra County? It was strange, but Ray had thought it sounded like Max Johnson. It was his father's old cabin—why would Max threaten him? No question it was time to consider retiring—maybe it should be somewhere that no one knew him.

CHAPTER 7

Oklahoma City, Oklahoma—June 1987

Joe was enjoying a much calmer schedule now that tax season was over. Every year he swore to himself he wouldn't do it again the following year, but so far, he had always broken that pledge. He didn't consider himself much of an expert on taxes, but it went with the job. If you said you were a CPA everyone assumed that you spent every waking hour keeping up with the huge, convoluted pile of crap that was the tax code. And, of course, tax season accounted for a substantial portion of his annual income. On the plus side, even though things were intense leading up to the filing deadline, for the most part after April fifteenth the whole mess disappeared for another nine months or so.

As part of his recent I-need-to-relax-more approach to life, Joe had taken up golf. He had never thought he'd get into it because he wasn't exactly a natural athlete and he was sure it would be humiliating. But after a few lessons he had gone out with some of his friends and realized that having golfing skills didn't seem to be a requirement. While he was really bad, some of his buddies—who had played for years—were actually worse. It was an odd game, and he was still unsure if he really enjoyed it, but it did give him an excuse to drink in the afternoon without the social stigma of hanging out in a bar.

He was playing today at Oakwood County Club as a

guest of one of his clients, who was in the used car business. Joe thought the guy was a little creepy, but he had turned out to be a well-paying, decent client. His client had brought two employees along to make sure he was playing with people who would hold him in the highest esteem—and would let him win. Joe didn't care. He tried to enjoy the day and the setting. The game went as expected, with his client being the easy winner. They invited Joe to have drinks with them at the clubhouse, but he begged off, saying he still had some business to take care of before the day ended. They said their goodbyes.

The truth was that just before he left, he had received a message that Mike had called and needed to talk to him later that day. The message said to meet him at the usual place around 4:30. Of course the usual place was Triples. Joe was headed that way.

"You're not going to believe this!" First words out of Mike's mouth as Joe slid into the booth.

"First, I need a drink. Then you can tell me what I won't believe." Joe signaled to the bartender and got a finger wave indicating that his drink was on the way.

"First thing this morning, I got a call from some realtor guy from someplace in New Mexico asking me about a property that was owned by Elizabeth Ruth Hall of Oklahoma City. He said it had taken him months to track her down to this phone number. Well, I wasn't real sure what to say—I told him that was my mother's maiden name and she was no longer living."

Mike's mom had died suddenly of breast cancer about six years after his father died. His mother's death had been a crushing blow to Mike. She had always been the one who he knew cared about how he was and what happened to him. Mike had great difficulty at the time, dealing with her death. He was still grieving four years later.

"What—what are you talking about? Your mother—I thought her name was Bugs?"

"Yeah, that's the only name she used, but her legal name was Elizabeth. My mother didn't have any property in New Mexico, or anywhere else for that matter."

Mike had been about ready to tell the guy he must have the wrong person when the guy had mentioned that it also looked like there was a bank account that was paying the taxes on the property, and that it might also be part of his mother's assets.

"It just doesn't make any sense. My mother was a stay-at-home-mom who had absolutely nothing to do with money or business. It doesn't seem possible. My dad took care of everything—there's no way she owned real estate and had bank accounts in New Mexico. But, anyway, I got the guy's name and number and told him I'd get back to him to find out more. Mostly I just wanted to get off the phone so I could have time to think. I really don't get it."

Joe got a strange feeling. He had known Mike's mom, and there was no way she owned secret property or had secret bank accounts. This woman was an almost perfect "normal" mom. She scolded children for keeping secrets—she would never have any herself. It would be against her mom code.

"It has to do some way with your dad. That's the only explanation. Maybe this is connected to the other stuff."

Joe hadn't thought this through very well—just kind of spit it out. But, no doubt, that had to be what it was—Pat Allen, the bootlegger, had a secret cabin located in New Mexico, hidden under his wife's maiden name. Now if that wasn't a mystery, what the hell was?

"Mike, you had said your dad went on business trips a lot—where did he go?"

"Not real sure. I guess I always thought it was some place in Texas. He would be gone for a few days at a time. My mom and I had adjusted to those trips, so we hardly paid any attention to when or how long he was gone. He never discussed them with us, as far as I can remember. Although I do remember one thing. After one trip he brought my mom and me some stuff from New Mexico. I'd completely forgotten that until now. It was from some little town—Mesa, Mesilla, something like that. I remember now because my mom was so surprised—he'd never brought us anything from one of his trips before. It was tourist kind of stuff, souvenirs from this little town in New Mexico. It was strange—it didn't seem like something my dad would do."

It was odd to Joe that he seemed to be more curious about Mike's father's past than Mike was. Joe hadn't been really close to his own father, who had always been predictable and reliable—there were no mysteries in his dad's past. He had worked at the post office until one day he dropped dead. Joe would have considered it a wonderful day if he had suddenly learned that his dad had been more than he seemed. But Mike's dad was involved in *multiple* mysteries. He was, or maybe was not, a bootlegger who had hidden millions. There was the strange key to nothing and now a cabin in New Mexico nobody knew about, not to mention the bank account. From Joe's point of view this was just great.

"Trinkets from New Mexico would at least *seem* to suggest that he had been there, right?"

"Well, I guess that would support the idea of my father having business dealings in New Mexico, at least. As you say, he was there once. So that probably means he was the one who owned the cabin. Still doesn't explain why he owned a cabin he never mentioned, or why it was in my mother's maiden name. Guess I'll call the realtor back and ask some more questions."

"Of course, you should, Mike! Who knows, maybe this is somehow a clue to his letter or the key."

A few days later Mike did call the New Mexico real estate person to get more information. And Joe did some research and determined where Las Cruces and T or C were. He also found the town of Mesilla, or Old Mesilla, which was right next to Las Cruces.

Any time Mike and Joe got together they would discuss every possibility they could think of about the cabin and Mike's dad's travels to New Mexico. The mystery seemed to loom larger every day, even without much more concrete information. Joe was very anxious to find out more, while Mike seemed hesitant. Joe began to realize that, for Mike, there was a fear of finding out something he didn't want to know. The mysteries surrounding Mike's father were thrilling to Joe, but not to Mike, who couldn't be sure where they might lead.

"I think we should go there and see that cabin ourselves and also check out Las Cruces. What do you think?" Mike had finally reached the conclusion that he needed to find out the truth about the cabin, no matter what that truth might be. He was broke, but he would worry about that later—he still had room on at least one credit card. And if the cabin was legally his mother's, it should now be his. Maybe he could sell it and use the money to help dig himself out of his financial mess.

"Mike, count me in." Joe thought getting out of town sounded like a good plan.

PART TWO: 1952

Most Americans were very optimistic in 1952. The end of World War II had brought a sense that the world would be a better place, especially for Americans. Harry S. Truman was president, and with his no-nonsense style he was popular despite the war in Korea. Soon-to-be President-elect Dwight Eisenhower was a hero to almost everyone, which enhanced the sense that great things would come under his leadership. The average worker made $3,400 per year, and the average house cost $9,800. Many families owned cars, telephones, and even television sets. The average woman was married by twenty, and if she worked, she would stop once there were children. For most, it was a good time to be an American and dream about the future.

CHAPTER 8

Oklahoma City, Oklahoma

Shit—it was his kid's birthday. Pat Allen always forgot his kid's birthday. Maybe it was some kind a masochistic thing—he sure as hell was going to hear about it from Bugs. Jeez, just what he needed was some more bullshit about what kind of father he was. Pat was approaching sixty-two and sure as hell did not need an eight-year-old kid—or maybe he was nine—messing with his lifestyle. Young wives had some real advantages, but this was one of the disadvantages: children.

Pat had married Elizabeth Ruth Hall—known to everyone as Bugs—twelve years before. Pat had been fifty and she had been twenty-nine. Bugs was tall at five feet seven, and very slender, with long dark hair. She had only one goal in life: to be someone's wife. Once she was pregnant, she discovered her other talent: being a mother. She never involved herself in "man stuff" and seemed to always be happy.

Pat was almost the perfect husband for Bugs—he left her alone. He went about his business and she went about hers. She had a complete life devoted to her social activities and her son's needs. She was on various committees at church and at Mike's school. She managed the house with military precision—meals were preplanned for weeks.

Bugs lived in an orderly world under her control, or so

she thought.

Even in his sixties, Patrick Allen was still a very handsome man. He was six feet one, with a muscular body. His hair was full, though completely grey. Pat had never made any extra effort to stay in shape—it was mostly just good genes. He had always been aware of his appearance and he spent a considerable sum on clothes in order to look his best. The role in life that defined him was salesman—not husband or father—and a salesman had to look successful to be successful.

Pat's son, Mike, was an okay kid. Pat just wasn't all that interested in hanging out with the boy. He was busy putting together the next big money-making deal. He felt like he owned Oklahoma City and much of the state. Every day it seemed like more good things fell his way. For many years it had seemed to Pat that everything he touched turned to crap, but lately he had the old Midas touch—it was all golden, all the time. He had fallen into the bootlegging business almost by accident, supplying some of his friends. Now he was riding high.

For many years Pat had been an insurance salesman. He had traveled extensively all over Oklahoma selling insurance policies to farmers, town officials, and sheriffs. He knew everybody in the state who mattered. He had made a connection with a guy in New Mexico and started bringing in some booze, using it as a sales incentive to get people to buy insurance. Buy a big life insurance policy and Pat would show up with a case of hooch. Before he knew it, he was spending more time selling whisky than insurance. He had always been a good salesman, so selling people something they already wanted wasn't much of a challenge. Soon he was moving a lot of booze and it just kept growing.

He had become the number one bootlegger in Oklahoma. Prohibition had ended many years before, but with a wisdom rooted in spiritual values, all of Oklahoma and many parts of Texas remained dry. From Pat's point of view this was absolutely divine intervention. Glory be to the Bible Belt's penchant for screwing things up for the ordinary sap while praising misery and pain as the path to salvation.

Pat didn't think too much about whether what he was doing was right. He knew it was illegal, but in Pat's view that was just because the politicians lacked the backbone to stand up to religious groups. The rest of the country had legal liquor—it was stupid that Oklahoma didn't. He felt almost like he was providing a public service, giving his customers what they wanted and could have had if they lived just over the state line.

Bugs and he, along with the boy, lived a modest lifestyle. No need to flash the bucks. But Pat was stockpiling a shitload of cash. One of his challenges was what to do with it without looking like a big spender. He wanted the money, there was no question about that—and he found some interesting ways to spend his ill-gotten gains—but he also wanted a stable life for his family. Bugs was not involved in his real life. She seemed oblivious to where the money came from. If he jumped into the big bucks lifestyle he could now afford, she wouldn't understand. And there was no question that she would be shocked to know what he really did for a living. Jeez, why did he put up with this shit? The answer, as corny as it was, was that he loved her.

Pat and Bugs had never had a fight. She was always attentive, and she was pretty damn sexy when she wanted to be. They didn't talk much about anything except the house and the kid. She never asked him where he was or what he was doing. If he forgot to tell her he wasn't going to be home, she never got upset. If he showed up for dinner after he had said he was going to be out, she acted happy to see him. He couldn't imagine a more perfect person to be his wife and the mother of his child.

Pat bought Mike a too-expensive gift for his birthday and had it wrapped at John A. Browns, his favorite place to shop. The gift was the largest Erector set they sold. Since his knowledge was a little limited, Pat wasn't sure if it was something his son would like or not, but it was big and impressive—the perfect gift from a traveling dad, seldom home.

John A. Browns & Company was the largest department store in Oklahoma and, excluding Dallas, probably in the region. Pat guessed it was 300,000 or 400,000 square feet, on five floors, right in the middle of downtown. There were even rumors that Browns was going to take over the building next door and connect the two, which would almost double the square footage. He couldn't imagine what they would add to fill that much space. It seemed like they already had everything one could want.

Pat's sometime companion worked at the restaurant in the basement, The Colonial Lunchroom. Browns' somewhat hidden restaurant was a favorite of daytime shoppers for its selection of special sandwiches and cream sodas.

He thought he might as well drop in and test the waters. You could never tell with Sally exactly what sort of mood she would be in. If it was bad, he would quickly move on to calmer waters.

"Hey Sally, how's the world treating you?"

"Well, if it isn't Mr. Patrick Allen, world famous asshole. And you know how the world is treating me? Like shit!"

Sally was about five feet two, blonde, and gorgeous, with a body to die for—and she was used to being treated better by younger, better looking men. Every aspect of Sally attracted attention from men—her looks, her smile, her walk, her laugh—she was what men dreamed about when their wives weren't around. Pat knew that one of these days she was going to tell him to take a hike.

"Sally, you should watch your mouth. Browns is a respectable business."

Apparently, that was not the thing to have said. Pat's smile didn't help either. She gave him the finger and went into the kitchen. Fearing that she might be retrieving something sharp, he gathered his bags and quickly headed for the elevator.

Once on the main floor, Pat exited through a side door into an alley where Browns had valet parking service. He gave his parking ticket to the attendant. Within a few minutes the parking attendant pulled around his pride and joy: a 1952 Cadillac Series 62 Convertible—cream outside, with a burgundy interior. Pat just stood there and stared. Other people in the area also glanced over with admiring looks.

Of all the things he had spent his money on, this was the one that meant the most. He knew it was a little over the top and didn't fit his "modest means" lifestyle. He just couldn't help it—he loved this car. He had told Bugs that it was a special bonus from the insurance company because he had closed a large deal, and said that if she thought they should sell it and spend the money on something else they could. She didn't hesitate for a moment, saying that he deserved the car, that he had always taken good care of his cars, and that she was pleased he was so happy. She was easy to manipulate on this kind of stuff, but he felt bad that her reaction was always the same—whatever made him happy made her happy.

His wife was almost too good. Pat wanted to scream at her "Bugs, honey, I was just down at Browns to see my girlfriend and I decided to buy you a little something." My goodness, he was such an asshole. He didn't even know why he did the things he did. He liked to go out and raise hell occasionally with a little drinking and dancing, and it had never seemed right to take his wife—and the mother of his child—to the places he liked to go to. So, there was Sally. He was just getting too old to be doing this sort of nonsense.

Pat lived off of Walker Avenue and 17th. This was an area of nice homes, some pretty large. As a matter of fact, the mayor lived in the neighborhood. Pat and Bugs' house was one of the smallest in the area, but it was convenient, and it felt like home.

Pat went into the house through the back and stopped in the kitchen to fix himself a bourbon and water. Naturally, only the best bourbon for the number one bootlegger in Oklahoma City: Wild Turkey. It had just been introduced and had become an immediate success. Pat thought it was the best Kentucky bourbon he had ever tasted—and he had tasted a lot.

Not hearing any movement in the house, Pat figured Bugs and Mike were out, probably getting something for Mike's birthday. He went into his office and shut the door. Opening his small safe, he took out the ledger where he kept track of the payoffs to various officials that ensured that his business ran smoothly. He had made a run to El Reno today and given Sheriff Tubbs a nice little present and wanted to enter it into his book before it slipped his mind. He hated keeping anything in writing, but there was no way he could keep all of the bribes and kickbacks straight if he didn't have some kind of system. He had recently hired a new guy in Las Cruces, New Mexico, Emerson, who could maybe take over some of this record-keeping shit—once Pat decided if he could trust him.

That was one of several reasons to get back to Las Cruces in the next few weeks. His primary source of product was currently in Juarez, Mexico, and Pat had established a base of operation in Las Cruces, a quiet little college town of about 25,000 people. Just perfect for his needs—and it wasn't in Texas. He had a few employees there and, in El Paso, Texas, who helped him manage the shipments coming from Mexico. The operation had just become too big for Pat to keep it all in his head. This was very troubling—

he felt like he was becoming too visible.

After he had outgrown his original supplier he had started dealing with an Italian Texas family, headed by John Giovanni. He knew almost from the moment the deal was set up that this was probably a mistake. The Giovanni Texas group made him nervous—very nervous. He was sure they knew he was buying from the Mexicans and no doubt didn't like it. The Texas guys were different. Pat realized a little late that he should have stayed away from them. While most of his dealings were casual and friendly, these guys were really bad people. If it hadn't been for the network of county, state, and city officials who would only deal with him, he was sure those crooks would have buried him a long time ago. His operation ran smoothly, with little interference from the feds or the state cops, all because he greased a lot of wheels. As a matter of fact, Pat's business was probably one of the biggest contributors to government corruption—right after the oil industry.

His Texas connection was the reason he was starting to plan a way to get out. Those hoods seemed more like New Yorkers than Texans, and it was making Pat really nervous. The Mexican guys, by contrast, seemed like gentlemen. They were always very gracious, and they seemed to genuinely care that everything was going the way he wanted. He had been to the homes of the two main owners down in Juarez and met their families. He thoroughly enjoyed their company.

As it turned out, the kid was nine and the birthday party was—well, a birthday party. Cake and ice cream, gifts—Mike liked the Erector set—relatives, neighbors and a bunch of other kids being annoying. Bugs was in her element, as excited as the kids were. Pat snuck off into his office and poured another Wild Turkey, straight up. Much better way to enjoy a kid's birthday party.

While sitting and enjoying his drink Pat decided that he would go to Las Cruces the following week. He had his own plane—a Beech Twin Bonanza, a model that had just been introduced the year before. After World War II, it had taken some time for the domestic aircraft industry to come back to life. Pat had learned to fly in the early thirties and seemed to have a knack for it. The plane was something of a secret—Bugs knew nothing about it. It was registered in the name of his company, Blue Devils Development, and it was kept in a hangar at Wiley Post Airport, just a little northwest of the city.

On his business trips, he always told Bugs he was flying out of Will Rogers Field on Braniff. She never questioned this and had no idea he was flying himself in his own plane—she would have worried herself sick. The plane also usually held some special cargo on the return trip for some of his more discerning customers.

The next few days were uneventful for Pat—boring, really. He made some rounds to be sure all of his big customers were getting timely shipments, and everyone was happy. He called Sally and begged forgiveness for whatever he had done wrong. He suggested they should go out on the town that night and visit some nightclubs. Sally played hard to get, but eventually relented and said she would meet him at the Lincoln Club—her favorite club and one of his top customers. It was located a couple of blocks from the state capital, and there was always a big delegation of politicians and celebrities.

Pat pulled his big Cadillac into the Lincoln's parking lot. Passing up the valet service, he parked the car himself. He wanted to make sure the idiot kid who parked at the Lincoln didn't dent his pride and joy. Entering the Lincoln, he headed toward the bar. While Oklahoma was dry and selling liquor was illegal, the bar at the Lincoln couldn't have been more out in the open. It always amazed Pat that there wasn't more scandal about this than there was. Cops, politicians, and rich businessmen—especially the oil industry tycoons—openly flouted the law without suffering any consequences.

There were probably more liquor-selling clubs in Oklahoma City per capita than in Vegas or New York City. The newspaper people didn't care and never reported on this double standard. The bulk of the population was religious, with a strong belief that alcohol was evil and ruined the lives of good people. Many of them were shocked when *Look Magazine* listed the twenty-four worst cities in the nation for "vice and sin" and included Oklahoma City on the list. It was as if two entirely separate worlds existed in the same place, ignoring one another.

He immediately spotted Sally. My, oh my, that was one good lookin' woman. As he got closer, she turned and gave him a smile that sent chills down his old body. Sally had only been in the city a short while when Pat had met her at this bar. She was a knockout. One night they started talking and she told him that she had come to OKC to have some fun. Said she was working at the

John A. Brown's basement restaurant while she looked for something better. Pat was not real sure if he was being conned or not—she had the appearance of a hustler looking to have a good time with wealthy gentlemen. In their first chat Pat had told her he was married but did a lot of business in the clubs and was usually alone. That first night they had talked for hours, and Pat began to realize he was not only attracted to her beauty, he actually liked her.

After that they had met a few more times and always seemed to enjoy each other's company. On their third "date," Pat had offered Sally some money. Well, all hell broke loose. "What do you think I am—some kind of whore? Listen, you dumb son-of-a-bitch, I don't want your money and I don't want your company." She had stomped off to the ladies' room, leaving Pat embarrassed and humiliated. He had figured that was that, and that he wouldn't see her again given that he had been so vile. But after about fifteen minutes she returned to the booth where Pat was soothing his wounds. After some time, she said she was sorry for her outburst and began to be friendlier. Pat was confused. He understood her earlier anger. Now he didn't know what was happening at all. Sally said, "Look, Pat, I care about you a lot. I know you're married, and I don't expect this to be anything but two people enjoying each other's company and having some fun. I also know you think you're too old for me and the only reason I go out with you is money—well, that's not true. I like you, okay? I enjoy going out—and it makes it a lot easier for me if you're buying—is that so horrible? I'm not taking money from you—that would make me something

I'm not. I know this is a fling and it won't last, but I say, hey, let's enjoy it while we can." Pat thought, *wow what a woman.* "And Pat, I want to make it clear I won't take money from you—but dinners and drinks are just fine, and an occasional gift wouldn't be frowned upon." The rules of the game had been laid out. The only remaining question was whether he wanted to play—he did.

After that, Pat had rented an apartment and Sally moved in. He bought her a car, and he bought her clothes and jewelry—but she kept her job and didn't take money from him. This logic worked for Sally and Pat never complained.

Pat never took Sally for granted. He knew she had options and he always tried to treat her like a lady. There were times when Sally could make that difficult, but they quickly passed. She was funny and he loved being with her. For an old man she was like a fountain of youth. He dressed better. His clothes became more stylish and he paid three times what he had before for his haircuts. He thought he was looking pretty good.

"You're looking lovelier than ever." Pat still felt a little funny saying these kinds of things, but he sure meant it.

"Thanks, Pat. Look, I'm sorry about my little fit at Browns. You know, I haven't seen you much lately and I guess it was starting to feel like you were losing interest. Well, I don't know, I just lost it."

Pat was impressed at how well Sally handled herself. She was quite young, but she seemed so mature. It occurred to him that some people were just older than others, no matter their age. Sally had a mature wisdom, but also a little girl's joy in life. He was finding that he wanted more and more to be with her. Fully recognizing the folly in this, he still found he couldn't help himself.

"Sally, I'm sorry. I've been so busy with my business customers I haven't had much time. That's going to change. Why don't you come with me on a trip to New Mexico? We can see each other more and have a lot of fun drinking margaritas and eating enchiladas. Maybe we can even find a place to go dancing—what do you say?"

Sally let out a scream of joy that got everyone's attention, and after some enthusiastic hugs and a few kisses she said, "Yes!"

CHAPTER 9

Dallas, Texas—Some Years Earlier

Sally Thompson had to get away from her brother, Hank. Because either Hank was going to make her permanently crazy or she was going to kill him. Her brother thought he knew everything, and since their mother had died, he had taken it on as his personal responsibility, as the head of the family, to make Sally miserable.

Sally lived in a rather shabby part of Dallas with her brother and sister in the apartment once occupied by their mother. Things had been different when her mother was alive. Her mother had loved all of her children, although she seemed to favor the girls. She fussed with them and hugged them—she had been wonderful. Every day she made them feel special and loved. But then she had become ill—they had said it was the flu—and in a matter of a few weeks she had died.

The sadness Sally felt was physically painful. She had trouble just getting out of bed. Soon her brother started acting like he was in charge. He would yell at Sally that she had to find another job. He made her miserable. She had been fired from her previous job because she had stayed home with her mom while she was sick. Her sister had helped, but she was still in school and said she couldn't miss any more classes, or their brother would kill her.

Sally was an extremely attractive young woman. She

had just turned twenty-three when her mother died. Her best years had been in high school, when it seemed every boy in school was attracted to her. She felt like she was a queen or something, with all of that attention. But even with all the adulation, Sally had remained aloof. She felt she was destined for something very special. After high school, Sally had no option but to find work to help support her family. She had never known her father, who apparently had left when Sally was very young. Her mother never discussed him.

During the years after high school, Sally had been a waitress at several restaurants in her neighborhood. She gave most of her money to her mother, who would waste it on her big, useless brother. Sally always thought her mother seemed intimated by him—he had a meanness about him. Sally didn't mind the work, even though she got tired of all the men making a play for her. There were many days when she deliberately didn't make any effort to look good, just so maybe those lugs would leave her alone—it didn't help.

To appease her brother, she decided to go out to see if she could get another job. She thought she might go back to the last place and explain why she hadn't been able to work, and they might hire her back—but for some reason that felt like begging, and she didn't beg.

Sally knew she was beautiful. What most people didn't realize, although Sally knew it, was that she was also smart. In the illogic of the times, people simply thought that a good-looking woman *couldn't* be smart. Sally knew that she wanted something better for herself than just marrying some guy and becoming a household slave, cooking, cleaning, and putting up with the sexual advances of some ape, just to have a place to live. She thought that with her looks and brains she should be able to do anything she wanted. Although the world seemed ready to disagree.

Sally got a waitressing job at another greasy spoon diner close to her apartment. Same job, same grabby boss, same foul-mouthed cook—and, it would appear, the same goddamn customers. It was more than she could deal with. She lasted two weeks at the new job, told her boss to go to hell, and walked out.

She went home, fell onto her bed, and cried. Why was everything so hard? She knew she had options—men were always making lewd propositions to her—but her own moral code wouldn't let her take them up on it. There were times when she didn't understand why she said no.

Hank had become religious during his senior year in high school, and religion seemed to give him a new power. Almost everything he said was based on some strange interpretation of the Bible. He constantly berated Sally about the evils of sin, and the biggest sin of all was sex. It seemed all Hank thought about was sex. In the last year or so, Hank had started to look at Sally in an unhealthy way. Sally knew Hank was having sex with the girl next door, mostly because you could hear them for some distance, and it happened almost every day. Sally didn't understand how that fit with Hank's view of morality, but she really didn't care as long as he left her alone.

Lying on her bed, she made a decision: she was leaving. She worried about her sister, but by this point she felt a sense of desperation. She had a premonition that if she didn't leave something bad would happen. She wrote a note to her sister.

Dear Sis,

I hope you understand why I am doing this. Remember that I love you, but I have to leave. I cannot live in the same place with Hank. Something bad would happen. You should also leave as soon as you can.

I'm going to Oklahoma City. Do not tell Hank. Once I get there, I'll let you know how to get hold of me.

Please be careful. I love you very much.

Sally

She put the note on her sister's bed and began packing what little she had. It didn't even fill her one small suitcase.

Sally had a little bit of money. Not much, but probably enough to buy a bus ticket somewhere. The Greyhound bus station was only a few blocks from her downtown slum apartment. She walked.

"How much for a ticket to Oklahoma City—one way?" She was both scared and excited. She had decided on Oklahoma City because it was the closest big city that wasn't in Texas. It was an act of rebellion: she wanted out of Texas because her brother thought it was so great.

The man in the ticket window gave her the amount. "Wow that's cheap." She paid and he gave her a ticket.

Sally found the right bus number and got on board, giving the driver her ticket. Greyhound had buses leaving for OKC almost every hour—hers would leave in twenty minutes. She went to the back, still holding her small suitcase, and sat down. The bus filled up. A couple of men gave her glances, but she just stared out the window and tried to ignore them.

Sally had never been anywhere. She had been born in Dallas and had never left. She knew Oklahoma City was just up the road—she thought it was a couple hundred miles—but at least she was going *somewhere*. She was sorry about her sister, but she felt she had no choice—she simply couldn't deal with Hank any longer. If she never saw him again, that would be fine. The bus started and the door shut. Pulling away Sally almost cried, but she didn't.

The scenery was not a whole lot different whether you were in Texas or Oklahoma. The trip was only about four hours or so. They pulled into the Oklahoma City bus station, and if it hadn't been for the signs she could have been in Dallas. Maybe you had to travel farther for it to look different. Sally got off the bus. *Now what?*

Within a few blocks she found a hotel. It looked like something she might be able to afford—it was cheap. She paid cash for one week's rent. Now she was almost out of money. The room had a bed and a small dresser with one drawer that wouldn't open. Sally unpacked her few possessions and had a good cry. On her own at last. She felt some relief, but she was also frightened.

The next day Sally put on her best outfit and walked toward downtown Oklahoma City, only a few blocks from where she was staying. There had to be restaurants there where she could get a job. Once she was in the middle of downtown, what caught her eye were the display windows in John A. Browns—huge windows with some of the most beautiful clothes she had ever seen, like the designer outfits she saw in magazines. She had passed windows like this in Dallas, but somehow being on her own made everything more alive.

She postponed her job hunt for a while and decided to go into Browns to see what it was like. Unfortunately, it wasn't open yet. But there was a sign announcing that the Colonial Lunch Room was now serving breakfast—it pointed toward a staircase that led to the basement. Sally went down, sat at the counter, and had a cup of coffee. She asked the waitress if she knew of any places that were hiring.

"Sure, they're always hiring right here. These people are hard to work for, so there's always an opening."

Not much of a recommendation, but beggars can't be choosers. She was hired and she started at eleven that same day. Sally was ready for some fun.

She quickly made friends, especially male friends. These were mostly young men with no money who were after one thing. Sally wasn't going to end up with any of these losers—she wanted something better. She quickly developed a reputation as a prude and a snob, but that suited her just fine.

After a few months, the gentlemen hanging around Browns' lunch counter became a little older—and definitely richer. Sally liked them better. This improvement was a direct result of what might be called the gentlemen's downtown grapevine. The offices in downtown Oklahoma City were full of executives and junior executives who gossiped about women with little shame. She started going out with three or four of these guys, rotating her attention from one to the other. It was fun going out to clubs and dancing. But it was tiring to deal with all of these male egos.

Sally had become an attraction at the lunch counter and was making a nice amount of money in tips. She spent everything she could get on clothes since she knew she had to be "classier" to attract the type of man she wanted.

During her time off, Sally actually fantasized about the type of man she wished she could be with. She developed a mental picture of who this person would be: someone older, in their fifties probably, maybe even married. She knew that Hank would have had a heart attack if she had said that to him. She wanted someone who would treat her like a lady, but who didn't want to marry her. Sally had thought about this a lot and thought her best chances of having the kind of success she wanted was as a single woman.

She understood that her plans conflicted with her morals, but it was a very difficult world for young women. She was alone, and *she* was the only one who knew or cared if she was okay. She would look out for herself.

And then there was the number one requirement for her man: he had to be rich. It was obvious that everywhere you looked the only truly happy people were rich, and she was dirt poor. That had to change.

Sally saved her money for several months to buy some special clothes. Then she manipulated one of the younger men who was always chasing her to take her to the Lincoln

Club. She had heard people talk about this club, where politicians and big-time executives hung out with their girlfriends. Sally didn't know if that was true or not, but it sure sounded like a place she needed to visit.

Her young date was astonished at the prices. He whispered to Sally, "We've got to get out of here, I'm not sure I have enough money for a glass of water."

Sally gave him one of her amazing smiles, "You go ahead and leave, I'll be fine. Don't worry—if I have any trouble, I have enough money for a cab. Please, just go before you embarrass me."

He gave her a look that suggested she was a real bitch and that if she got killed it sure as hell wasn't his fault. In a totally unnecessary huff, he left.

Sally moved to the bar and asked for a glass of water. She wasn't entirely sure whether they charged for water or not, but she would risk it. Soon Sally had company and a free drink: champagne.

That first evening she met several gentlemen who were close to what she was looking for, but she chose no one. Sally enjoyed some delicious food at the bar, champagne, and plenty of company. When it was approaching time that she felt she should leave, she excused herself, stepped outside, and asked the doorman to call a cab for her. It cost her several days' tips to get a ride home, but it felt like she had made a statement.

Within a short time, she was being entertained by several men who roughly fit her model. She hadn't found the right one yet, but she was confident he was out there somewhere, waiting for her.

CHAPTER 10

Oklahoma City, Oklahoma

It took a couple of days to work out the logistics and circumstances for their trip to New Mexico. Sally could easily get off work—by all accounts she had more real authority at the restaurant than the manager. Pat would collect her and her luggage early in the morning at her apartment, avoiding any issues with her finding the hangar or a spot to park her car. It also meant they could get an early start on their trip. Pat preferred to fly in the morning.

Sally wasn't thrilled with the airplane. She had never flown before, not even on what she called a "real plane," referring to large commercial airplanes with a captain and staff in uniform. This little plane, flown by Pat, was causing her some serious concern.

Pat was a good pilot and took his responsibilities very seriously, especially with a passenger. He let Sally watch as he inspected the plane and did his pre-flight checklist. He told her what everything did and pointed out the safety features that were built into the plane and the flight process. They walked around the airplane together as he inspected it and he took time to explain each checklist item and why it was important. The more she learned, the more relaxed she became, and the more excited about the trip she was.

Pat had filed a flight plan that took them to Lubbock,

then El Paso, and then Las Cruces. Total flying time would be five or six hours. Las Cruces had a small airstrip with no services, so he would refuel in El Paso before the jump to Cruces. He had made arrangements with Emerson, his employee in Cruces, to meet them at the airstrip and take them to the hotel.

He had packed the plane with a lot of snacks that Sally loved, including chocolate, strawberries, cheese, and crusty bread, along with pastries from the bakery at Browns. The stops in Lubbock and El Paso would avoid any embarrassing issues arising from not having a restroom on the airplane. Pat was used to flying alone, but he was looking forward to having Sally's company. He really wanted to impress her, and he was hoping everything would go well.

The first leg of the journey, stopping in Lubbock, was smooth. Sally was chatty and seemed to enjoy herself. After the stop in Lubbock, the air was choppier. This was normal as the morning air got warmer, but Sally wasn't pleased. Pat encouraged her to try to take a nap—that way they would be in El Paso before she knew it. The turbulence wasn't too bad, and it finally seemed to lull Sally to sleep.

The landing at the El Paso Airport was smooth. This was a much larger airport, with both civil and commercial operations. Pat was very focused on what he was doing to make sure he didn't make any mistakes. They taxied to the FBO area and parked the plane as directed by the ground crew. After a bathroom break and refueling, they took to the air again and headed to Las Cruces. This would only take fifteen or twenty minutes, so Pat stayed at a low altitude. Even though this made it a little choppier, being closer to the ground made Sally calmer. She was definitely enjoying the scenery, looking at the mountains to the east that appeared to be higher than they were. She had turned out to be a good co-pilot.

"There's the little airstrip for Las Cruces—do you see it?" Pat was pointing out of the cockpit window in front of them.

"Oh, yeah, I see it. We're getting close. This has been great, but I'm ready to be out of this plane for a while. I bet you are too?" Sally gave him one of her great smiles.

"Yeah, I 'm ready for some libations and maybe some Mexican food." Pat was tired, but he wasn't going to admit it. This trip was right at his time limit for flying. Flying a small plane with visual flight rules wasn't usually stressful, but it was tiring.

Pat lined the plane up with the runway and settled in for a slow descent into Las Cruces. The landing was smooth. The small airstrip was well taken care of and had good markings. He followed some flags that guided him to an area where he could park the plane. As he looked out of the cockpit, he saw Emerson standing by an old car, waving.

Once the plane was parked, Pat told Sally he was going to walk over and talk to his man and she should wait there for a minute.

"Hey, Pat—you're right on time. How was the flight?"

"It was good, Jim—no problems with weather and not very bumpy."

"Great. I made reservations for you at the Meson de Mesilla—they have a great bar and restaurant right in the hotel in case you're too tired to go out."

Pat had heard of the hotel and had been wanting to try it. That was a plus for Emerson, taking the initiative to make reservations. Maybe he was going to work out after all.

"That sounds good, Jim. I need to tie down the plane and lock it up, but once I'm through you can take us to the hotel. I'd like to meet with you in the morning to go over some things, but I think for tonight we'll just stay in. Maybe tomorrow we can have dinner together." Pat still wasn't sure about Emerson—didn't even know if he was married. He told himself he would decide on this trip if this was the right guy or if he should look for someone else. There was a lot of sensitive information he would have to share, so he needed to be sure.

Emerson helped Pat secure the plane and load the luggage into the car. Pat didn't recognize the make of the car, but he thought it might be a late thirties Buick. Anyway, all the luggage fit into the large trunk and Sally slid into the back seat. Pat caught a glimpse of her great legs and wanted to follow her, but he got into the front and carried on a meaningless conversation with Emerson as they took about ten minutes to reach the hotel in Old Mesilla. Emerson never acknowledged or mentioned Sally. What a dumb son-of-a-bitch. Was he blind, or afraid of offending Pat? *I guess that might actually make him smart.*

Old Mesilla consisted of the remnants of an old town right next to Las Cruces, the original settlement in the region and part of the land acquired from Mexico in the Gadsden Purchase in 1853. The United States had bought the 30,000-square-mile region, which included southern

Arizona and southwestern New Mexico, for $10 million, establishing the border between the two countries, and history was all around them. What was left of Mesilla was mostly an old town plaza with an even older church.

The area had become a tourist attraction, with Mexican goods and some of the best Mexican food Pat had ever eaten. The hotel was small, somewhat hidden under towering trees, with a lot of charm—he thought Sally would like the feeling of the place, and she did. The colors were like a festival. Of course, the main attraction for Pat was Sally herself.

The exterior of the Meson de Mesilla lived up to Pat's expectations. It was an adobe structure that could have been in Santa Fe. There were beautiful red flowers blooming around the hotel's entrance, and soft music in the air.

"Pat this place is wonderful. If feels like we're in a foreign country." Sally was enchanted and eager to get out of the car. She explored the hotel while Pat and Emerson unloaded.

They checked in without any hassles. Pat said goodbye to Emerson, reminding him about the next day. Sally wanted to take a bath in the beautiful suite and have a siesta. Pat said he would go to the bar for a quick drink, then come back and take a shower before they went out to dinner. Even though he had told Emerson they were going to stay in, Pat was looking forward to a night out with his beautiful Sally. And he certainly didn't want the evening to be spoiled by Emerson's attitude.

Pat told Sally, "We'll go to La Posta—some of the best Mexican food I've ever tasted—plus some of the biggest and best margaritas in the world. How does that sound?"

"Pat, it sounds wonderful. What was with that guy? He acted like I wasn't there."

The more Pat thought about it, the more he thought that maybe Emerson didn't approve of Sally. He knew Pat was married, and Emerson was probably one of those people who could rob and murder all day long but didn't approve of sexual infidelity. To hell with him.

"I know—not sure what that was about. But let's not think about him. I want you to have a great time. I also know a little place right on the plaza where they play great music that we can dance to—how about that?"

"Are you sure you're okay with doing all of this after a day of flying the plane?"

"Is that an old man comment?"

"Shut up, Pat."

Pat made a little face, then smiled. "Take your bath and I'll be back in a little while. We'll go have some fun—until I collapse. Then you can bring me back and have your way with me."

"Oh, my goodness, how did I ever get mixed up with you? Now go!"

Dinner at La Posta was fantastic. Everything from the décor to the food was authentic. Sally enjoyed her margarita and consumed an unbelievable number of red enchiladas. Pat was right with her on both the margaritas and the food—he had the chili rellenos, a La Posta specialty. After almost two hours of eating and drinking, Pat was questioning the logic of going dancing but, of course, by this time Sally insisted. She felt the music in her feet and was eager to try some of the steps she had been watching other dancers do.

It was a short walk to the El Patio Bar, just a little off the plaza. Obviously not the swankiest of bars, but the music was loud, and the crowd was happy. They settled in and ordered drinks while listening to the music. After a few songs, awareness set in quickly that you can't be in a small plane all day, have a gigantic meal of Mexican food and a prodigious amount of alcohol, and not be close to dead tired. They glanced at one another and smiled. "Maybe we can come back tomorrow a little earlier and try the dancing—that okay?" Pat said with a certain amount of pleading in his voice. He was absolutely beat.

"Sure. I was just about to ask you if we could call it a night. I've had a full day." With that, Pat got one of those famous smiles and he decided it was a wonderful night. They headed back to enjoy a little loving time and some heavy sleeping.

CHAPTER 11

Mesilla, New Mexico

Pat woke up feeling amazingly good. Sally was probably going to be the cause of his demise, but as of right now she made him feel twenty years younger. He knew this couldn't be anything but a fling, but he still didn't want it to end. Lingering in his mind were all of the reasons this was wrong, not only for him but for Sally and Bugs and Mike—Jeez, who was it right for? Knowing all of that gave him pause—but then Sally came in from the veranda and took his breath away. She was beautiful, smiling, young, and alive like no one he had ever known—it was so exhilarating to be with her.

"Good morning, beautiful."

"Well, good morning to you sleepyhead. I was beginning to wonder if you were going to get up before noon or not." Sally smiled, enjoying teasing him as she twirled her skirt and sashayed around the room.

"I tell you what, I feel much better than I would have thought after the day we had yesterday. I want to thank you again for a wonderful day—and night."

"Aren't you sweet? I think this New Mexico air agrees with you, Pat."

"I think you agree with me."

Her smile lit the room as she approached him with a playfully seductive set of dance steps. After a little snuggling, Pat decided he needed to redirect his attention to the things he had to get done that day. He would play with Sally later. Gently easing Sally into one of the chairs in the room, he gave her his schedule for the morning. "Headed into Cruces to meet with Emerson. My guess is that it will take about two hours. After that I'm going to drop by to meet with a new attorney I'm hiring to deal with some business stuff down here for me. So, probably be back by one or so if you want to get a late lunch around that time?"

"That's perfect, Pat. How long are we going to stay in Las Cruces?"

"I think I can finish everything today, so we should head back tomorrow morning. I'm going to meet one of my associates from Texas in Oklahoma City on Friday, so I'll need to get back. I told you it would be a short trip."

"No, that's fine, I was just wondering. I kind of like flying in, doing stuff, and then flying out—like we're big shots."

"Hey, I *am* a big shot!"

"Really Pat, give me a break."

He loved the way she never let him take himself too seriously. Pat really wanted to cancel his meeting with Emerson and stay and play, but duty called. He called Emerson and asked to be picked up in front of the hotel in about thirty minutes. Sally gave him a quick peck and said she was going to sun a little on the veranda—maybe even have a siesta.

After taking a quick shower and getting dressed, Pat got a cup of coffee and walked outside. He really did like it here—something about the air, the mountains, and the friendly people just made it feel comfortable to him.

Emerson was right on time. Pat got in and they headed into downtown to the little office where Blue Devils Development was located. The office included a reception area, two offices, a conference room, and a storage room with a bathroom. They settled into the conference room, which was furnished in a no-nonsense style—just a worktable and serviceable chairs—no wasted money here. Pat liked that approach to business.

"Jim, we've only worked together a short while, and so far, you've done well. You seem to have a real knack for this record-keeping stuff. Also, your dealings with my friends in Juarez have been smooth, and they've said very good things about you." They actually hadn't said much, but Pat was feeling generous. "Coordinating the shipments from El Paso into Oklahoma has gone without a hitch for the nine months you've been overseeing things. All in all, I would say you deserve a promotion."

Jim looked pleased, although Pat still had a problem reading exactly what he was thinking. Jim had been introduced to Pat by an acquaintance in El Paso who had gone to school with him. He had recommended Jim and said he could be trusted—exactly what that meant, Pat was still trying to figure out. The guy in El Paso was someone who knew Pat's Juarez suppliers and they had given the man a good recommendation, which had given Pat the confidence to hire Jim in the first place.

Their first meetings covered what Pat did and how it could be viewed as both illegal and dangerous. Jim seemed to accept and understand that most of the business information would have to be kept quiet.

"I'm going to put all properties and operations under BDD. I want you to be an officer of the company and keep all of the records here in Las Cruces. Obviously, that gives you more responsibility, and considering what drives all of this, also creates more risk for you. With the risk will be more reward. Starting immediately, you'll be vice president, and I'm increasing your pay thirty percent." Pat watched Emerson closely, but saw very little reaction.

"What do you think, Jim, is this something that you want to do?"

"Absolutely, Mr. Allen. This has been a great opportunity for me, and I won't let you down."

Well, at least he said the right things. Maybe this cold fish exterior was a good thing—nobody could tell if he was lying or not. Pat was still not a hundred percent sure, but he really didn't have any options. He couldn't run an ad in the paper: *right-hand man for bootlegger, must be detail oriented, keep his mouth shut, and be willing to lie if necessary—please send resume to Bootlegger Pat.* At this point Pat was comfortable moving forward with Emerson—if it didn't work, he would figure out something else.

"Okay, let's get this working. I'm headed over to Bill Bates' office to discuss some legal matters with him. I'm going to ask him to put together the paperwork for your promotion and then get it back to you for your signature. I think this is going to work for both of us. Just remember to keep me informed, and the most important thing is keep me informed when things go wrong—never hide the bad news—okay?"

Emerson agreed. Pat borrowed Emerson's car and headed over to the attorney's office. Pat had requested on his last trip that Bates put all of his holdings under the umbrella company Blue Devils Development, Inc. All the ownership certificates were in Pat's name. The only officers were Pat and Emerson. And Pat had made an offer on a cabin in T or C owned by a local man whom Pat had met at a dinner party during his last trip to Las Cruces. Bud Johnson was the guy's name and he was in the same business as Pat, sort of, but he was mostly selling booze illegally to the Indians. Pat thought he was a moron.

Pat wanted Bates to finalize the purchase and put the property in his wife's maiden name: Elizabeth Ruth Hall. Pat was not really sure what he was going to do with it, although in the back of his mind he thought it might be a little hideaway he could use after he got out of the booze business. He was thinking maybe he could bring his wife and son to enjoy a real vacation without worrying about being killed or arrested.

This was happening more and more with Pat. He was managing his business activities, and at the same time, he was planning how he would get out. This trip with Sally had been a blast, but he couldn't ignore his increased risk from the Texans, the rumors that the feds were looking to bust up the bootlegging business in Oklahoma, and of course his desire for a slower, more sane life. His fantasies about rowdy adventures were becoming fewer and were more commonly about tranquil family time. He was as surprised as anybody at this turn of events. But then he thought about Sally and decided maybe he would give up rowdy in a month or two—not right now.

After wrapping up his business with Bates, Pat drove back to the office and had Emerson take him to the hotel. He told Emerson he would take him to dinner next time he was in Las Cruces—tonight he was going to bed early. He would have to be up early in the morning to fly back to OKC. He also let Emerson know that he had arranged to have the hotel staff take him to the airstrip in the morning. Pat and Emerson both knew that the dinner wouldn't happen next time—they were both too involved in their own thoughts to notice that neither of them cared.

Pat found Sally resting in their suite. The setting was lovely, and the mood prompted some spontaneous love making. Sex in the middle of the day with the most beautiful woman in the world had Pat smiling so large as to possibly risk injury. He ordered some appetizers from room service and they spent the rest of the afternoon in bed.

Sally and Pat had another great dinner, this time at the hotel restaurant. The hotel staff was extremely attentive and made them feel like royalty. After dinner they went for a leisurely walk around the plaza, music all around them. They decided not to go dancing tonight. Pat appreciated Sally's subtle understanding that he was no spring chicken. She said she just wanted to buy some souvenirs from the shops on the Plaza and go back to the hotel to rest. She bought—or Pat bought for her—a variety of trinkets that all seemed to please her. She even got a couple of things for Pat's wife and son. Sally was a strange contradiction, and Pat found himself always just a little bit confused around her.

As they walked around the Plaza, a mariachi band began to play in the gazebo. The music was enticing, and before long a crowd had gathered. Sally was beaming, and soon she began to dance. Pat stood back and watched—as did several other people. Sally dancing was a joy to all manhood. She laughed as she twirled, and Pat thought he had better step in before she caused a riot—but she grabbed his hand and he danced with her. Soon much of the crowd was dancing to the beautiful, exotic mariachi music.

Pat and Sally danced until her sudden, contagious laugh had them both laughing and dancing and hugging and kissing—he had never felt so alive.

They returned to the hotel and sat on the patio to enjoy the flower-scented night air and have a nightcap.

"Sally, what are your dreams?"

"My dreams? Sounds like a very serious conversation."

"I'd like to know." Pat thought this could be some dangerous ground, but he really did want to know. Plus, he was feeling pretty mellow.

"When I was little, I wanted to get married and have children. I wanted a great big wedding with hundreds of people there—it would have been beautiful." Sally giggled a little. "Then I got older and marriage didn't seem all that good. There were plenty of women around our neighborhood who were married and had kids and they seemed to be miserable. I began to think that maybe I wanted something else."

Pat cautiously interjected, "Yeah, not real sure marriage and kids is all that great for most women."

"Most of the women I saw looked all washed out—like

they hadn't smiled in months. They worked hard all of the time and mostly just got yelled at. That wasn't for me. Now you can't laugh—okay?"

"Sure, okay."

"I decided I wanted to be a famous businesswoman. I know it sounds stupid—so few women are in business. I should want to be a movie star or something. But I don't. I want to move to New York City and live in a tall building and run a major business—maybe something like John A. Browns. Crazy sounding isn't it?"

"It's not crazy. I'm just surprised. I would have guessed movie star—you sure are gorgeous enough. Never would have thought about business."

"I know. Women are stupid—but Pat, I'm not stupid. In school I knew I was smarter than every boy in my class. Now I want to do something that requires me to think, not just be pretty. Hey, maybe I could be your partner?" She began to laugh.

Pat sure hoped she was kidding.

"Sally, you are the most exciting person I have ever known."

"Well, thank you, Mr. Allen. I think you are pretty great yourself." They laughed and went inside to be together.

CHAPTER 12

Las Cruces, New Mexico

Their early departure was rewarded by gorgeous flying weather: a cool morning with no wind made for a turbulence-free flight, first into El Paso for a quick refuel. Taking the same route up to Lubbock, everything was calm and stress-free all the way to Wiley Post in Oklahoma City.

Sally was almost shy when Pat dropped her off at her apartment. She seemed happy but subdued, lost in her own thoughts—mostly, no doubt, they were about Pat and her. The trip had been wonderful, and it felt like their relationship was changing, becoming more serious.

She was going in to work the next day, a Friday, and agreed to go out with Pat to meet his Texas business associate for dinner that night.

Pat drove away from her apartment, also in a thoughtful mood. He already missed her, although he also felt an odd sense of relief to be alone and headed home. Pat was not a complicated guy, but lately he seemed to be having complicated thoughts. He wasn't sure he liked it.

Trying to imagine a life that included Sally was easy short-term, but impossible long-term. He knew she was the most appealing person he had ever been around, but it just wouldn't work. He was an old man, with a wife and child—what was he going to do, run off with Sally? Well, maybe he wanted to—it just didn't make any sense. What was he going to do?

Pat was home by late afternoon, but nobody was there. Mike would still be at some kind of after-school activity and Bugs was probably shopping. He went upstairs and decided to take a short nap.

That evening he had an enjoyable dinner with his wife and son, both of whom seemed glad to see him. He was happy to see them too and gave them the gifts from Old Mesilla. Bugs seemed very surprised by the gifts and gave Pat a suspicious eye but said nothing. Mike seemed only a little interested.

The next day, Pat was occupied with various business tasks that required his personal attention. The first was a collection call to one of his older customers who had not paid for his last delivery. Pat always hated this stuff. Everybody knew what was expected: you paid when the product was delivered. Pat wasn't in the banking business, handing out credit. His old customer begged for some extra time because he was short on cash. Pat made it clear he didn't care whether they were old friends or not—that wasn't the way he did business. There would be no more deliveries until he paid, which of course would put him out of business. And Pat would sell the receivable to his business partners in Texas, whom this customer knew of, and thereafter *they* would handle collections. Suddenly his old friend found the cash. Their friendship was over, but business was business.

He couldn't get Sally off his mind. Pat was still confused by Sally and had no real answers. All he knew was that he couldn't wait to see her. The afternoon dragged on, and then finally it was time. Pat picked Sally up at her apartment for their evening out, and as soon as he saw her, he felt happy. She was ravishing. Sally was so striking—most everywhere she went she turned heads, both men and women. Pat often found himself just staring at her—she didn't seem to mind.

They were headed to the Deep Deuce area. This was the predominantly black part of downtown Oklahoma City. There were lots of clubs and live music in this part of town, and it was an area where Pat had a lot of customers. He always felt welcome and enjoyed the party atmosphere of people having a good time. Sally was very excited about going into this somewhat forbidden zone to meet the Texas Italian, John Giovanni.

Pat had told her about some of the history of the neighborhood. That it had been a distinct section of town since the 1920s. It had become a regional center of jazz music, featuring some of the best big band music of the era, including the Oklahoma City Blue Devils. The name came from a gang of fence cutters infamous in the early American West. The Blue Devils had several prominent musicians, including Lester Young and William "Count" Basie.

The area was mostly black during the day, although at night the clubs attracted a mixed-race crowd. The music was some of the best live music most anywhere—but for damn sure the best in Oklahoma City.

Pat pulled up in front of Trevas Supper Club and handed his car off to the valet attendant. His entrance with Sally on his arm created quite a stir. Most people didn't openly stare, but they watched surreptitiously all the same. The club owner, Willy Trevas, was there to greet Pat and Sally warmly. Willy owned the club, but what many people didn't know was that he leased the building from Pat. This was one of several real estate investments Pat had made in his hometown. Willy immediately showed them into a private room where Giovanni—and a couple of bodyguards—were waiting. To say that Sally made an impression on Giovanni would be a serious understatement. Pat wasn't sure, but John might have been drooling.

Pat and Sally greeted Giovanni like old friends and settled in with drinks and menus. In the background, from the main room, they could hear the Billy Parker Band playing some restful jazz. The mood was full of promise and anxiety. The bodyguards remained standing in the background, never acknowledged by Pat, Sally, or Giovanni, but their presence was felt by everyone.

Their dinners were delicious. The Trevas Supper Club was famous for serving the best steaks in town. Oklahoma prime beef, direct from the local stockyards, cooked to perfection over a huge open pit with leaping flames. The club also featured the largest baked potatoes ever seen, topped with a full assortment of enhancements. Everyone commented on how good the food was and really seemed to enjoy their meal. After dinner, over drinks, Giovanni got to the point.

"Pat, I hope it is alright to discuss our business in front of Sally?"

"Sure, John. After all, Sally's the brains of the outfit."

Sally gave Pat a quick jab, a little harder than necessary. Giovanni continued with a slight grin on his face, "I always suspected there was someone other than you, Pat, pulling the strings."

This little exchange seemed to remove some of the tension, although no one thought they were really being friendly. The bodyguards did not smile.

"Pat, I'll get to the point. I think it's time for you to retire. And I want to help set you up for your retirement years. I'm prepared to offer you a very sweet deal for your Oklahoma and Texas business connections and contacts. How does that sound to you?"

Pat paused. He knew Giovanni wanted his business. He had always suspected the thug would just kill him and take it—buying it seemed out of character. "Well, John, I appreciate the thought, but you know I'm not sure I'm ready to call it quits quite yet." The previous level of tension returned. Not too many people said no to Giovanni.

Giovanni's unhappiness seemed to actually darken his skin. This was a very unpleasant person.

"Let's cut through the bullshit—you know, and I know, I could just take the business and you would get nothing. Or, maybe you would get less than nothing." Giovanni's voice was rising along with a slight flush to his face. "So, let's not pretend there's a decision to make here—you'll sell me your contacts and operations, or things will get real ugly for you."

Pat had a quick decision to make. He could say yes and probably be dead within a month, or he could say no and still probably be dead within a month—maybe even the next hour. He wanted out of the business but dealing with Giovanni was literally a dead end—nobody in their right mind would trust the man. He had to try to prevent Giovanni from taking any immediate action while he figured out what other options he might have—one hell of a mess.

"John, let me cut through the bullshit, as you put it. My business runs smoothly because of the connections I have and the things I do to make it work without a hitch. You can take over the business, shoot me, or whatever you and your goons do—but you wouldn't have a business left. You'd have lost the wholesale business on what you sell to me—which I would think is quite profitable—and you'd have lost the opportunity to take over my business, because if the state thinks you're moving in they'll push to legalize booze. They'd rather deal with the Bible-thumpers and sin than deal with the likes of you."

Giovanni looked more than pissed, and Pat suddenly wondered if he had gone too far. He was a stupid old bootlegger who had just pissed off a serious hoodlum with two pet thugs—he probably deserved to be shot. But Sally sure as hell didn't. What was he thinking?

Giovanni gradually began to smile. "Pat, I like a man who has the balls to tell me to my face to go piss up a rope, but no matter what you may think, we're not negotiating. I'll take over your business one way or another. I'll give you a little time to think about this—but know for damn sure this is not over." The smile was gone. Giovanni got up, picked up Sally's hand and kissed it, gave Pat a look that could have killed, and walked out with bodyguards trailing.

"My god—what the hell just happened?" Sally seemed more than a little upset.

Pat didn't have a good answer. But there was no question things were going to change, whether he wanted them to or not. He tried to reassure Sally that this was just a little business misunderstanding and that everything would work out. She gave him one of her do-you-think-I'm-an-idiot looks. She wasn't an idiot, and he had no idea what was going to happen.

Pat and Sally went to the bar area and had some more drinks. The music softened out the mood, and soon they were dancing to the great music of the Parker band. They tried to forget Giovanni's implied threat, but it hung over their heads.

Pat didn't hear anything from Giovanni after their confrontation. His shipments were still moving. It was business as usual, but obviously what happened that night in Trevas Supper Club wasn't over. Giovanni was a real threat—it was obvious to Pat that the man had no morals and wouldn't hesitate to harm whoever he had to in order to get his way. He was increasingly alert and concerned that Giovanni's goons would show up and start blasting.

Months passed. Pat still saw Sally, though a little less frequently. He was concerned that something would happen to her if she were with him at the wrong time. The business continued to run smoothly, keeping him in high demand. Emerson had proven to be very capable of handling the day-to-day operations from Las Cruces. Pat was still dealing with local officials and making contributions to the local economy. Everything seemed normal, but it wasn't—tension was always in the air. They were waiting on something; they just didn't know what it was.

Pat had given a lot of thought to what he should do. He decided that he wanted out—that was for sure. But he didn't want to get out by being killed. He didn't want to get out and still have to deal with Giovanni or corrupt government officials. If he was out, he was out. He still didn't know how to do that. Procrastination set in. He didn't have answers, so he just waited.

CHAPTER 13

Oklahoma City, Oklahoma

Bugs knew Pat was seeing other women. She didn't know if it was one or many, but she knew it was happening. She could feel it, smell it, and she hated this side of Pat. She knew, though, that if she confronted Pat their marriage would be over.

Bugs had devoted most of her married life to pleasing her husband. Even as a girl, her only goal in life had been to be a wife. Her devotion to her husband was based on her love for Pat and her religious convictions. Obeying and pleasing your husband were in Bugs' nature. There had been times when she did this with an abundance of joy. Lately, though, it had felt more like a difficult chore. How do you continue to love a man who seems to want to be with other women rather than you?

Pat had provided a wonderful home and given Bugs the joy of her life, her son. Her child had become her focus. She could not control Pat, but she could make sure that their son wasn't going to be like his father. Bugs, of course, recognized the conflict she was creating, and because of that she made an effort to praise Pat in front of Mike, but all the while she was bringing up their son to be a devoted husband to whomever he married. She taught him her Christian values and made sure he understood the consequences of failing to meet these standards.

Bugs didn't know the details about what Pat did for a living, other than that he was in insurance, but she didn't believe for a minute that he wasn't doing other things. She had heard the whispers about him being a bootlegger. She just chose not to confront him about it—if he didn't want to tell her then she didn't want to know. Over the years she had never been sure how much of their income had come from insurance or booze. This troubled her, but on some level it was Pat's concern how he supported his family and she wouldn't judge him.

The First Baptist Church had become a source of solace for Bugs. It was a big, impressive church not far from her house. She felt a sense of pride when she saw the church of which she was a member. Of course, Pat had nothing to do with it.

As Mike grew and spent more time in school activities, Bugs had increased her volunteer work at the church. It was where she felt the most comfortable. Much of that was because of the minster, Reverend Todd Jenkins. Bugs and Todd had spent hours and hours together working on church projects. As they had become closer, Bugs had shared her concerns about Pat's activities with women and his bootlegging business. Todd was very sympathetic to Bugs' difficulties. He had given her special one-on-one counseling sessions to help her understand how this could be part of God's plan.

After a while, their relationship began taking on a different tone. They would make excuses to be together. Todd wasn't married, but he had a busy life dealing with the church and its congregation. Even so, he always found a reason to see Bugs. She began spending more and more time at the church. She and Mike often attended evening events, where Bugs acted as the hostess for the event, supporting Todd.

"Bugs, could I see you in my office?"

"Sure Todd." Todd's tone alerted her that something wasn't right. They would often meet in his office to discuss various church matters, but today he made it sound different.

They entered the office and Todd shut the door. There was a small couch on one side of the room and Todd went and sat down. Bugs wasn't sure where he expected her to sit and she started toward one of the desk chairs.

"No, sit here with me. I need to talk to you about something."

Bugs changed direction and sat at the opposite end of the couch. She was becoming nervous, sensing that something was troubling Todd.

"Bugs, you know I'm a man of God—but you must know that I'm also a human being, with all of the faults and desires of any other human."

Bugs was cringing on the inside. She suddenly knew where this was heading.

"For months we've been spending more and more time together. I know you love this church as much as I do—I can see it in the work you do here and in your interactions with the congregation.

"Bugs, you've become more important to me than anything else. I can't stop thinking about you and your miserable marriage. I love you, Bugs. I know I shouldn't be saying any of this, but I can't help it—I want to be with you."

Oh, my goodness, her minister had just said that he loved her, wanted to be with her—what kind of sin was this? Bugs was speechless. She knew this was wrong. She knew she cared greatly for Todd, but not the same as she did for Pat. Why had Todd thought this, what had she done? She began to cry.

"Todd, I'm so sorry. I can't believe you mean these things. You belong to the church. I'm a married woman. Oh my, I'm so sorry."

"Bugs please, I know you're married—but it's a bad marriage. You should leave your husband and I will be here for you. I know it's wrong, but I love you."

Bugs couldn't handle it and ran out of the room. She found her car and went home. It was early afternoon, and no one was there. She knew Mike was still at school and she had no idea where Pat might be. She went upstairs to lay down for a while. She felt all mixed up. The church had been a safe place for her, but it couldn't be that now. It was so sad. She cried some more. After a while she went downstairs and fixed some tea.

Bugs' ambitions in life were small. She knew who she was—a wife and a mother—and that was all she wanted to be. She sure did not want to be someone's lover. It repulsed her. She thought about Pat. She thought about Todd. She knew Pat was ten times more the man than Todd was. It shamed her that she had let Todd think otherwise. She knew why—she wanted someone to pay attention to her, and maybe she wanted to hurt Pat. The phone rang.

"Hello."

"Hey Bugs. Just wanted to let you know I expect to be home pretty early tonight—thought maybe you and Mike might like to go out and have a hamburger, what do you say?"

"Sure, that sounds great. Mike's not home yet, but he never turns down eating out, especially a hamburger."

"Okay. See you a little later."

What was that about? Pat almost never took them out to eat, and usually when he did it was a last-minute sort of thing because Bugs hadn't fixed what he wanted. This was preplanned and seemed joyful. While she was being propositioned by the minister of her church, Pat was planning a family outing—so who was the bad person? Sure as hell wasn't Pat. Bugs started crying again and went upstairs.

Bugs knew she could not go back to the church. It would be too embarrassing. She also wondered if other people had noticed that Todd was attracted to her. She knew what she had to do—she had to devote herself to Pat. She would forgive him everything he had done to hurt her. After all he was just a man, and apparently all men were weak and flawed. She would concentrate on being the best wife and mother anyone could ever be. These thoughts made Bugs feel a little better—she was back in control. She made a special effort to look her best for their evening out.

All of them enjoyed the evening, and Pat seemed to be having a really wonderful time. They went to Johnnie's Grill and had onion burgers and fries. Mike thought it was the best food he had ever eaten. Especially the french fries—with a huge amount of ketchup—and the Coca

Cola, a treat he was seldom allowed. The whole restaurant smelled of onions and wood smoke. Several people came up and said hello to Pat, but he actually seemed more interested in his family than in these business contacts. Bugs felt more and more guilty.

Pat drove them home in the Cadillac with the top down. The whole evening felt unreal—like something from a storybook. Pat carried Mike into the house and up to his room. He came back down and gave Bugs a kiss on the cheek and said he had some office work to finish.

Bugs felt elated. She went upstairs and kissed Mike good night. She went into her room and changed into her most alluring lingerie and got into bed. She fell asleep. When she awoke it was morning and Pat wasn't in bed— it appeared he hadn't slept in the bed at all.

Bugs got dressed and went downstairs. Pat was gone. She didn't know if he had left that morning or the night before. There was a note on the kitchen table.

> *Bugs Honey,*
>
> *Sorry I didn't get to say goodbye. Forgot to mention I had a business trip to Texas. Be gone a few days. See ya when I get back.*
>
> *Pat*

Bugs wondered if she was going insane.

CHAPTER 14

Oklahoma City, Oklahoma

It was time for another trip to Las Cruces. Pat debated with himself about Giovanni's threat and whether the trip put him closer to danger, but decided he had to go. He also decided he really wanted to invite Sally. She had been a little cooler to him lately, no doubt because of the Giovanni incident, but he still craved her company. The trip to Las Cruces would be a lot more appealing if she were with him. He asked her, and while there was obvious reluctance, she agreed to go.

Pat had given more thought to Sally than to his business. He knew he wanted to have Sally in his life, but also knew it was impossible to continue this double existence. He had to make a decision of some kind about the business and about Sally. He needed to get on with whatever in the hell he was going to do. But he was reluctant—he wanted it all and knew he couldn't have it.

Pat picked Sally up at her apartment and they had headed to Wiley Post. It looked like a nice day to be flying, the morning bright and sunny as they became airborne. Pat was happy just thinking about flying, so the moment the plane left the ground was always exhilarating to him. While he understood the concept behind flight, it was still very exciting for that huge, heavy machine to lift off the ground and climb smoothly into the sky.

The flight was uneventful. Sally napped. Maybe it was a way to avoid conversation. They had discussed the Giovanni mess very little and it seemed to hang over their heads. Pat knew that something would have to happen and that his days with Sally were about over, but he hadn't voiced any of this to her. He also knew that she was more than likely thinking some of the same things. Their relationship was now different. They had pretended before that they could go on in this playful way without worrying about it ending, but now they knew it would last only a little while longer.

Pat had been trying to think about all the ramifications of any course he decided to take. He knew a decision could not be avoided. His business had been important to him, and in many ways had defined who he was, but he was ready for that to be over. Add Giovanni's threats, and he was sure he wanted nothing more to do with this kind of life. But the decision about Sally was harder, and he couldn't seem to settle on an answer. He knew what was right, but it wasn't what he wanted.

They chatted during the flight about clouds, about various landmarks they could pick out, and about the remaining time to reach El Paso—but said nothing about what was really on their minds. Once in El Paso, they had a late lunch at the terminal while the plane was being refueled, then quickly lifted off for the short flight to Las Cruces. Emerson was supposed to leave a car at the airstrip with the keys hidden under the seat—not much crime in Las Cruces, so it was probably still there. Sally was relieved that they would have the car waiting so she wouldn't have to be around Emerson again.

Pat was aware that some weather issues had come up around the Las Cruces and El Paso area, but they were just rain showers, so he didn't anticipate any problems. As he approached Las Cruces, though, the weather thickened. Clouds could be a serious problem in being able to get low enough to get a visual on the airstrip and Pat was getting a little worried. He was a good pilot, but he was still an amateur who made a point not to fly in bad weather conditions. He knew he had plenty of fuel and could head back to El Paso or up to Albuquerque if Las Cruces was socked in.

As they continued to Las Cruces, the clouds became too thick to see anything on the ground. "Looks like we may have to turn around and go back to El Paso—don't worry we're not in any danger." His monotone announcement didn't seem to settle Sally's nerves. She was glued to her seat and her eyes never left the cockpit windows.

Once they reach the area above Las Cruces, there seemed to be a break in the clouds. Pat banked the plane over a large clear circle where he could see the ground below. "Sally, I believe we can spin down through that hole in the clouds and land in Las Cruces. This is going to feel a lot more dangerous to you than it is. I practiced just this type of maneuver when I was in flight school. Are you okay with that?" The answer in her expression was *no*, but she said she was—as she gripped the armrests with all of her strength.

The break in the clouds looked like it was closing. If Pat was going to do this, it would have to be now.

"Sally, you're sure you're okay with this?"

"Yes, damn it—do it, I'm ready."

She sounded tense, but Pat thought it was the right decision, so he began his maneuver.

Many planes are equipped with alarms to warn pilots if they're about to stall or if their descent or ascent is too steep. Pat's plane had those alarms, but he had forgotten about them and hadn't told Sally about any sort of alarm. As he was starting the spiral maneuver to spin down into the hole in the clouds, the descent alarm went off. It was loud—very loud and very disconcerting, as it was designed to be—and suddenly, along with the alarm, came the sound of Sally screaming. She had been doing just fine until the alarm started and then—sort of like a dog howling at a fire truck siren—she had begun shrieking in a strange accompaniment to the plane's alarm. Pat concentrated very hard on the task at hand, but the combination of the alarm and Sally's screaming unnerved him, and for reasons he would never be able to fully explain, he started singing his high school fight song.

Alarm, alarm, alarm.

Scream, scream, scream.

"Go team go. Fight team fight."

The spin through the clouds to the tune of this unholy clamor lasted only a few minutes, but it seemed like hours. As the ground began to come up at them, Pat backed off the spiral. They were closer to the ground than Pat wanted, but he still had room to level the plane and line up the airstrip, which was off in the distance about a mile. Once the plane was leveled and lined up, he let out a deep breath. "Son of a bitch—are you okay Sally?"

Sally was wide-eyed, staring straight ahead. After a moment she began to laugh. It was contagious, and within a few seconds they were both laughing. They laughed so hard that it edged toward being painful. And even with the laughter, the landing was silk smooth—best landing he had ever made. They continued to laugh uncontrollably all the way to the plane parking area. Once parked, they simply sat while tears streamed down their faces.

"You know, Pat, I am going to miss you." She gave him a peck on the cheek—and one of her famous smiles. They were both happy to be alive.

They hauled their luggage out to the car. *Where's Emerson when you need him?* Even though the clouds were thick, there was only a slight mist falling. They found the key where it was supposed to be and headed to the hotel. They checked into the same room as the previous time and cleaned themselves up a little. Pat said he needed to run downtown to Citizens Bank to check on something, then would be back in about an hour and they could go get something to drink. Sally reminded him that she hadn't even been to Las Cruces yet and wondered if she could go along for the ride. Pat saw no problem with it, so they headed out to the bank.

Sally was surprised at how small Las Cruces was. She liked the look of it, but there wasn't much here. Although when Pat drove past New Mexico State University it was bigger than Sally had thought it would be. They circled around town some, even though there wasn't a lot to see. At the bank, Sally went in with Pat but waited in the lobby while Pat went into an office to meet with one of the staff. The lobby seemed more like it belonged in a hotel than in a bank, and Sally remembered Pat telling her that the building had housed a brothel many years before. She chuckled at the thought of the same building housing both a brothel and a bank—somehow it seemed appropriate. Sally didn't have a lot of respect for banks or bankers.

Pat quickly completed his business and they returned to Old Mesilla. Having a drink before dinner sounded inviting and the atmosphere of the lobby bar was particularly enjoyable, with its old-world charm. It had a calming effect on their frayed nerves, and they were soon enjoying a more intimate conversation.

Over drinks, Pat told Sally about the cabin he had purchased in Hot Springs, or as it was now known, Truth or Consequences. The cabin was located just outside T or C, on a large lake called Elephant Butte. The name made Sally laugh—he loved it when she laughed. They made plans to go see the cabin the next day. Pat would have time in the morning to drop in on Emerson and sign some papers first.

While it would have been logical to try a new place for dinner, they decided to stick with the familiar, and that meant La Posta—hello margaritas and heartburn. They held hands as they walked the short distance to the restaurant and the evening air seemed especially fresh and wonderful. Maybe the spinning dive in the plane that day wasn't exactly cheating death, but the emotions and the adrenaline sure made it feel that way. They had shared something that gave them a whole new appreciation of being alive and being with someone they loved.

CHAPTER 15

Las Cruces, New Mexico

The next morning, they made a quick stop at the downtown office, where Pat met with Emerson just long enough to read and sign the papers. During this time Sally walked down the street a short way and bought an assortment of Pan Dulce—Mexican sweet breads—at a bakery she had been lured into by the enticing aromas that leaked out into the street.

Bringing the breads back to the office, she sampled some while she waited. The meeting was over in less than an hour, and they headed out to T or C. Once in the car, Pat had some of the sweat bread and, giving Sally a kiss as a reward, declared them to be delicious. The small town of T or C was located about sixty miles north of Las Cruces. Pat tried to make it more interesting by passing along some of the history.

The name had been changed in 1950 when a radio quiz show ran a contest looking for a town that would be willing to change its name to match the show's name: *Truth or Consequences.* Apparently, the town leaders were willing to be bought, or maybe they didn't like the old name, which was Hot Springs. Anyway, they got a lot of publicity and a new name. Seemed kind of stupid to Pat. The publicity dried up quick, while the town was stuck with a nonsensical moniker. He figured they would change it back to Hot

Springs pretty soon. At least the old name had referenced the town's main attraction—other than the lake—which had drawn tourists for many years, coming to soak in its warm waters. Sally loved it when he took the time to make her feel a part of whatever they were doing.

After a quick spin down Main Street, they headed north of town a few miles, toward the lake. Pat gave Sally some brochures about the area he had picked up at the hotel and she began to tell him some of the tidbits of information she found.

"Elephant Butte Lake was created in the early 1900's when a dam was built on the Rio Grande River. At the time, the dam was considered an engineering marvel. The reason for building it was to be able to harness a year-round water supply for agriculture in the Mesilla valley below. The lake grew and shrank over the years as water was siphoned off for agricultural use in the valley. The reservoir allowed much of southern-central New Mexico to irrigate, and thereby grow water-intensive crops in the desert. From this area came the area's world-famous chilies and equally famous pecans. There was great agricultural dependence on the water from Elephant Butte. Hey, I've turned into a tour guide."

"I always had a thing for tour guides," Pat said, reaching over and squeezing her leg.

"Pay attention to where you're going," Sally said, smiling.

The area around the lake was hilly, with rocky outcroppings and some areas of trees and scrub bush. While it wasn't exotic, there was an outdoorsy quality to it that made the area feel different from Las Cruces, as if you were far away from everything.

Following a rough map that Pat had gotten from Emerson, they quickly found the road to the cabin. It led to a slight hill, with an impressive view of the lake below. Pat liked what he saw and felt better having bought the property sight unseen. It had a private, unobserved feeling.

The cabin itself was rustic, but in a good way. It was built from hewn logs, and its two-story structure gave an impression of great size. The logs were impressive and obviously had been hand-worked by skilled craftsman builders. Sally marveled at the grandeur of such a simple structure. There was an impressive wrap-around porch that gave it a very welcoming feel and that came ready with a couple of rocking chairs. After a quick search they found the key hidden where it was supposed to be, below the second step leading up to the porch, and went inside.

The cabin needed a little airing out, but had a majestic two-story layout with a bedroom loft. The massive stone fireplace—which soared to the full height of the cabin, dominating the room—promised a very impressive show once it was fired up.

Pat and Sally unloaded the cleaning supplies they had brought with them and found brooms and mops stored in a closet. Pat thought Sally might not be too enthused about cleaning, but Sally—always a surprise—jumped right in and began sweeping the main room. He might even have heard her humming. Pat opened windows to let in some air, and between them they had the place looking pretty good in a fairly short time. The electricity was working, and the kitchen had all of the necessary appliances, which also worked. It was a great place.

Pat took a walk around the outside perimeter, inspecting the cabin's condition, then came back inside. "Sally, I think I may have bought a bargain without even knowing it." He was very pleased with his purchase and happy to be able to share it with her.

They had brought some groceries along with the cleaning supplies, which they now stored in the kitchen. It was only a little cool, but Pat decided to light a fire for the atmosphere. They had brought overnight bags as well as sleeping bags, just in case they decided to stay, and after examining their handiwork they brought them into the cabin. Pat had an ice chest with some beer and offered one to Sally. They settled down in front of the fire, satisfied with their work and with their surroundings.

Darkness set in. They nibbled on some cheese and crackers that Sally had packed. The fire gave off plenty of heat and before long they were feeling a little drowsy and extremely comfortable.

"Pat what's going to happen with us?" Well, there went the good mood. Pat knew he would have this conversation with Sally, but he would be more comfortable doing it sometime in the future—not right now.

"You're very important to me, Sally. Being around you has been one of the greatest things that's happened to me in a long time. But—you knew there was going to be a *but*—my world is getting ready to change and it could be dangerous." Pat was rambling.

"That doesn't answer my question." Sally wasn't going to make this easy.

"No, it doesn't. Sally, it is hard for me to talk about my feelings. It's just not in my nature. If we could just go on as we have been forever, that would be great with me—I want to be with you and take care of you. The world isn't going to let that happen. Giovanni wants me out, and I don't have too many options other than to give him what he wants. That's one problem, but the bigger problem is us. I'm thirty years older than you. There's no future for you with me. You know that, and I know that. We've had some great times—and without a doubt I love you." Sally listened intently but did not react. Pat was starting to feel like he was not real sure what was happening—his words were coming out without a lot of thought.

"Every day we've been together has been a gift I'll never forget. But it has to end. You need to be with people your own age—not some ancient bootlegger. You need to be around good people, not hoodlums. You're smart and beautiful and your life is all in front of you—not like me, with everything in the past. I want you to be happy."

There was a long pause. Pat had no idea what was going to happen next.

"Pat, you are so full of shit. I see, you're dumping me for my own good. Isn't that just wonderful. We're in the middle of fucking nowhere and you're saying *adios*. Thanks a lot. You didn't mention your wife and kid. Are you dumping them too?" Sally stormed out, slamming the heavy front door as best she could. *Well, that went well.* Pat sat in front of the fire in a daze.

After a while, Pat realized Sally had gone out into the dark and he went out to find her. He found her sitting in one of the chairs on the porch and felt immediate relief that she hadn't wandered off. She was smart as well as beautiful.

"Sally, please forgive me. I should have never gotten you involved in my life. I know you don't want to hear it now—but I love you. I only wish that things were different, but they aren't. We can't ignore the real world. And, yes, that does involve my wife and my son, Mike. I've messed up a lot, and now I need to try to fix some things. You can't imagine how much I'd rather have you in my life—but it can't be that way. For me and also for you. I'm sorry." Pat turned to go back into the cabin.

"Don't go. I shouldn't have yelled at you for just telling me the truth. Pat, you know, most of the time I don't even think about our ages—but you're right, it's there. You've been good to me. You make me feel good about myself. I hate this, but I knew it was going to happen. Just not now." Sally was crying, but just a little. She was sad, but no longer mad. They sat on the porch for a while, saying very little.

It was incredibly dark away from city lights. After a while they started to hear the sounds of birds, mostly owls, as well as other movements farther away from the cabin. They didn't feel threatened, but they became increasingly aware they were not alone.

Pat stood up, gently took Sally's hand, and led her back into the cabin. Their time was almost over. They both knew they loved one another. That night the cabin was full of love and caring—and also dread and fear of what was going to happen next. Once Sally fell asleep, Pat sat down in front of the fire and wrote her a letter. He had said a lot to her that night, and he wanted her to have something from him that made it clear this wasn't just a fling, but something very important to him—and, he hoped, to her. He wasn't sure when, but he wanted her to have this letter from him.

They returned to Las Cruces the next morning and went to the hotel. They made plans to leave the following day for Oklahoma City. Pat told Sally that he had to go to Juarez to meet with his suppliers for the rest of the day. She decided she would just hang out at the hotel, or go shopping on the plaza, until he got back.

The mood was subdued. They now knew how much they each cared about the other, but also knew that it was coming to an end. Sally was still a little weepy but hadn't let Pat see her cry since the night before. She knew that once he left for Juarez she would lie down and cry her eyes out. Pat had become more important to her than anyone else in her life—she couldn't imagine how she would ever fill that void. It made her terribly sad and it frightened her. Sally's sister lived in Chicago now, and, of course there was her brother in Dallas. Maybe she would go see one of them and start over. But her brother wanted to tell her how to live her life—that had been the reason she had left Dallas for Oklahoma City in the first place. It would probably be better to go to Chicago and see if her sister would let her stay with her a while. She missed her sister and wanted to be sure she was okay.

As predicted, once Pat left, she had a good cry and tried to take a nap. She hadn't felt this blue in a long time.

Pat stopped by the bank on the way out of town to add some papers to his new lock box and to withdraw some cash. He was sad and happy at the same time. He knew this was for the best and, after the initial blast, things had gone well with Sally. The trip to Juarez was uneventful. He crossed the bridge and entered Mexico without having to interact with anyone official. He supposed it must be normal, but it seemed odd to have an international border that was so loosely guarded.

There were parts of Juarez he was definitely not going to visit, but the area he was headed for was very upscale. The buildings, cars, and people all looked upper class and very happy. Pat hadn't thought too much about Mexico until he had started to buy some of his liquor there, but it was an odd mixture of very poor and very rich people who seemed to get along without conflict. And by very rich, he meant superrich. His destination was an office building that was classier than any he had ever seen. He hadn't been to many places outside of his little world, but he couldn't imagine a more expensive building than the one that housed Altos Internacional de Mexico. Everything was plush.

Feeling a little like an intruder, Pat entered the posh building, went straight to the receptionist, and gave her his name. Within seconds his two contacts—the brothers, Juan and Francisco Martinez—appeared and greeted him like a long-lost relative. Both gentlemen were impeccably dressed, making Pat feel somewhat shabby. But their greeting was warm and seemed sincere. Pat joined them in a huge conference room to begin their meeting.

Meanwhile, Sally felt better after a short nap. She had gotten dressed and was ready to head to the Plaza to do a little shopping when there was a knock on the door. Not expecting anyone, but without any reason to think she should be concerned, she opened the door.

"Hey, how you doin', Sally?" John Giovanni seemed out of place and frightfully sinister. If she could, she would have slammed the door and run, but he was already partially inside. Sally backed away.

"Pat just left, but he'll be back in a little while if you need to see him." Sally knew in her gut that something was wrong, and that Giovanni wasn't here to see Pat.

"Sally, I need you to stay calm. I'm not going to harm you. I have a disagreement with your boyfriend and, unfortunately, you're caught in the middle. So, you just stay quiet and everything's going to be fine."

As Giovanni finished his speech, his two goons entered the room and shut the door. Sally realized she was in real danger. She began backing toward the sliding door to the outside, but before she could make a move one of the ugly gorillas grabbed her arm and pushed her down onto the bed. The other pulled out duct tape and put it over her mouth, and then they tied her hands behind her back. She started to panic. What the hell was happening? Why were they doing this to her? They flipped her over onto her back on the bed. Oh, my God, were they going to rape her? Oh shit, this was too much. She felt faint.

Giovanni told his goons to stop being so rough. They backed off but didn't look happy about it.

Giovanni bent down close to Sally, "Look, Sally, if you

cooperate this could be over very quickly. I don't want to hurt you, but if I have to, I'll let my boys here have their fun. Do you understand?" Sally nodded her head. She was thinking that if she ever got the chance, she would kill this son-of-a-bitch and the stupid apes with him.

Giovanni and his men huddled in the corner whispering, no doubt discussing what they would do next. One of the men went out of the room. After a short conversation with the remaining one, Giovanni came over to the bed. "We're going to take you out to the car. We're going to put a coat and scarf on you. If you don't cooperate, or if you make any noise or try to run, it'll get real ugly real fast. We'll hurt you Sally—you need to know that's what'll happen unless you do exactly what we say. If you follow our orders, nothing will happen to you. We're going to take you to El Paso, where you'll stay while we contact Pat. If Pat does what we tell him to do, we'll release you to him in El Paso. Sally, for everybody's sake, you just need to do as you're told, and this'll be over soon."

They stood her up, placed a man's trench coat over her shoulders, and belted it around her waist. Then they tied a large, flowery scarf over her head, covering much of her face. There was a knock at the door and Giovanni said that it was his man, indicating that it was time to leave. Giovanni and his goon grabbed Sally and hauled her to the door. They opened the door, where the other goon was waiting. The two thugs grabbed Sally and started out to the parking lot. Giovanni followed behind them. They quickly came to an old limousine, probably from the thirties, with curtains on all of the rear windows. Sally was shoved into the back and one of the goons followed her in. Giovanni got in the front and the other man got in to drive.

Sally couldn't believe it—she was being kidnapped. She knew they would not hurt her for the moment, or they wouldn't get Pat to do whatever it was they wanted him to do. She also knew that either one of the goons would be a living nightmare if he were turned loose on her. She was terrified and royally pissed off at the same time. She started thinking about Pat and what he would do when he found out she had been taken. This didn't feel like it was going to end well. Maybe someone had seen her being taken to the car and had called the police, but that thought seemed more like a prayer than anything else. She closed her eyes and cried.

CHAPTER 16

Ciudad Juarez, Chihuahua, Mexico

Pat had concluded the business portion of his meeting with Juan and Francisco and was enjoying some conversation with the two men. While to say they were friends probably stretched the meaning, Pat felt close to them, both in business and in their personal relationships. The contrast with the hoodlums from Texas was amazing. They were just shaking hands in farewell when the receptionist came in and whispered something to Juan.

"Is he still on the line?" Juan asked the receptionist. She nodded.

"This is very strange Pat—there is a man on the line wanting to speak to you. He has given Maria the message to tell you that this is about Sally and whether you will ever see her again or not—does that make sense to you?" Juan looked very concerned.

Pat felt a panic. There was only one asshole who would even talk like that—it had to be Giovanni.

"Yes, it does Juan. I'm afraid I've gotten myself mixed up with some bad people, and the guy on the phone is one of them. I need to talk to him and find out exactly what he's talking about, but I'm afraid this isn't good."

Juan and Francisco both looked worried. Juan asked Maria to transfer the call into one of the offices. Juan showed Pat into the office and said he could pick up the phone and his call should be on the line. Juan left and shut the door.

"This is Patrick Allen. Who is this?"

"Well, well, how the hell is Mexico, Pat?"

Pat's fears were confirmed. Giovanni, the asshole.

"If you've done anything to Sally, I will track you down and kill you—do you understand me?"

"Pat, why would I hurt Sally? She's a lovely person. It's just that you've decided to put her at risk, because you're too fucking stupid to understand how things stand. You're going to take my offer or see a lot of bad shit happen to you—and everybody you know. Do you understand what's happening here, Pat? You said no to me. I don't like that, so we're going to reopen our discussion about the future of your business. And guess what—you're going to say yes."

"Where is she—have you hurt her?" Pat wanted to scream—to find the son-of-a-bitch and kill him—but he needed to remain calm and try to make this end without Sally getting hurt.

"I already told you asshole—she's not hurt, yet. Two things are going to happen, unless you do what you should have done in OKC and take my offer. One is that your wife is going to learn all about Sally, with some nice photos of the two of you. That's going to be a special moment for her. And two, if you don't do what I want, Sally is going to suffer—real bad."

"You're a real low-life piece of shit aren't you, Giovanni."

"You know Pat I could hang up right now and a lot of bad shit would fall into your lap—so why don't you watch your mouth and let's figure out how we can conclude our business. Okay?"

"What do you want me to do?"

"That's more like it, chum."

Giovanni told Pat to meet him in an hour at an old hotel near downtown El Paso. He wanted Pat to give him the names of all his contacts with local, state, and federal officials, and he wanted to know how much each was being paid. He wanted a list of all of Pat's customers in Oklahoma and Texas. He wanted all the details on Pat's operation in New Mexico. He said Pat would stay in the room where they were meeting until he finished listing everything. Then Pat would sign a document confessing to bribing officials and bootlegging. Finally, if Giovanni was satisfied, he would tell Pat where to find Sally and he could go get her. Otherwise, they would both die.

Pat didn't see a choice open to him, so he agreed but told Giovanni it would take him at least two hours to get there and Giovanni accepted this small change to the plan.

Pat had no idea how Giovanni had known where he was or how he had gotten the phone number. It seemed odd that Giovanni didn't mention anything about the Mexicans—did he not want to mess with them or just think they weren't worth discussing? Pat felt out of his element—he was just a booze salesman, not a gangster.

After thinking for a while, Pat joined the Martinez brothers in the conference room. They were curious and concerned about his phone call. Pat shared everything with them. The reaction was quick and violent. "We know Giovanni—he is the worst kind of scum and extremely dangerous. I cannot believe he would try to take over your operation. He has been mostly unsuccessful in Texas because he sees every business deal as a threat. His idea of taking care of a customer is to shoot him if he is not doing what Giovanni wants."

"Actually, Pat, we may be part of your problem. We have heard, since we have started to sell you some product, your Texas friends have decided that we are getting ready to take over your business and expand into Texas—which is just stupid."

Pat couldn't believe it. Was he caught in the middle of something that he wasn't even aware of?

"Guys, I'm a booze salesman. You knew that when we first met. I'm not running some kind of hoodlum enterprise; I'm just trying to sell some hooch to the folks who want it. It's not my fault these ridiculous politicians appease their Christian supporters with this 'stop drinking stop sin' campaign. I just want to make a little easy money and live what's left of my life in peace."

"We know who you are, Pat—you are our friend. We will help you with Giovanni. We know his kind and what has to be done to stop him."

Pat's head was spinning. The Martinez brothers, two of nicest people Pat had ever met, were now ready to go to war against this evil pile of shit Giovanni because of him—what was going on? There was something missing—what was it?

"Why would they think you were going to take over my business in Oklahoma? That doesn't make any sense at all."

"At one time Giovanni was selling in El Paso, San Antonio, and Houston. Those areas are now being supplied by us. This has led to a small feud between our two organizations. We never had any designs on your business, and we recognize that without you there probably would not be much going on in Oklahoma. Our analysis was that if we took over, or for that matter if Giovanni took over, the officials would move quickly to legalize alcohol and the bootlegging days would be over. Giovanni, on the other hand, probably thinks he can threaten everybody—from the governor on down—and everything will be just fine."

"You know, I was and am willing to let Giovanni have my business. I just didn't want to have to deal with him in maintaining the kickbacks and keeping things running. He misunderstood what I wanted. He can have everything. I just want to be done. No further contact with him."

"Maybe we can help."

Juan gave Pat a slip of paper with a name on it, Manuel Reyes, along with a phone number. Juan said Pat could trust Manuel completely, with his life if it came to that—words that didn't exactly comfort Pat. Francisco had left the room, but now returned. He indicated to Pat that Manuel had been told where Pat was meeting Giovanni and that arrangements were being made. Everything would be ready by the time Pat got to the hotel. The meeting was to be at Hotel Cortez on Mesa at Mills. Pat wasn't completely sure where that was, but Juan gave him directions.

Pat thanked the Martinez brothers and left. Heading back across the bridge into the USA, things were only slightly more secure than when he had crossed the other way. He did have to stop, and a border guard asked him if he was a US citizen. Pat said yes, asking rhetorically where else he would get an Okie accent. The guard waved him through. Juarez and El Paso sure didn't seem to worry much about who crossed the border.

Once across, it was just a short drive into downtown. Pat quickly found Mesa Street and headed in the direction Francisco had indicated. Within a few blocks he found Mills Avenue, with the hotel on the corner. There was parking across the street and Pat pulled in. Sitting there for a moment, he gathered his thoughts, and the pause seemed to calm him. His fears were all about Sally and how horrible he felt that she had been caught up in this mess. He knew it was his fault, and that just made it worse. He was afraid of Giovanni, and of what he might do to Sally—but he was also very angry. He didn't have a gun, although Juan had offered him one. Pat wasn't a gun person, and no doubt would have ended up shooting himself or some innocent bystander. Unarmed and scared shitless, Pat wasn't much of a threat to Giovanni and his goons.

His plan was not about violence, it was about negotiation. Pat had been negotiating all his life, and it was something he was good at. All he wanted was to get Sally out of there and someplace safe—he would agree to anything Giovanni wanted to accomplish that. After that he didn't know what he would do, but she had to be safe.

Pat got out of the car, cut across the street, and entered the hotel. He would meet Giovanni in the lobby. When Pat entered it was so dark, he couldn't see well enough to determine whether anyone was waiting or not. He stood still for a minute to let his eyes adjust. While he was standing there, Giovanni walked up to his side.

"Nice to see you, Pat. If you don't mind let's step over here to see if you were dumb enough to bring a weapon." Pat let Giovanni direct him into the shadows of the lobby. The mobster quickly checked to see if Pat had a gun.

"Stand here and keep fuckin' quiet while my guys check to see if you were followed."

Pat was terrified, but he didn't know what to do. The Mexicans had said they would help but had not told him how or when. He felt helpless and that made him angry. What should he do? What *could* he do?

"John, you need to release Sally now. I'll agree to whatever you want. You can have the damn business. All I want is to get Sally back safe and unharmed."

"Well, that sounds very good Pat. I guess we both want the same thing. I'm sure we can make that happen once we agree on the details and I get what I need from you. And let me assure you, my little escapade with Sally was just to get your attention. She'll be safe as long as you do what you're told, shithead."

In a very ugly part of his primate brain Pat regretted not bringing a gun or a knife—or maybe a big rock. His whole being was telling him to destroy this vile man. But he did nothing, wanting only to get Sally released and safe.

One of Giovanni's men came into the lobby and gave Giovanni a thumbs up, apparently indicating that Pat had come alone.

Giovanni gave Pat a shove and said they were going upstairs. Pat headed toward the elevator, but Giovanni said they would use the stairs. Climbing to the third floor, they exited into a hall. Giovanni told Pat to head to room 308. Pat arrived at the door and waited while Giovanni took out his key. After opening the door, Giovanni pushed him inside. The room was empty. Pat had been hoping that Sally might be in the room—not knowing what he was up to, he was becoming more and more worried about Giovanni.

"Just sit down over here at the desk. My guys will bring Sally to us in just a minute. In the meantime, you need to start writing a list of your contacts and how much each is being paid."

Pat sat. "Listen, John, if you try to strong arm these ol' country boys in Oklahoma, it won't work. They'll either take up arms against you or force the legislature to pass laws to legalize booze. Your tactics won't work in my state."

"Pat, you're a backward hick. Let me tell you something. Even your hick friends will start to pay attention once a couple of them are found dead with no balls."

Well, he might have a point there.

There was a knock on the door, no doubt Giovanni's two goons, maybe with Sally in tow. Giovanni got up and started to open the door when it was suddenly shoved into him, knocking him across the room. Pushing their way into the room were two immense Mexicans. Each one had to weigh three-hundred pounds at least. They almost literally filled up the room. One of them had a gun, which was pointed at Giovanni. Giovanni started to reach into his coat, but one of the giants gave him a backhanded slap across the face with such force that it knocked him against the wall and left him only semi-conscious. They searched

Giovanni and took his gun. Then they taped his mouth shut and tied his hands behind his back.

An elegantly dressed man followed the giants into the room once Giovanni was incapacitated. "Pat Allen, my name is Manuel Reyes—I believe we have mutual friends." He reached out and shook Pat's hand. "Mr. Giovanni's friends are upstairs in room 410. I have two additional men up there with them. Your friend Sally is also upstairs waiting for you—she is unharmed."

Pat wanted to run immediately to Sally, but things were changing fast and he wasn't sure of himself. "Can I go and see her?"

"Let's step out into the hall for a minute." Reyes moved aside and followed Pat into the hall. "Our friends, the Martinez brothers, told me that you should leave now with Sally and return to Oklahoma City. We will clean up this little mess. Once everything is under control, they will contact you. Do you need me to do anything further to assist you?"

Pat wasn't sure he understood what was happening, but at that moment he just wanted to find Sally and get the hell out of Dodge. "No, I don't need anything else. Thank you so much and be sure and thank Juan and Francisco for me."

"Yes sir, I will let them know. Goodbye."

Pat went up the one flight of stairs and entered room 410. There was no one there—except Sally. Pat was so relieved that he excitedly hugged her so hard he thought it might crush her. She cried and hugged him back just as hard.

"Where are the goons?" he asked her. "I thought there were some Mexicans here holding them—what happened?"

"They just left. They told me to stay here, that you would be here in just a minute. The Mexicans took the goons with them. Pat, I have never in my life been so scared. If I ever get the chance, I am going to put a bullet in that asshole Giovanni. Oh, Pat, I am so glad to see you!"

They hugged again, as if they might hang on to each other and never let go. After a while, though, Pat said they needed to get downstairs to the car and get back to Las Cruces. He told Sally that, if possible, they were going to leave that day for OKC.

CHAPTER 17

El Paso, Texas

They practically flew down the stairs but saw no one. They walked through the lobby and out to the street, where they found Pat's car. He took the most direct route to get back onto the highway and headed toward Las Cruces. As they left El Paso, Pat felt both a sense of relief and a feeling of dread. He wasn't sure what was happening. He sure as hell hoped he hadn't gone from bad to worse.

Pat and Sally didn't talk much on the drive to Las Cruces. They were both coming down from a huge adrenaline rush. They needed a nap—or maybe one very big drink.

"Sally, I'm so sorry this has happened to you. I had no idea that Giovanni would be so stupid as to try to hurt you to get to me—it just never crossed my mind. I just should never have gotten you involved in this in any way—I'm so sorry."

Sally just grinned. Pat was a little worried that maybe she had been so traumatized that something had snapped.

"Pat, I know you didn't mean for that to happen. I was scared to death, but right now I feel more alive than I ever have. I think I may have become addicted to these life and death situations, what do you think?" She was smiling. Okay, she *had* lost it. Addicted to life and death situations? This girl had gone off the deep end.

"Sally, I think it's time you find a more normal life—

actually, I think *I* need to find a more normal life."

This struck them both in the funny bone, and they began to laugh and laugh. The release of anxiety had a physical reaction and made them giddy.

After a good laugh the tension was reduced to a more livable level by the time they pulled into the hotel parking lot. They locked the car and went straight to their room. Sally didn't have a key, but Pat still had his. Once in the room, they sat down, and Pat explained what he thought they should do.

"I think we file a flight plan to go up to Albuquerque this afternoon. Spend the night there, refuel the plane in the morning, and then head to Oklahoma City. Does that sound okay to you?"

Sally agreed that she would sleep better tonight if they were somewhere else—hopefully somewhere that no one could find them. She was acting brave, but her nerves were on edge.

While Pat was on the phone filing his flight plan, Sally packed. They would leave the car at the Las Cruces airstrip with the key hidden in the same place as they had found it. He would call Emerson that night and let him know to pick it up.

It would be late afternoon before they were airborne, but they would be in Albuquerque before sunset with time to spare. Pat wasn't comfortable making a night landing, which was why they would stay in Albuquerque before they headed out to OKC in the morning. The Albuquerque airport had an FBO, so Pat called and arranged for the plane to stay overnight, with refueling in the morning, and also gave their ETA. The FBO offered to arrange a hotel room at a nearby hotel and give them a ride to the hotel, then pick them up in the morning. Pat appreciated their customer service.

They loaded the car and headed to the airstrip. The weather wasn't going to be a problem—not a cloud in the sky. They hauled their luggage from the car to the plane and Pat began his pre-flight check list. Sally climbed aboard like an old pro and settled in with her headphones on. Pat's pre-flight went without a hitch. He taxied to the run-up area, tested his gauges, and confirmed the engine's various pressure readings.

Visually checking to make sure there was no one on a path into the airstrip and announcing over the public radio frequency that he was entering the airstrip for take-off, Pat was ready to go. He gave the plane full power, and while the strip was a little bumpy, they were airborne in no time at all. He quickly banked to the right, heading north toward Albuquerque. Both Pat and Sally gave a sigh of relief.

The flight to Albuquerque was smooth and their path took them over thousands of acres of very dense, impressive forests. Sally's old fear of flying had been replaced by curiosity and she gave a running commentary on the terrain below.

The Albuquerque airport was on the south edge of town and it was within sight in less than an hour. It was used by both commercial and civil aircraft and required Pat to follow a set of flight procedures and take directions from the control tower. There was no traffic in the area, so Pat was given permission to land and instructions on taking a direct path to the runway. Making a slow and easy descent, he landed with a bounce so slight it would have made his old flight instructor proud. Once they left the runway, they saw a truck with a flag and sign saying "follow me," which led them to the FBO parking area. Pat secured the plane as the FBO employee helped Sally with their bags. Sally went over to Pat, said "Great landing, captain," and gave him a big kiss with one of those soon-to-be-missed smiles. Pat's knees felt weak.

They checked into the hotel with no hassles. Neither one of them commented on the fact that he had registered them in separate rooms. He was still not sure how to be with her. He knew they cared about each other, but it was important not to make assumptions one way or the other so two rooms seemed like the gentlemanly thing to do. And as far as Sally was concerned, he wanted to be a gentleman.

As they headed to their respective rooms, Pat suggested they meet in the lobby in about an hour to have some dinner, and Sally agreed. Pat called Emerson and told him that the car was at the airstrip. He also said that they would need to talk in a few days about some changes he was going to make. Pat wasn't sure what that was going to be, but one way or another something was going to change. He gathered an envelope he had prepared earlier and headed to the lobby bar.

Pat spent some time alone nursing a drink. All in all, it seemed things had worked out. He had no idea what had happened to Giovanni and his henchmen—and really didn't care. He was still somewhat unsure what to think about the Martinez brothers. Obviously, they were more than just the mild-mannered businessmen he had thought they were—he would have to give that more thought later. Soon Sally entered the bar and he escorted her to a table.

Even after all of the trauma she looked great. He could tell she was very tired, and her nerves were still on edge, but she was smiling. Pat realized how much character there was behind her lovely facade.

"We'll leave for Oklahoma City tomorrow morning. The flight won't be too long—we actually follow Route 66 east to the city. Once we get there, I have no idea what's going to happen. The people who helped us are my suppliers in Mexico. I guess they took Giovanni and his goons somewhere, but I don't know what actually happened." He paused. Sally was paying attention.

"I guess it's possible that Giovanni's still a problem and will show up in Oklahoma City, but my gut tells me that's not the case. I don't want you to worry about this, but you need to know what the risks might be. I think it would be best if you left Oklahoma City for a while, just until we can see what's actually going on."

Sally looked thoughtful but not particularly concerned. "Well, I guess I was thinking along the same lines. I'm not sure I could handle anymore gangster action, with Giovanni or anyone else. I never want to be that terrified ever again. Plus, you and I have things to work out. You have to figure out what's going on with your business, and I think you need to find out what's going on with your family. Me, I need to figure out what the hell's going on with me. I've already decided to move to Chicago and will stay with my sister. I can get a job up there—waitress or something—and lick my wounds a little until I can decide what I want to be when I grow up." That came with a smile.

Pat was sad. He had told her to leave, but that didn't mean he actually wanted her to be out of his life. What a mess. He cared so much about her and now she was going to disappear. He knew he had to be strong or he was going to cause great harm to Sally, his family, and himself. It might be coming a little late since he was in his sixties, but it was time for him to show some maturity.

"I'm sad you're leaving even though I know it's for the best for everyone—especially you, Sally." He pulled the envelope from his coat and handed it to her. "Listen, when you see what's in that envelope, please don't scream at me. I love you Sally, and if we were in a different place in our lives, I'd fight to have you stay and be with me. That's not an old bootlegger's bullshit—it's the truth. But you have to go. You've suffered all kinds of bad stuff since getting involved with me, and I want to give you the means to get started somewhere else."

Sally picked up the envelope and looked inside. She didn't count it. It was a considerable sum in hundred-dollar bills. She stared at him for a while—then began to chuckle. "I see why you were picking your words carefully. The last time you offered me money, I think I threatened to do you in—although, I let you know gifts were okay. Well, Pat, some of my delusions are gone. I need this money, and I appreciate you thinking enough of me to want to help me. I'll just consider this tidy sum as my wages for being a hostage on your behalf."

"You really are an amazing woman, Sally Thompson."

Dinner was pleasant and uneventful. They chatted about the weather, the trip to OKC the next day, the food, the waiter—about anything except themselves or what was going to happen. Each dealt with that subject in his or her private thoughts. Returning to their rooms, they both slept soundly in an exhausted, deep sleep.

CHAPTER 18

Oklahoma City, Oklahoma

The next day brought a glorious New Mexico sunrise. Pat paid the bill for the plane and quickly ran through his pre-flight checklist. In a short time, the plane was airborne and headed into the beautiful sunrise, toward Oklahoma.

Like most early morning flights, there was little turbulence. They took a more or less direct route due east, following the highway, which they could see below. Since they were enjoying the flight and dreading it being over, it naturally seemed to go by quickly.

The landing into Wiley Post was not one of Pat's best, but no one complained. He taxied into the hangar area and waited for one of the field hands to open his hangar so he could park the plane. His Cadillac was parked inside, so they transferred their luggage from the plane to the car—all the while not saying much.

After a short trip to downtown, they pulled up in front of Sally's apartment. She got out and began unloading her luggage. Pat came around to help her. She put her hand on his arm. "I can handle it from here, Pat. I'll just leave the key with the apartment manager and tell him that you'll be by to pick it up. I guess, you know, we should probably just say goodbye and not drag this out."

Sally seemed to be fine, but Pat was starting to tear up a little. "Sally I wish—"

Sally stopped him by placing a kiss on his cheek. "Yeah, I wish things could be different too, but they can't. I'll always remember you, Pat. And our great adventures. Now you need to go. Please."

Pat kissed her gently and got into the car. He drove off without looking back. He sure hoped he was doing the right thing because he felt like shit right now.

The next few days seemed like a blur to Pat. He went about his business without giving it much thought. Bugs and Mike seemed glad to see him, but they weren't aware of all of the things that had happened—it was just him coming back after one more of his business trips. They acted normal, and after he had been home a few hours, started to ignore him, just like usual.

Emerson called him and said he had a message from the Mexicans—they wanted to see Pat in a couple of days and would be in Oklahoma City. Pat called Juan Martinez. He said he and his brother, along with Manuel Reyes, would be in Oklahoma City on Saturday and wondered if they could get together. Pat agreed. They would be staying at the Skirvin, and they agreed to meet in the lobby at about four on Saturday afternoon.

Pat was anxious to know what they wanted, but also reluctant to deal with all the issues of the last week. He knew he couldn't hide from what was happening, and at the same time wasn't very eager to jump back into the snake pit that his business dealings had created. He was now one hundred percent sure that he needed to get out—find a life that would never include the kind of tension he had gone through for the last several days. He had an old acquaintance who was trying to sell his hardware store—maybe that was something he should think about. He knew for damn sure he couldn't sit at home and listen to Bugs assign him home projects.

He didn't know anything about the hardware business, but the store had been in Oklahoma City forever and was an institution— "the best little hardware store in OKC." It would give him a new identity and a place to go. The more he thought about it, the more he liked it. He got on the phone, called the buddy who owned the store, and set up a meeting for the next week. Now the hard part. He had to get out of the booze business—before it killed him.

The Skirvin was an Oklahoma City landmark. Opened in 1911, it was the most glamorous hotel in Oklahoma City, located right downtown on Park Avenue. The lobby alone was worth the price of admission—soaring ceilings with amazing chandeliers. It was elegance far beyond anything most of the local cowboys had ever seen. Pat was in awe whenever he entered.

Walking into the lobby, Pat immediately saw Manuel Reyes. Looking very much at home in the splendor of the hotel, he was sipping something and reading the paper. Pat walked over and Manuel jumped up and shook his hand. "So good to see you, Mr. Pat. Let me call Juan and Francisco and let them know you have arrived."

Pat couldn't help himself; he really liked the Mexicans' manners. For all he knew they might be bad guys—like Giovanni, but more polite—and their next move would be to drop his body in the hotel pool. But there was no question that they sure seemed nicer.

Manuel came back and told Pat that the Martinez brothers wanted him to join them in the presidential suite, where they would be able to conduct their business in private.

Well, maybe not the pool. They would just shove him out the fourteenth story window. They headed to the elevator to ride up to the top floor.

The presidential suite was something to behold. It looked like something out of a movie and it was a little hard to believe that he was still in Oklahoma City. The Martinez brothers greeted him and seemed genuinely glad to see him. There was a large, round table in the middle of the room, and they all took seats.

"Pat, we are so sorry you and your lovely companion had such a bad time in El Paso. We feel especially bad that you had been in town to see us."

Pat said he appreciated their concern. In some ways he was reluctant to ask, but it would seem odd not to inquire about Giovanni. "Do you think Giovanni will give up trying to get my business, or is he still out there waiting?" He was nervous and it showed.

"Mr. Giovanni will not be bothering you any further, Pat. You can just forget about him."

There was a tone to that statement that led Pat to believe that he shouldn't make any further inquiries about Mr. Giovanni.

"Pat, you have been a good customer of ours for many years, and we have appreciated your business. During some of the recent unpleasantness you indicated that you were ready to sell and that all you wanted was to be left out of any future business dealings—isn't that correct?"

"Well, yes, Juan. That's what I was thinking when I had Giovanni threatening me. Time for me to retire and enjoy my remaining years—why, what are you thinking?"

"We would like to buy your business."

Pat was a little stunned. He wasn't sure what that might mean. "Well, I am a bit surprised. How could you guys run the business in Oklahoma?"

"Our friend Manuel Reyes will be the manager. We are going to ask you to assist us in a transition for maybe six months or so—and then maybe be available if we have questions. We are not the hard-nosed type of businesspeople like Giovanni. We believe that customer service and a good product will work better than strong-arm tactics. We will not come in here and try to disrupt things. We will want everything to stay very much like it is now. Manuel has spent a lot of time in Oklahoma and has many relatives in the bar business here and in Texas—we think he will do an excellent job." Sitting at the table Manuel just smiled.

"Sounds like you've thought this through. My main concern is that we don't turn this into a booze war in the state."

"Giovanni was a thug. He didn't know how to do business except by threatening and hurting people. I hope you know, Pat—we do not do business that way. The last thing we want is conflict. We know that we need to keep paying the cost of doing business with the fees you are paying to the officials. We need your help to make a transition. But we guarantee you that if anything goes wrong, we will not cause problems. If for some reason it turns ugly, we will just pack up and head home—we will not drag you or anyone you care about into any kind of violence."

"You've both always been fair with me, and I trust you. I'm agreeable in principle to sell you my business. How about the details?"

"Could it be we are talking about money?"

"Yeah, it could be." Pat was grinning.

"We are going to take your business in good faith with the expectation that we will be able to continue operating the system that you have built over the years, so it makes sense to pay you out of what comes in the future. We propose paying you five percent of the gross revenues for five years. And, let me mention, that we feel we can expand the business from where you have it today. That could be a lot of money, Pat, for your retirement."

Wow. Pat was quickly calculating in his head. Wow. Without much effort, Pat would reach over a million in that span of time. This was better than anything he had thought.

"I probably owe you my life—and the life of my friend, Sally. This deal is almost too good. Are you sure you want to pay me this much?"

Juan and Francisco laughed. Manuel smiled—he probably thought it was too much also.

"Pat, we will make a handsome profit from what you have built here and in Texas. Plus, we want your goodwill. We want you to be willing to assist us in the transition and also to have a vested interest in helping with any problems that might happen in the future. We think it is a fair price.

We appreciate your attitude and think we can make very good business partners. We are ready to do the deal, are you?"

"Yes!" Pat was joyously happy. If only Sally were here to help celebrate. He couldn't call his wife—she wouldn't even know what it was they were celebrating. He just sat at the table, grinning.

They sat around the table and discussed details of the deal. Pat told them that he owned buildings in Oklahoma City, El Paso, and Las Cruces. He would continue to operate that part of the business. They said they had understood all along that the buildings would not be included in any deal. They agreed that a handshake was sufficient to close the deal. They would follow up with a vague legal document that would give them both some protection against anyone changing their mind and from any misunderstandings that might come up.

Pat told them about the buildings he owned in Deep Deuce, and they agreed that they would send Pat's share of revenues to him each month at the address he provided them in Deep Deuce. He suggested they celebrate this new beginning at Trevas Supper Club, one of the buildings he owned, and they agreed.

Trevas Supper Club was rocking with a new jazz band from Chicago. They entered, and Pat and his friends were treated like royalty. The dinner was one of the best Pat had ever had at Trevas. His guests were impressed and seemed to enjoy the music. They were not a rowdy crowd though. His new partners were much more laid back than Pat was used to, but they had a very enjoyable dinner together and then he left them at the hotel at a very early hour. They agreed to stay in touch to finalize any last-minute issues. He and Manuel Reyes agreed to meet Monday morning at the hotel to begin the first steps for the Martinez brothers to take over Pat's business. Pat was elated.

The next week Pat spent quite a lot of time with Manuel, and he was very impressed with the man's understanding of the bar business, as well as his rapport with the customers. Pat didn't care much about people's ethnic backgrounds, so he hadn't really paid attention to how many of his customers were Mexican, but it was more than he would have guessed, and they warmed up to Manuel immediately.

The first month passed and the paperwork was signed. Pat spent less and less time with Manuel, and after only a month he was starting to think that his sense of being indispensable to the business had been exaggerated. In another month they might not remember his name.

Pat had contacted Willy Trevas and told him that he was expecting personal shipments of supplies to arrive at the restaurant on a semi-regular basis. When a shipment came, he requested that they place it in the basement and then to let him know it was there. Good news came quickly: within a few weeks he was notified of the first shipment. In the future he needed to think about how to handle these deliveries, but for now this approach would work.

Pat drove over to Deep Deuce to see what they had sent. He always got a kick out of taking his Cadillac into the Deep Deuce—it created quite a stir of envy. But lately he had been thinking about getting something a bit lower key. Maybe a Ford. He parked in an open spot and went into the building. The shipment had been placed in the basement.

The crate was well sealed and indicated on the outside that it contained restaurant supplies. Once Pat was alone, he broke it open—and could not believe his eyes. Stacks and stacks of bills, mostly hundreds and twenties. Exactly how much, he really didn't care—it was a lot, and in only one month. He was going to have to figure out a way to keep this secure. He had some ideas, but he needed to get it done soon because it looked like the Martinez commissions could add up quickly.

Pat had purchased two buildings in Deep Deuce. One was the building leased to Willy Trevas for his nightclub—the other was a vacant building next door. He had bought the one next door for pennies on the dollar because of its history. He thought that Willy might want to expand into the vacant building, but that hadn't happened. The vacant building was going to be his solution to the need for a more secure location for his commissions.

The second building had at one time been a high-class hotel. In the 20s it had been one of the nicest small hotels in Oklahoma City—and one of only a few where blacks were welcome. Over the years it had fallen on hard times and operated as a brothel for a while. The police had the property closed when they discovered that a major drug running operation was headquartered there. Since then the city had denied all building permit applications for renovations to it, and it had remained vacant. When Pat purchased it, he had thought if he found a tenant, he would be able to handle the political battle—but no tenant had emerged, so he had just left it vacant. Now it would be a perfect place to store his fortune.

CHAPTER 19

Oklahoma City, Oklahoma

Sally was alone and pregnant. She could have told Pat that she was pregnant, and he would have done anything she asked, but it would have been wrong. She loved him more than anyone she had ever known, but she couldn't trap him with a baby.

A smartass might say she had some sort of father fixation on Pat. Well, maybe. How the hell would she know? What she knew was that he was funny, kind, generous, and cared about her a bunch. If he had asked her to stay and just be his mistress she would have done it in a heartbeat, but of course there would have been the child.

She did not hate his family—she didn't know them, so how could she hate them? —but she hated that they seemed to take him for granted. Sure, he was the one out chasing girls. But that didn't happen unless there were problems at home. Maybe Bugs—what a stupid name— was a cold fish or something. Sally sure knew Pat was a wonderful lover, but maybe Bugs hated that stuff.

Sally had called her sister, Molly. How had her mother come up with these names? Sally told her she was driving out the next day and would call her when she got to Chicago. Her sister didn't sound thrilled.

God, I wish I had a better option. Sally was dreading starting over. She had the money, and she could live on her own, at least for a while. But she needed a quick place to stay to give her time to sort out her next move. And she was pregnant. Sally had not mentioned that to her sister—she was afraid Molly might not want her to come. She had a big decision to make, and she needed her sister's support. But her sister had always seemed to be a little more like Hank than Sally when they were growing up, so who knew how she was going to react?

At least she was leaving Oklahoma City with a hell of a lot more than when she had arrived. Sally spent a large portion of the day packing her car. She thought about Pat a lot and had a few crying breaks. She had a lot of clothes now, as well as many other things he had bought her. Each thing seemed to have a memory attached to it, so it was a slow process with all the emotional breaks she took.

Once she had the car loaded, she went back to the apartment and looked around. This had been home for a while, and she had been wonderfully happy. It was hard to think about what was next without feeling like it would never be this good again.

She had a restless night and woke early. After fixing coffee and toast, she sat at the small kitchen table with a map and planned her route. She was going to take as many as three days to reach Chicago. She knew it could be done quicker than that, but she really wasn't in a hurry.

Sally had never driven anywhere, like a family vacation or anything, and she was excited. She would head out early in the morning and probably stop in Springfield, Missouri. Her plan was to stay at inexpensive motels along the highway, just as if she were on a vacation.

Her car was a 1953 Chevrolet Bel Air, which Pat had bought brand new. It wasn't as snazzy as his big ol' Cadillac, but Sally loved her car. She washed and waxed it almost every week—giving the teen boys in the neighborhood quite a treat. The car was light blue, with a dark blue fabric interior. She felt very sophisticated driving in her new Chevy.

Before she left, she locked up the apartment, went by the manager's unit, and left the key in his mailbox with a little note that Pat would pick it up. For a moment she just stood on the manager's porch, as if she weren't sure what to do next—than she snapped out of it and headed toward her car.

Once she got moving, she started to feel better. The first part of the drive took her up to Tulsa. What she saw of it seemed different than Oklahoma City—greener, and maybe cleaner. She kind of liked what she saw. It crossed her mind that maybe she should just stop and find a place here. Did she really want to go live with her sister? Of course, the answer that always came back to her was: you're pregnant. She was going to need help and she didn't know anyone who lived in Tulsa. *So, keep driving.* She did.

After Tulsa, the landscape started to change to hills and tall trees. She had not realized that Oklahoma had places with mountains, but there they were. Not quite Rocky Mountain peaks, but a lot more than she had ever seen in Dallas. She was enjoying being a tourist.

She could not help but think about Pat as she drove. She thought about the first time he had offered her money and how she bit his head off, or the time he sent the plane into a dive through those clouds—was he crazy or what? Then, of course, her kidnapping experience with that hoodlum Giovanni. Even now the thought of Giovanni gave her chills. What a creep that guy was. But mostly she thought of Pat and smiled. She loved him so much.

She got to Springfield while it was still daylight. She debated continuing since she wasn't tired. A road sign said that a place called Marshfield was about thirty more miles ahead and had five motels. She decided to continue on that far. It turned out that Marshfield wasn't much, and there were now only four motels. One of those had been boarded up, one she wouldn't go near, which left two. She arbitrarily selected the Traveler's Inn.

Pulling into the lot, Sally saw the office just ahead. She went in, but there was no one there. "Hello." No response. She looked for a bell or something but found nothing. After waiting a few minutes, she left. She got back in her car and headed toward the Rest Haven Court. Once again, she pulled into the lot and went into the office. As soon as she entered: "Well hello, dear, looking for a room? You aren't traveling alone are you? Gracious, dear, you better be careful. Now let's see what we have available." All of this came from the most pleasant-looking woman Sally had ever seen, although she was rather large. She looked like an image an artist would paint of a grandmother.

"Thank you very much. I am traveling alone—I'm meeting my husband in Chicago." Sally knew it was wrong to lie, but sometimes it just made things easier.

"I just got into town, and for no particular reason I pulled into the Traveler's Inn, but no one ever came out to help me, so I decided to come over here."

"You're talking about Beth Higgins. She and her husband own the Inn. They both have a drinking problem, so after five sometimes it's a little hard to get their attention. Then—if you can believe it—she'll complain and moan about not having enough guests. My lands, the poor woman just doesn't seem to have good sense."

"Here we go dear. Room number twenty-four was just cleaned this morning by my granddaughter. She does a better job than Patsy, who normally cleans. But Patsy's always sick. How can you keep a job if you're always sick? I have no idea."

"Well, I'm sure the room will be very nice. Thank you so much. How much will it be for one night?"

She gave Sally the price. Maybe she should just stay in Marshfield. At these rates she could last a long time on her "Pat money." She could even offer some cleaning competition to Patsy. No, not a good idea.

"That sounds very reasonable. Also, is there a place around here I could get a bite to eat?"

"Of course, my dear. This here is the highway. If you go down to the next street and turn left, that's going to be Main Street. Just go about a block and on the right will be Jackson's Diner—best food in town."

Sally thanked her again and paid her bill. She pulled the car around and parked in front of number twenty-four, then unpacked just a few things for the night and left everything else in the car. She followed the directions to Jackson's Diner, where she was greeted warmly and enjoyed what amounted to a home-cooked meal of fried chicken and mashed potatoes.

Sally got unwelcome stares from a couple of farm workers, but she ignored them. As she was leaving, one of the jerks made an offensive remark.

"Man, that is one goddamn sweet ass on you baby. Maybe you'd like to show me more? What do you say, sugar?" The moron smiled to his friend like he had said something clever.

Sally walked over to the lady who had greeted her when she arrived and asked if they had a police department or a sheriff's department. The lady looked a little surprised at the question but told her there was a sheriff's department. Sally asked if she would call them. The jerks got the hint and left.

Sally waited for the sheriff's deputy. He arrived in a matter of minutes. Sally told him what they had said and that it concerned her. He asked her where she was staying and told her that they would make sure the clowns didn't cause her any problems. The deputy went on to say that they were harmless little punks anyway. He seemed to want to talk further with Sally, but she excused herself and thanked him for his help.

She returned to the Court and entered her room. She had dealt with men like the guys at the diner her entire life and was getting sick of it. She knew her good looks had helped her a lot in life, but sometimes it was just exhausting. She forgot about the incident and slept well. In the morning she woke early and repacked her car.

Sally decided she needed a good breakfast to start her day of travel and went back to the Jackson Diner. The same lady was working and greeted her like a long-lost daughter. It was a very warm feeling. Sally enjoyed the best breakfast she had ever had—if the Jackson Diner *wasn't* the best food in town, she'd like to try the place that was.

She got back on the highway and headed off toward St. Louis. As she drove, she could see a large area of forest off to her right. She couldn't judge just how big the area was, but it had to be huge. She drove from one little town to the next, most of them looking a lot like the one she had just passed through. Of course, the people living there would have disagreed, but from Sally's perspective they all seemed the same.

The trip had been fun, and she was getting to see a lot of things, but she was still very worried. She kept thinking of Pat and what would happen with him and his family. Then she would think about herself and how she would manage a child. My goodness, a child. Sally almost couldn't think about it—it was just too big. Sometimes while thinking she would get so upset and frightened that she would have to pull off the road and calm herself.

The emotional breaks were slowing her down and she willed herself not to take these short crying sessions on the side of the road anymore. With determination, she kept herself on the go and started making good time. She decided to stay in a larger motel this time, one that had a restaurant. She found a Holiday Inn on the north side of St. Louis and checked in. The room was nice, and it felt safer to eat in the motel than to have to go out. She rested well and was up early again in the morning.

Sally had called her sister but hadn't reached her. She

had Molly's address, but she wanted to make sure everything was still okay for her to be there today.

On the road, she tried to stop worrying about her sister and just enjoy the scenery. As she got closer to Chicago, the traffic got a lot heavier. She knew Chicago was a big town, but maybe she hadn't realized how big. Everything slowed down. It was going to take some time to get to downtown where Molly lived.

Sally exited from the highway and followed her sister's directions to the neighborhood. As she drove around looking for the street, she was astounded at how bad the whole area looked. In Dallas she had always thought they lived in a slum, but it hadn't been nearly as bad as this. She was getting nervous.

She found the right street and, she thought, the building in which Molly had an apartment. She parked her car and locked it—though it still didn't feel safe. After a little hesitation she went into the building and located apartment number 210. Sally knocked. The door was opened by a very thin, shirtless teenager with a serious acne problem. "Who the hell are you?" Ugly and a moron.

"I'm looking for my sister, Molly—is this her apartment?"

"Her apartment—that's a good one. This is my apartment and sometimes she stays here." Well shit. This was not what was supposed to be happening at all.

"Is she here?"

"Nope."

"Do you know where she is?"

"Yep."

Sally had no idea how the guy had lived this long, but she was about thirty seconds away from helping all humanity by killing the little shit.

"Look. I'm her sister I'd like to see her—if you know where she is, tell me—*now!*"

"Hell, you don't have to get upset. She's at work. Ed's Deli, just around the corner. My god you're just as nuts as she is."

Sally left. She had come here to get support from her sister, but it looked like Molly was the one who needed some help. She couldn't believe that her little sister was living with that creep. Sally quickly found Ed's Deli. Molly was busing tables.

"Molly."

"Oh my god, Sally. Why didn't you call and let me know you were going to be here today? I would have taken off work or something. Oh my God—you look great." They hugged.

Molly asked the guy behind the counter, no doubt Ed, if she could talk to her sister for a minute and he said yes—a very generous sort.

They chatted a while about how her trip had gone and how she had been. Sally asked Molly if she was staying at the address she had for her and living with the guy she'd just met there. Molly acted a little sheepish, but said she was. Sally told her she was going to get a room somewhere and asked if Molly could come there and meet with her. Molly said she couldn't—that if it was close, maybe, but she didn't have a car or much money.

After more we-are-getting-nowhere discussion, Sally

asked the man at the counter if there was a reasonably priced hotel close by. Turned out there was what he described, a very nice hotel about two blocks down the street. Sally talked to Molly, told her about the hotel, and that she was going there now to see if she could get a room. Sally wanted her to call the hotel in about an hour and ask for her room and they could make arrangements to meet. If she couldn't get a room, she would come back to the deli.

As it turned out, it really was a nice hotel and Sally had no problem getting a room. The two blocks seemed to make a significant difference in the overall feel of the neighborhood. Sally was able to park her car in the underground hotel parking. Molly called, and they decided to meet at eight that night—Sally told her not to bring her boyfriend.

They met in the hotel lobby, then went up to Sally's room rather than the bar or restaurant. Molly wasn't dressed very well. They talked a lot that night, and Sally began to realize that Molly was in need of a big sister. It made her sad, but also it got her mind off of herself, which was good.

Over the next week, Sally found a very reasonably priced apartment in a nice neighborhood not far from the hotel. She asked Molly to move in with her, but Molly hesitated. Of course, Molly thought she loved the skinny jerk—although in time she did move in with Sally. Sally purchased some used furniture and a couple of beds and got the apartment looking respectable.

Sally also had found a job as a waitress in one of the upscale restaurants downtown. She knew how to wait tables, and after a couple of weeks her tips were covering Molly's and her living expenses. She had spent a good chunk of the "Pat money," but not all, so she was feeling good.

Months went by, and she and Molly got into a good routine. Molly was still working at Ed's, but she wasn't seeing the skinny creep any longer. She was taking better care of herself, and she was being noticed by a better class of creep.

As happens in life, though, it didn't stay good for long. Sally started feeling bad. She was only showing a little, but there was no doubt in her mind that it had to do with the baby. She went to a doctor, who said he couldn't find anything wrong with her. He recommended that she stop working and just rest. Thanks a lot Doc.

Sally missed work more and more because she was ill. At first the restaurant manager was very supportive—after all, she was his most popular waitress—but soon he said he was going to have to hire someone else if she couldn't work more often. Then he fired her.

Calculating how much money she had and what they were spending, Sally figured she could stay home and rest for the last month or so of the pregnancy, and then once she had the baby she could go back to work. She also thought she could call Pat. She decided she would never put the child at risk, so if she had to, she would call Pat—she also knew he would want her to. Once she had decided what to do if worse came to worst, she stopped worrying about money.

Sally spent most of the last month in bed. She didn't

know what was wrong, but she knew something was—and she was scared. Molly seemed more attentive. She stayed with Sally as much as she could and only left to go to work. She and Sally became close again.

"Sally, how are you, can you hear me?" This was from a doctor that Molly had called after she couldn't get Sally to respond to her. Molly was terrified. The doctor examined Sally.

"She's not in good shape. She needs to go to a hospital. I'm going to call an ambulance and she'll be taken to St. Joseph." He went to the phone and, in a very businesslike manner, called for an ambulance.

"What's wrong—is she going to lose the baby?" Molly was almost hysterical.

"I really don't know what's wrong with her at this point. They'll have to do some tests at the hospital, but she's very sick. I'm very concerned for her life and the life of the baby."

About that time, they heard the ambulance siren. Sally was rushed to the hospital and immediately placed in intensive care—out of concern for the baby, the nurses told Molly.

Molly stayed at the hospital for three days, never leaving. She slept on benches and chairs in the waiting room, almost mad with worry. The nurses were very kind to her and kept her informed about Sally—the doctors just seemed to ignore her. She was told that Sally had some kind of an infection and that the baby would need to be delivered soon or it might not live.

On the third night, the baby was born. Surprisingly,

the doctors and nurses reported that the baby was by all accounts a very healthy girl. Whatever was ravaging Sally seemed not to have affected the little girl's health.

Sally went into a coma.

Molly continued to live at the hospital. She thought about the things she and Sally had talked about over the last few months. They had talked about their names and wondered how their mom had come up with them. Sally had told Molly that if her baby was a girl, she was going to name her Michelle, and if a boy Patrick. They had giggled about how Michelle sounded so much more "sophisticated" than their own names. They didn't discuss the boy's name much. Sally had also told Molly that she hoped it was a girl since she wasn't sure she knew how to raise a boy.

The baby was well taken care of by the nurses, with help from Molly, and after two weeks Molly took the child back to the apartment. She was doing her best every day to do what she thought Sally would want her to do. She had matured years in a matter of months.

Sally stayed in a coma for almost two months and then she died. Everyone at the hospital was immensely affected by the untimely death of this beautiful woman—it made no sense at all. The tears were real.

Molly did the best she could for a few months, but when the money Sally had left was almost gone, she had no choice but to take baby Michelle to their brother in Dallas. She was sorry, and hoped Sally would forgive her, because she loved Sally and she loved Michelle.

CHAPTER 20

Oklahoma City, Oklahoma

It had been almost a year since Pat had purchased the hardware store. It was a different kind of life. There was a routine to the operation of the store that was comforting to him. He would open the store by seven every morning, Monday through Friday, and immediately have a few customers, often regulars from the immediate neighborhood.

Pat would have coffee made, and the regulars would stand and sit around the store discussing the topics of the day—usually politics and weather. They were all elderly men and most of them lived alone, and these morning sessions in the store were the most important part of their day. They had also been the source of most of his knowledge about how to operate the store. As a group they had been observing the ebb and flow of the business for many years. If Pat had a question, this was his resource team.

He hadn't had any contact with the Martinez operation. They continued to send crates of supplies like clockwork, but they hadn't needed him to handle any business matters. While Pat was pleased that the transition had apparently been smooth, he was actually a little disappointed that he hadn't been needed to solve some sort of problem. But he would never complain about the Martinez brothers—they were honoring every aspect of their agreement with him.

Pat stayed in the store most days. He had a few employees who helped run things and, of course, his son Mike was a big help. The store closed every day at five, just as it had for years. Pat knew he would have a lot more business if he stayed opened longer hours, but he didn't want to. Maybe the next owner would have to, but Pat was fine with closing and going home for dinner.

Since retiring from his bootlegging business, there had been only a few days that Pat hadn't been in the store. On one of those occasions he had flown himself to Dallas to meet with some new attorneys he was hiring.

When he got in the plane, he thought he could still smell Sally's scent. He sat in the cockpit for some time and felt a huge sadness overcome him. Most days he didn't think about her, or at least not much. It had been over a year since he had last seen her, and the pain was still strong. It seemed to Pat an odd thing for an old man to have such strong feelings—that was something for young people. But he hurt and he missed her greatly.

During most of his working days at the store he stayed busy with customers and stocking and didn't have much time to dwell on what had happened. Sitting in the plane, it snuck up on him and for a moment it overwhelmed him. He got out and went through the pre-flight check list. He knew this would be his last time flying the plane. While he loved it, he was getting close to the age where it would be difficult to get his license renewed, so he listed it with an aircraft broker. He had received two offers and was going to take one of them as soon as he came back from Dallas. Plus, it just wasn't that easy to be gone anymore—he was now expected to be home every day.

One of the ground crew helped him pull the plane out of the hangar. He finished his checklist and taxied out to a warmup area. He was cleared for takeoff almost immediately. Powering the plane down the runway gave him a thrill that had been absent from his life for a while. The plane jumped into the air with tremendous power, and in that moment, Pat didn't feel old at all.

The flight to Dallas was smooth for the first half of the way and bumpy the last half. His landing was textbook, although there was no one to see how well he did. He parked the plane at the FBO and took a taxi to his meeting with the attorneys.

Pat was making some arrangements for a variety of things that would need to be handled once he was gone. He had a plan, but he didn't know if it would work. The law firm had a reputation for being discreet and knowledgeable, and they had drafted the necessary paperwork for his signature with practiced ease, as well as providing him with funding instructions. Pat had great confidence that they would carry out his wishes as instructed, but it still felt odd relying on someone to do something after you were dead.

The flight back to Oklahoma City was smooth, and the plane was running great—he was definitely going to miss it. About halfway to OKC he started thinking about the time he and Sally had made the spin maneuver through the hole in the clouds in Las Cruces. Now, all alone and thousands of feet above the ground, he started laughing. He laughed until he cried, and then he just cried.

Pat made an okay landing at Wiley Post—definitely not one of his best. He parked the plane in the FBO parking and left instructions with them to clean it up, service it, and then turn it over to the broker, who had an office in their building. He wasn't going to be flying anymore.

Sitting alone that night in his home office, sipping a little Wild Turkey, Pat wondered if he had done the right thing. He knew he was right to have gotten out of the bootlegging racket before he got killed, and he knew spending more time with Bugs and Mike was right, but he wasn't sure about Sally. He didn't want to be old and he didn't want to not be with Sally.

In a crazy moment, maybe fueled by the Wild Turkey, he thought he had to see her again. Tomorrow he would find out where she was, and he would go see her. He felt elated just thinking about it. In the middle of the night, he sat alone, grinning at the thought. Why couldn't he be with Sally? He loved her so much.

The moment passed. He knew why—it would ruin her. He had to be strong for her. And he was.

The routine of that first year at Allen's Hardware became the routine for every year thereafter. Not much changed in the hardware business. His regulars changed occasionally, usually because one died, but it always seemed that there was someone new to come in and gossip.

Pat became such an institution, he heard people say he had run the business since the thirties—how old did they think he was? He enjoyed his life at the store and at home with his family. The sadness grew less.

"Didn't you used to be Pat Allen?" This question was

from an elderly man who had been in the store for a few minutes and had glanced at Pat several times.

"Well I guess I still am." Pat chuckled a bit.

"Well I'll be dammed. I sure thought you were dead."

"Not yet."

"Hey, I used to see you when you visited my uncle, Sheriff Tubbs in El Reno."

"Well yeah, I remember Sheriff Tubbs. How is he doing?"

"Oh, my uncle died many years ago. I can't believe you're working at this hardware store. That's really something. You know my uncle was shocked when you sold out to them Mexican people—but that worked out great for everybody. I helped my uncle as he got older, so I knew all about that shit."

Pat was sure he didn't want to have this conversation. He steered the guy away from the regulars and just nodded his head as he talked.

"Yeah, I tell you those were sure some nice gangsters—it was like they really cared if everything was working out. We need those damn people running the telephone company—they sure as shit knew what they were doing. Of course, you probably know about them pulling out."

"I wasn't aware."

"Yeah, must have been seven, eight years after you retired—they just up and quit. Of course, that was about the time the state started their own liquor stores. Guess you can't compete with the goddamn state, even if you're a gangster. Anyway, we heard that they were having trouble in Mexico with gangs and bandits and that they moved their whole operation to Miami. Man, how would you like to live like that—go from one foreign place to another at the drop of a hat?"

Pat found the part that the guy had come in for and shooed him out the door. What a blowhard. But Pat thought that sounded like the Martinez brothers—once it got too ugly, they moved on to something else. Those guys sure did treat him right. There was never another sighting of Giovanni—the Mexicans must have done the world a favor and ended his vile existence. If Pat had been a little bit younger, he sure would have liked to go to Miami and visit Juan and Francisco Martinez, two of the nicest gangsters he had ever met.

Pat woke up one day and everything seemed different. He had always been a strong man—sick occasionally, but never really ill. But this time something was wrong. He had trouble rising and could only sit on the edge of the bed. Bugs had already gone downstairs, so he just sat there for a while. It crossed his mind that he should talk to Mike about the money—but then it seemed to leave his mind. He knew he would never be the same.

PART THREE:
1987

CHAPTER 21

Oklahoma City, Oklahoma—July 1987

Joe was to meet Mike at the check-in counter for Continental Airlines. A little excited and somewhat apprehensive about their planned trip to Las Cruces, Joe was uncertain of what they would find, and therefore not entirely comfortable. Joe was not the adventuresome sort and liked to know in advance where things were headed. Mike, on the other hand, seemed more carefree and was willing to step into a situation without a clue as to what would happen.

They had a direct flight to El Paso, where they would rent a car and drive to Las Cruces. Joe had looked up information about El Paso and Las Cruces and was intrigued by the history of the area, and the connection to Mike's dad only made it more fascinating.

Joe said goodbye to Liz that morning after one of her lengthy diatribes about his faults and overall lack of character. Either she was becoming increasingly harsh or he was becoming more thin-skinned. He knew she did not love him, but he was beginning to realize that she didn't like him much either. The look in her eyes when she was berating him was one of disgust. She wanted a husband who would provide for her and the kids, but she also wanted a husband who would participate in her social activities. Most of these centered on her church, the Church of Christ. Joe was a reasonable provider, but he just couldn't participate in her social life, and was definitely not interested in church functions, which had made him an outsider in his own family.

Joe hated the unknown, so it had been easier to just put up with Liz than to move out and venture into a new life with no assurances as to what it might be like. It was becoming clear to Joe that he didn't like himself much either.

Mike came into the waiting area as the plane was boarding. Joe was punctual to a fault—Mike was perpetually late to everything.

"Sorry, I'm so late. Sam's the world's worst driver. She drives five miles per hour, pissing off everybody on the road, and claims she's the safest driver in the state. I thought we'd never get here. We'll probably be in El Paso before she gets back home." Mike smiled through most of his outburst. For reasons that maybe only Mike could understand, ever since the phone call about the cabin in New Mexico he had been upbeat. An old cabin in T or C couldn't be worth enough to solve his financial problems, but it was a connection with his father, and that seemed to cheer him up.

"She's probably trying to compensate for the way you drive." Joe had been with Mike many times when it seemed like they would soon be dead on the highway. The man knew only one speed: faster. Not always paying attention, and always going full tilt.

They boarded the plane and took an aisle and window seat, hoping no one would take the middle one. It wasn't a problem—the plane was only about half full. Continental had been having some financial problems lately, and that probably compounded the problem of attracting custom-ers. But they were the only airline that had a direct flight to El Paso, and they were cheap—all of which were good things as long as they didn't crash.

They pushed back from the gate and were airborne within minutes. Financial problems or not, the flight was excellent. The service couldn't have been better—having a half-empty plane helped with that—and the flight was smooth all the way. As they approached El Paso the air became choppy, and the pilot came on to ask the passengers to buckle up. He said it was always bumpy coming into El Paso.

The contrast was striking. Oklahoma had lots of green trees and beautiful blue lakes. El Paso was brown. Every-thing seemed dead. Even the mountains looked stark. The land gave off a message of hardness—not a place for the weak.

Peering out the window, Joe said, "This is one of the ugliest places I've ever seen."

"Maybe it looks better close up?" Mike's earlier enthu-siasm wavered a little.

As they descended, they could see that they were in the middle of a desert. Of course, they had known that this part of the country was desert-like, but it was still a surprise to see the vastness of this barren landscape. The landing was smooth, and there was brief applause for the pilot.

Being in the El Paso terminal felt like being in another country. The contrast with the Oklahoma City terminal was striking, and Joe felt like he had landed in Mexico.

As he looked around, he was aware of the way that bright colors had been used to make the terminal feel vibrant and alive. The people were different, too, browner, and there were also more smiles—everyone seemed happier. He thought it must be his imagination. Why would you be happier living in this barren land? Maybe they were leaving.

They had no hassles at the car rental booth and were quickly settled into their vehicle. Always frugal, Joe had rented a compact car that would likely be comfortable for the first ten minutes or so on their hour-plus trip to Las Cruces. He had also rented it in his own name, without adding Mike—he didn't want to die on the highway in a foreign land. Of course, he knew it wasn't really a foreign land, but it sounded more dramatic that way when he explained it to Mike.

Everything was hot. They didn't know what the temperature was, but there was no question that it was hot, and the compact's air conditioning was clearly not adequate. Mike gave Joe some dirty looks. "Next time, at least try to get something that has decent AC."

Probably wouldn't be a next time, although Joe had to agree that the heat was uncomfortable. It took about fifteen minutes for the car to finally begin to cool, at which point they began to relax.

The scenery was still dominated by brown. But at ground level there was more contrast and color than they had been able to see from the plane. The area had many mountains, which were rocky, with a minimum of vegetation, but were also very interesting to look at, with dramatic angles. Their drive took them north toward Las Cruces, and they began to pass large agricultural areas— huge areas of green in what seemed a tree farm, as well as large dairy farms lining the highway. Obviously, water was coming from somewhere, either wells or reservoirs. While still very different from Oklahoma, the land was more interesting and varied on the ground than it had appeared from the air.

Enjoying and commenting on the new things they were seeing made the time pass quickly. They got off the highway at the exit they needed and were almost immediately at the Holiday Inn. The hotel had been described as one of the nicest Holiday Inns in the country—although Mike suspected that Joe had made reservations here just because it was cheap—they were pleasantly surprised to find that it had a unique hacienda feel. As they entered the colorful lobby, they could see an enticing combination bar and restaurant, as well as an outdoor pool. The overall effect was nothing like one would expect from a Holiday Inn.

They checked in, found their rooms, then made plans to meet in thirty minutes and have a drink or two before dinner.

Joe was the first to hit the bar. No doubt Mike had called Sam and they were busy discussing whatever it was that happily married couples talked about. Joe hadn't called Liz.

Debating his choices, Joe decided to go local and ordered a margarita on the rocks. The bartender asked if he wanted an El Grande and Joe said, "why not?" The result of that decision turned out to be the largest glass Joe had ever seen. While he thought he could probably lift it, he elected to take a few sips through the straw first to lighten it a little. A huge glass and very, very tasty drink—what a perfect combination.

Joe was about halfway through his El Grande when Mike showed up. Being halfway through an El Grande probably represented more tequila than Joe had ever consumed—he was already feeling no pain.

"I love this place, Mike. Sit down and let me get you an El Grande." His words were not slurred, but they seemed to come out at odd speeds.

"My god, Joe. I think that drink is for more than one person."

"Maybe so—but I'm not sharing."

Mike ordered his own El Grande and any chance of serious discussion was over for the night. They settled in. Joe and Mike laughed and sang and made a nuisance of themselves. They had tacos for dinner and claimed to all who would listen that they were the best damn tacos in the whole damn world. After dinner, when they were contemplating another round of something, the bartender very diplomatically suggested it might be best if they found their rooms. Considering the size of the bartender and the glares from other guests, they made the wise decision to call it a night.

The next morning was a little gloomy. Not only did Mike and Joe both have hangovers—intensified by embarrassment over some of their behavior—but it was raining in sunny Las Cruces. They met at the same place as the night before. Fortunately, it had been converted over to a breakfast buffet and the hostess and waitress had not been there the night before, so Joe and Mike weren't publicly chastised for their previous behavior.

The breakfast, with lots of coffee, was definitely what they needed. Their plan for the day was to start at Chuck Owen's office to discuss the cabin and maybe pick up some keys. Next, they would see a local attorney about matters related to Mike's mother's will. Neither meeting sounded like something they wanted to deal with while suffering a hangover, but it would have been more helpful to think about that the night before, rather than the morning after.

After breakfast they both felt more like meeting people. They dashed to the car amid a rain shower. At least the showers cooled things down some. They could no longer see the mountains due to the clouds, and the whole area seemed different in the rain. They retrieved a map of the city from the front desk, so they had a good idea of where they were headed. As it turned out, it was only a short drive to the center of town.

It took only a little time to find the Owen Real Estate offices. Joe parked next to the building and they entered the office to find Owen enjoying a donut and coffee. After introductions they took seats in front of his desk.

"Well, how was the trip from Oklahoma City?"

"So far everything's been very pleasant. Although we may have had a little more margarita than we should have last night." Joe offered this candid assessment with a wry smile.

"Must be the curse of the El Grande?"

"I see. This is a famous tourist trap set up by the Holiday Inn."

"I wish it only trapped tourists—I'm probably a few inches shorter than I should be because of the El Grande." Everyone had a good laugh—Chuck wasn't a tall guy.

"Mike let's get down to business. I guess once you get all of the legal aspects straightened out, the cabin in T or C will be yours—and I have a buyer who is interested in purchasing. What do you have in mind?"

"Not completely sure right now. When you called it was a total surprise to me that my mother had a cabin in New Mexico. I'll be meeting Mr. Young of Bates and Young here in town later today, so maybe then I'll have a better idea how long it'll take to clean up the legal aspects. But I imagine, Chuck, that I'll want to sell the cabin. How much do you think it's worth?"

"The value of anything is based on what a buyer is willing to pay. But first you'll need to understand the problems with the cabin. It's been vacant for a long time. Also, there's no easy access. The primary road into that area was washed out some years ago and never repaired. And the county has no current plans to make those repairs. Obviously, that will have a negative effect on value. The cabin can be accessed either on foot or using an existing trail with an ATV. The person interested in purchasing the cabin is our current County sheriff who's retiring. He's aware of all of the issues and has told me he would offer $17,000. That may not seem like much to you, but you'll have to see the place to fully understand. I can tell you that I think, under the circumstances, that might be the best offer you're going to get."

Mike had no idea what the property was worth but $17,000 would help him a lot more than owning an old abandoned cabin in New Mexico. "I guess the first thing I need to do is find out how complicated it's going to be for me to clear up the ownership issue. Once I have that done, as I said before, I'm sure I'll want to sell it. I'd like to make sure that the sheriff's offer is a fair value—maybe get an appraisal or something."

"That makes perfect sense, Mike. There are a couple appraisers here in Las Cruces and one that I know of in T or C. Let me know if you decide to hire someone and I'll give you some names."

Owen handed Mike a map with a circle indicating where the cabin was located. "There doesn't appear to be a key that anyone knows of. I've asked Max, whose father used to own the place, if he happened to have a key but he said no. The sheriff was up there not long ago and looked around, but he didn't go inside. I think, if you can get something from your attorney stating that you own the cabin, you may be able to have a locksmith go up there and unlock it and put on new locks. And, of course, the sheriff's offer is based on the inside not being a big hole in the ground. Sheriff Pacheco told me he couldn't tell what the inside might look like, although the outside was in surprisingly good condition considering how long it's been since there had been any sort of upkeep."

"Well, thanks, Chuck, you've been very helpful. Sounds like I have a few things to get done before we can transact any business. Joe and I will be in Las Cruces for a few days, but my guess is that we will have to come back once the attorney gets all the paperwork in place. Oh, by the way, Chuck, you had mentioned something about a bank account paying the property taxes and you thought that might be my mother's?"

"Yeah. Sorry about that. I got that wrong. The property taxes have been paid every year and the clerk I talked to said it was probably something set up by the owner of the property. But I talked to the clerk again and she said the tax bills were being sent to a law firm in Dallas and they paid the taxes."

"Okay, thanks Chuck. Here's my card with my work number—if anything else comes up, just give me a call."

Owen reciprocated with his card and asked Mike to keep him informed about progress on the legal stuff. They shook hands and agreed to stay in touch.

Once they were in the car, Joe had a few thoughts. "Not sure how much I would trust old Chuck. Something about him seemed a little too eager to please—don't you think so?"

"I don't know. Yesterday, this all seemed like a dream, inheriting an old cabin, flying down to New Mexico— now it all seems like a bunch of work. No telling what it will cost in legal fees just to get to point where I can sell this old cabin. Now I probably need an appraisal and a locksmith. Plus, I guess I need to contact that damn Dallas law firm and find out what they've been doing all of these years. I just don't know Joe, I guess I just wanted it to be a bunch of fun, not a bunch of work."

"Hey, slow down Mike. Chuck said the sheriff would pay $17,000. So, you have a few expenses—you're still going to net out a nice little pile of cash. I think that helps."

"Yeah, you're right. Seems like all I do lately is deal with problems and complications—I guess I'm just a little on edge. Let's get over to the attorney's office and see what he has to say. Maybe this will be easier than it sounds."

They drove a few blocks and pulled into a parking lot adjacent to what appeared to be the tallest building in town—ten stories. Bates and Young was on the fifth floor. First National Bank of Las Cruces occupied the entire first floor and at least half of the rest of the building and by all accounts was the largest bank in town.

They entered the fifth-floor offices and asked the middle-aged receptionist if they could see Mr. Young. She looked like they were an unwelcome interruption in her day and held her stare a little too long. Mike was beginning to think that maybe they had come to the wrong office, when she finally responded, "Do you have an appointment?"

Joe wasn't paying much attention, but sure noticed the tone. Maybe these attorneys had all of the business they could handle, and they had hired this receptionist to run people off.

"Yes, my name is Mike Allen and I have an eleven o'clock appointment with Mr. Young—I know we're early and, if Mr. Young is not available, we can come back." While Joe could tell Mike was still feeling grumpy, he was being very polite.

"Please be seated and I will tell Mr. Young you're here." This was more of a command than a request. Joe and Mike took a seat.

After a short wait, a tall, handsome, youthful Mr. Young

came out to greet them.

"Mr. Allen, it's a pleasure to meet you."

"Thanks, this is my friend Joe Meadows." After handshakes Jeff Young showed them into his small but comfortable office. "My partner has a meeting going on in the conference room right now, but we can meet in my somewhat messy office if you don't mind?"

"No problem at all. This is very comfortable. And please call me Mike."

"Okay Mike, and call me Jeff. Now, how can I help you? You had said on the phone something about a piece of real estate that you'd inherited but hadn't known about—is that right?"

"Yes, sort of. The property is in my mother's maiden name, and I think she probably didn't know about it. My guess is that my father purchased this cabin many years ago and put it in my mother's maiden name for his own business reasons. My father had business dealings in Las Cruces and El Paso in the 40s and 50s. He passed away about ten years ago and my mother died about four years ago. When my father died, he apparently didn't have a will, or at least no one could find one. My mother had a will drawn up for herself after my father's death, in which everything was left to me. Apparently, this piece of real estate, a cabin in the T or C area, has been abandoned all this time. Your local sheriff heard about it from the son of the person who sold it to my father and is looking into buying it as a retirement spot. Anyway, that's how Chuck Owen got involved, and he did research on the owner—my mother, under her maiden name—and eventually tracked it to me. Now I need to find out what I have to do to claim ownership and sell the cabin."

"Wow. That's an interesting story. What kind of business was your father in?"

Now the good part. "Actually, my mother and I never really knew. He may have been in the insurance business. He quit that business in the early 50s and went into retail hardware in Oklahoma City. So, most of my life he was working in his own hardware store—obviously, that had nothing to do with Las Cruces or a cabin in T or C." Mike paused. He was not real comfortable spilling the family secrets, especially since he didn't know for sure if they were true.

"I see—I think. So, you believe your father was in the insurance business in Las Cruces?"

"Actually, I never really knew, and if my mother knew she never told me." A little evasive but what did that have to do with his current legal needs?

About this time an older man with a regal air about him entered the room. Jeff stood in a show of respect.

"Excuse me for interrupting, Jeff. Just wanted to let you know the conference room is available now."

"Okay, thanks Bill. Bill I'd like you to meet some people from Oklahoma. They're asking us to help them clear up some title issues on some property here in New Mexico."

"Joe Meadows and Mike Allen, this is my partner Bill Bates." Handshakes all around.

"Mike Allen from Oklahoma—any chance that you have a relative named Pat or Patrick who used to have business dealings in Las Cruces?"

Mike just stood there—this was too weird. Could it really be his dad? And if it was, what did this Bates guy know?

Mike chuckled. "My heavens, what a small world—that could be my father. Did you know him?"

"Yes, I did. I did legal work for him in the 50s, back when I was a young man. I didn't know him well because we only met a few times, but I remember him because he made such an impression on me. He was one of my first clients. I was never sure of the type of business activities your father was involved in—I was always curious. But I'm aware of the real estate I suspect you're inquiring about—if it's a cabin in T or C with the ownership in his wife's maiden name, because I handled that transaction for your dad."

Jeff looked stunned. "Maybe we should all go into the conference room and figure out what's going on."

With that they all headed to the conference room. Mike pulled Joe aside. "Where did you get this law firm's name?" Joe had done the research to select a law firm in Las Cruces for Mike.

"I just called the attorney I use and asked him to give me a name in Las Cruces—he looked it up in some directory that attorneys have. What are the odds of it being one your dad used a hundred years ago? I can't imagine what this means, but it has a very strange feel to it."

"I know. What should I tell them—should I tell them I suspect my father was a big-time bootlegger? How the hell is the sheriff going to feel about buying a hidden cabin from a bootlegger's son? Jeez, every day my life gets stranger. Tell me Joe. What should I do?"

"Number one, whatever your father was, it's obvious it didn't involve you or your mother. Number two—well hell, I forgot number two. You're just looking to clear up the legal mess, and as it turns out you're probably talking to the guy who can get that done the easiest. He already knows all about it—he did it! So, you need to go in there and tell them what you know and what you don't know but can only guess." Mike looked thoughtful, then agreed. Might as well just be truthful—after all, he wasn't hiding anything.

They sat around the large table in the conference room while Mike explained that he really didn't know what his father did before the hardware store. "The rumors were that he was a bootlegger. It never made sense to me and my mom because he was such a great husband and father. His only fault was that he was gone a lot. He would go on trips several times a month and would be out at night quite often. He told my mother he was in the insurance business and she never questioned him beyond that. Then in the early 50s he said he had retired from that business and had bought a hardware store in Oklahoma City. From that point on he was never gone. He spent all his time with his family. We lived well, but not extravagantly by any means. And the rumors about his days as a bootlegger just felt silly. My mom said people made up those stories because they were jealous that my father owned his own hardware store. He was my dad, for goodness sake, not a bootlegger. So, I never believed them. But I guess now, I realize, those stories could be true."

"A bootlegger in Oklahoma in the 50s—well I'll be.

That could easily make sense. One of the rumors I heard was that your father was doing business with some people in Juarez—that could have been his liquor supplier. My word, isn't that interesting?" Bates seemed more intrigued than upset.

"Do you know Jim Emerson?" Bill Bates asked this directly to Mike.

"No. Don't believe I've heard that name, why?"

"There may be some legal confidentialities here—but I would suggest that you communicate with Mr. Emerson about the company he operates, Blue Devils Development, and about his dealings with your dad. You should be aware that Mr. Emerson is the richest man in southern New Mexico and not someone you want as an enemy. One of his biggest holdings is Citizens Bank, here in Cruces."

"Are you saying he was in business with my dad?"

"I think it'd be best if you asked him that question. Once you've talked to him, we should probably meet again. Regarding the property, we can begin work immediately to get the legal questions resolved. If you can provide us with a copy of your mother's will and maybe the name of the attorney in Oklahoma who handled the probate, I think we can get something done pretty quickly."

"Sounds great. We're staying at the Holiday Inn and we'll be in town at least two days. Also, if you think it's okay, we'd like to go up and look at the cabin. No one seems to have a key, and I guess it is boarded up and may take a little effort to get inside. We thought we could at least go up and see what it looks like from the outside."

"We don't have any problem with you doing that. I

would think that maybe even by tomorrow, if we can get some details from your attorney in Oklahoma, we would be comfortable with you accessing the inside and having the property secured with your locks. Why don't you give us a call tomorrow afternoon?"

With that they broke up the meeting and said their goodbyes. Back in the car, Joe and Mike just sat and stared for a time. Joe spoke first. "I guess you made the connection with Citizens Bank and the CB on the lock box key?"

"Yeah, I didn't say anything to Bates because I'm still nervous as hell about how all of this is related. But that just has to be the bank where the key belongs. Do you think there's any chance there's still something in the lock box after all these years?"

"Don't know Mike, but so far it sure seems like your father was a much more complicated man than you knew."

"No shit, Sherlock!"

Their next move wasn't obvious. They could try to find Emerson, but that sounded like it might easily turn into one big fuck-up, walking into the office of the richest man in the county and asking him if he used to be a bootlegger. Joe persuaded Mike that they should wait to see Emerson until they were clearer what their position was going to be. So, with nothing better to do, they decided to head toward T or C and see if they could find the cabin.

They got on I-25 and headed north. The country didn't change much, although there was a subtle increase in the amount of vegetation. The effect wasn't dramatic, but the tone of the land was greener the farther they went. The T or C exit took them into downtown. They made a pit stop at a local diner—this was Mike's choice. His preference was always something run by people, not corporations, especially when it came to food. Joe was more the fast food type guy where the food was made by a formula approved by a board of directors in New York City. Joe would say that at least it was always the same. Mike would say it was always bad.

The Lone Post Café was doing a booming business. That was good, as a testimony to the food, but bad if you wanted to get a table quickly. Since the pickings seemed slim as far as local food places went, Joe and Mike decided to wait to be seated. Sitting in the front on hard wooden chairs made the time pass as slowly as if they were waiting to be executed. But within a relatively short while a booth opened, and they were seated and served big glasses of sweet iced tea without being asked if they wanted any. Apparently, everyone was expected to want this sugary delight. It was delicious.

The menu covered breakfast, lunch, and dinner, with a lot of green chili items and a hefty dose of fried foods, all to the delight of Joe and Mike—your basic truck stop food kind of guys. Joe had chicken fried steak, Mike had the green chili cheeseburger, and they each had fries. If you had to die of something, might as well be a heart attack—at least it would be quick.

After a meal that they probably enjoyed way too much, they paid up and headed farther north, following the map. As they got closer to the lake, the terrain became hillier and there were more trees. It began to feel less like New Mexico and a lot more like Colorado. After several wrong turns, they eventually found the area drawn on the map and could identify where the road had been before it washed out.

After getting their bearings, they went on foot toward the spot on the map where there was supposed to be a gate. Walking was an effort after their mega-lunch, but it was also much-needed exercise. They began to relax a little and enjoy the scenery. The land was still harsh and rough looking. There were no gently flowing grass fields—everything was rocky and hard. But they were both getting used to the look of the New Mexico land. While not as green as they were used to, it had its own charm.

They had only walked a little while when they saw the gate. It was no effort at all to bypass it, hopping over the low fence. Beyond the gate were the obvious remains of a road. Off to the right there appeared to be some kind of outbuilding in the distance. They seemed entirely isolated. They hadn't given any thought to the possibility of running into anyone and they approached without any concern.

Once they got closer, they could see the cabin a little farther off. The outbuilding hadn't been mentioned by anyone—probably an oversight since it was no doubt part of the same property as the cabin. They decided to walk to the cabin along a roughly direct path through the underbrush. If they had given their plan a little more thought, they might have gone back to the partial road that looked as if it curved around the cabin and came up from behind. But they were feeling like adventurers, so off they went.

As they got closer, they could see that the cabin was originally a high-quality building. The logs and detail reflected craftsmanship. It was also obvious that it could use a little attention and clean-up. Mike started feeling a pride of ownership and had just turned to comment to Joe— when a shot knocked him to the ground. The sound was not very loud, but Joe immediately hit the ground, getting some scrapes along the way. He rolled over to where Mike was lying.

"Are you okay?"

"Hell, no, I am not okay. Somebody just shot me. What the fuck is happening?"

"I don't know. Can you move?"

"Yeah, I think so. Looks like I was just nicked on my shoulder. It's not even bleeding very much. It wasn't very loud—must have been a small caliber."

"Roll over this way and get behind this hill." Joe had scooted over behind a small rise and was lying flat against the ground. Mike, apparently not seriously harmed, joined him.

"Son-of-a-bitch, you know technically I think I've been shot for trespassing on my own property." Shouting now, he called out. "Hey, whoever's out there. I own this damn place. Do not shoot me again—understand asshole?" So much for diplomacy.

"Calm down, Mike. Let's not start calling people names when they have guns and we have dirt clods."

In the distance they heard a vehicle start up and begin moving away from them. They kept down for another ten minutes or so before Joe stood and declared the coast to be clear. Of course, he could have been shot at that point since actually he had no idea if the coast was clear or not, but apparently it was. Joe looked at Mike's shoulder and declared that he would live—good news for Mike.

Even though the wound appeared minor and the bleeding had stopped, they decided it would be best if they went to a hospital or something to get Mike looked at. They quickly reversed their path and got back to the car in much less time than it had taken to get to the cabin. Once they were back in T or C they stopped and asked a service station attendant where they could find a hospital. He directed them to Las Cruces. Well, it was a good thing Mike wasn't bleeding—he would probably have been dead by the time they got to Las Cruces. But by this point they were just as glad to say goodbye to T or C and head back down I-25 to Las Cruces. They saw a sign directing them to a hospital just a short distance off the interstate.

Mike was checked out from the emergency room and declared fit to travel, or something like that. He was bandaged up and given an ointment to apply when he changed the bandage the next day. The ER doctor said the wound was very superficial and looked like it was probably a 22. But, since it was a gunshot wound, they had reported it to the sheriff's office, who in turn had requested that Mike remain at the hospital until a deputy could come by and take his statement.

Mike completed the paperwork and paid for the hospital services with his credit card. He joined Joe in the waiting room. "Almost feels like a good excuse to revisit the El Grande—what do you think?"

"I think you're a glutton for punishment. I do think that a drink is in order, but I was thinking more along the lines of a gin and tonic." Joe had decided that maybe tequila was not his booze of choice.

Within a few minutes a Dona Ana County sheriff's deputy appeared in the waiting room and asked for Mike. After introductions, Mike told his story. Joe added his own comments and observations. They hadn't seen anyone. All they really knew was that Mike had been shot, and they had heard some kind of off-road vehicle leave the area. The Deputy asked Mike about the property. Mike related the story about it being his mother's cabin and explained that he was working with Bates and Young to get the legal issues resolved. He also told the deputy that he understood from Chuck Owen that Sheriff Pacheco was interested in buying the cabin as soon as all the inheritance issues were resolved.

The Deputy became more relaxed and friendly once they mentioned the names of familiar locals—especially his boss. He asked them where they were staying and how long they expected to be in town and said that someone would contact them the following day. He made sure he had their contact information so he could follow up if something turned up about who had shot at them, and then he left.

Joe and Mike headed back to the Holiday Inn which was only a mile or so from the hospital. Mike said he was going to his room to clean up a little and call Sam. Joe said he was going to the bar, but upon reflection decided that maybe he should go to his room and at least change his shirt—rolling around on the ground hadn't done it any favors.

The message light was blinking when he came into the room. It was Liz saying that she and the kids were going to a church function and wouldn't be home until late. She hoped he was having a good time and maybe she would talk to him tomorrow. She seemed almost pleasant, or maybe was she being sarcastic—Joe couldn't be sure. But he was now officially off the hook as far as calling her went. He changed his shirt and headed to the bar.

"Well, let me tell you—Samantha flipped out. Shot— she just kept screaming *shot!* Why in the hell was I shot— what was Joe doing while I was shot?" Mike had joined Joe at a table in the bar.

"I'm sure she'll decide that I'm the one who shot you— she's probably on the phone with the sheriff's office right now telling them to arrest me."

Mike laughed. "Yeah, her opinion of you is not really good. You know, she thinks the only reason I've lost so much money in the hardware store is because you're such a lousy accountant."

Mike thought it was funny, but Joe already knew exactly what Sam thought and it really pissed him off.

They sipped their drinks—neither of them having an El Grande—while discussing the events of the day. They agreed that it probably could have gone much worse. Why someone would take a pot-shot at Mike was anybody's guess. Maybe they thought Joe and Mike were trespassing. Could be someone had started squatting at the cabin and now considered it theirs, or maybe someone mistook them for somebody else and it had nothing to do with the cabin and nothing to do with them. They decided that they might never find out why it happened.

The news about the attorney knowing Mike's father was very interesting. How that might involve this Emerson guy, they still weren't sure. Of course, the mention of Citizens Bank and the fact that it was likely the source of the key was very intriguing.

They began to lay out a plan for the next day. They needed to determine whether there was a lock box in Mike's father's or mother's name at Citizens Bank. They decided that the best way to handle the issue was to ask Bill Bates to help them. They also needed the attorneys to continue with the legal transfer of the cabin. They decided that, rather than wait for someone in the sheriff's office to contact them, they would go see Sheriff Pacheco. Joe, especially, thought the best approach would be to see for themselves how interested he was in the cabin, and to establish a line of communication directly with the sheriff. He didn't want to say so to Mike, but he had started to worry that maybe the shooting was somehow tied to Mike's father's past.

The final thing they needed to accomplish the next day was a visit to Jim Emerson. They still weren't sure how he fit in, or even if he did, but they thought they shouldn't leave Las Cruces without meeting with him.

Since they seemed to have a plan of action for the next day, it was time to move on to the pressing matter of dinner. After a quick inquiry at the front desk, they settled on La Posta in Old Mesilla.

The short drive was pleasant and took them through the greenest area they had seen since landing in El Paso.

The area known as Mesilla was close to the Rio Grande River and was filled with large trees and stunning flowers, giving it the atmosphere of a Mexican village. They found the restaurant after only two wrong turns and parked in the lot next door.

They entered to wonderful aromas and the sounds of exotic birds. This was looking to be a great choice for dinner. They were seated in a colorful patio area and served chips and salsa. While still a little gun-shy, they stuck with tradition and had margaritas—not El Grandes though.

The meal was the best Mexican food either one of them had ever enjoyed—just gloriously delicious—naturally, they consumed way too much. Joe in particular seemed impressed with the cuisine, both the content and the presentation. He even asked for and got a tour of the kitchen.

They decided to take a quick walk around the Plaza instead of heading back to the hotel. The night air was crisp and there were only a few other people out. The plaza had many little shops selling tourist items and there were places to buy food, from homemade fudge to tacos. On one corner was a bar, but they were too tired to investigate.

"You know, this must have been where my father bought that stuff he brought home from the one trip." Mike said this with a melancholy voice.

Joe wasn't sure what Mike was thinking—maybe wondering what his dad had been doing here—but he didn't elaborate.

After one quick lap around the square they headed back to their car and returned to the hotel.

CHAPTER 22

Las Cruces, New Mexico

The weather had cleared by the next day and the sunny skies were back. They had called and made an appointment with Jeff Young for ten that morning. They enjoyed a simple, low-calorie breakfast at the buffet in the hotel and then they spent some time in their own rooms waiting until they needed to leave. With a little time to spare, they headed downtown for their first meeting of the day, where the receptionist showed them into the conference room. She still seemed unfriendly—it appeared to be her nature rather than anything to do with them.

"Good morning." Jeff entered the room in good spirits. "We were able to have most of what we'll need for the property faxed to us yesterday by your attorney in Oklahoma City. I'd say that within a week or two we should be able to get a judge to sign off on the transfer of the property into your name, Mike."

"That sounds great, Jeff. We also have a couple of things we'd like to discuss with you this morning. I didn't mention this yesterday because, quite frankly, I'm still trying to figure out who to trust. After my father died, I received a letter from him, along with a key. Joe and I have determined that the key is for a bank lock box. We did some searching in Oklahoma City and determined that it wasn't a bank there. On the back of the key it's marked with the initials CB. After the discussion with you and Mr. Bates yesterday, we thought it was very likely that the key is for a lock box in Citizens Bank. How can we go about finding out if that's right?"

"Interesting. So, you're saying you think maybe your dad opened a lock box back in—what was that, like 1952—and then arranged to have the key delivered to you after his death? With no information or instructions provided to you about this key." Jeff looked puzzled as he thought about the scenario.

"Boy, there are going to be a bunch of issues here. The first one I can think of is that even if he did open a lock box, how was the rental paid? And if it wasn't paid, then were the contents turned over to the state? If so, what happened to them? Or let's say, the lock box has been paid for all these years—was it in your father's name? Maybe this was also in your mother's maiden name? I think we have lots of questions to answer."

"How would we go about finding out if there's still a lock box?" Joe asked.

"My advice is to just be straightforward. I know the V.P. of Finance for the bank, so why don't I just call him, or we walk over there and see if he'll look it up in their records? How's that for straightforward?"

"Guess that is better than my plan B, which involved a late-night break-in." Mike was kidding—probably.

Jeff made the call and the bank officer agreed to meet in thirty minutes. Citizens Bank was only a short distance from the First National Bank building, so it was a quick walk. The building was impressive, very old and ornate with a legacy feel and, no doubt, many stories in its past. Its age made the experience all the more emotional, since this was clearly the same building that Mike's father, Pat, had entered to conduct his business.

Once in the V.P.'s office, Jeff quickly brought his friend up to speed on what they were looking for. The manger, a man named Rick Lopez, looked on his computer and called up the lock box database. He said they did have a lock box in the name of Patrick Allen and Mike Allen, and it had been there since 1952. The manager added that while the length of time was impressive, they had several family lock boxes that had been in place since the 30s.

Mike was a little stunned. The lock box was in both of their names. That was the clearest signal yet that his father intended whatever was inside to go to Mike.

The V.P. spoke, "Not one hundred percent sure of the legalities here—it's very unusual to have two names on a lock box. I think I can allow you to have access with adequate proof that you're Mike Allen, but just to be safe maybe I'd better clear this with the president of the bank. And maybe have something indicating that you are Patrick Allen's heir."

"That is not a problem." Jeff jumped in. "We're helping Mike work out another matter with some real estate and we've secured all of the legal paperwork related to his father's death and the subsequent death of his mother. I can get all of it over to you this afternoon. How about, if we plan on meeting again around three this afternoon and, if everything is agreeable, you can allow Mike to have access to the lock box?"

"As long as you have the key, Mike, and we can be comfortable with the inheritance there should be no problem opening the box. Interesting, I was looking at the record and it shows that the annual lock box fee has been paid for all these years by a law firm in Dallas. Guess your father made some long-term plans for things even after his death."

Mike felt a shiver. This was great news but also unsettling.

They thanked Lopez, agreeing to meet back at his office at three that afternoon. They walked back to the First National Bank building and said their goodbyes to Jeff, who assured them he would have all the documents to the bank within the hour. Joe and Mike headed toward their car.

"That's pretty neat isn't it? You're going to maybe find out what's in the lockbox today. Man, I had figured all along it was probably going to take some kind of legal action to get access to the contents, but here we are maybe only a few hours away from finding out what your dad left you. Are you pretty excited?"

"Shit. I don't know what I am. I guess I'm excited but also a little apprehensive. Just not sure Joe. Guess I need to think about what's happening a little bit more. Jeez, I hadn't expected this to happen right now—you know what I mean?"

"Sure. It's happening fast, that's for sure."

Joe said they should drop in at the sheriff's office, which was just a few miles down the same street the bank was on. Mike wasn't sure but said "why not."

The drive to the sheriff's office was another quick trip.

Las Cruces was a small town, so most everything was pretty close to everything else. They went in and asked to speak to Sheriff Pacheco. The deputy behind the counter said the sheriff was out at that moment and asked to take a message. Mike began giving her his name.

"Aren't you the guy who was shot?"

"Yeah, that's one of the reasons we dropped by—the deputy we talked to yesterday said that someone would contact us today so we thought we would just come in."

"I know Sheriff Pacheco wanted to talk to you. Give me just a minute and let me get him on the radio—hang on." She turned to the base radio and said some things that sounded like official police gibberish, with numbers and letters and the sheriff's name. Within a few minutes the sheriff called in. She told him that the two guys involved in the shooting yesterday were in the office and asked if he wanted them to wait. They could hear the entire conversation. The sheriff said he would be there in about ten minutes and to ask the gentlemen to wait.

"I guess you heard all of that—not much privacy around here. Can you wait for a minute for the sheriff to get here?"

"Oh, sure—we can wait." They thanked her for her help, went over to the small waiting area in the front, and had a seat. In about fifteen minutes the sheriff walked up to them from the office area—clearly there was a back entrance.

"Hello, my name is Sheriff Pacheco. I really appreciate you guys coming by today. Let's go into the conference room so we can talk." After entering the small conference room, Mike and Joe introduced themselves. They each shook hands with the sheriff.

"Well, I guess, you had quite a day yesterday—going up to see an old abandoned cabin and having someone shoot you. That's not our normal welcome to New Mexico."

"Yeah, that was something all right. I was lucky, it was a very minor injury, but for a while there I'll tell you we were pretty excited. Still can't imagine why somebody would just start shooting—I don't know if whoever it was even knew who we were."

The sheriff chuckled a bit. "There are a few oddballs living up around that lake—hard to know at this point what it was all about. I know you told the deputy yesterday that you didn't report anything, just headed back to the Cruces hospital, so we contacted the sheriff for that county and told him what we knew. He seemed to think it was probably a hunter shooting rabbits or something, who just didn't notice you until it was too late—got scared and took off."

Mike looked doubtful. "I guess it could have happened that way, but we sure were not being quiet. We hadn't anticipated anyone being up there, so we would have been pretty obvious I would think. I'm damn sure we don't look like rabbits."

The sheriff agreed with a smile. "I've got a few ideas of my own that I need to run to ground to see if they check out. One way or another we'll figure out what was going on. I guess Chuck Owen has told you that I was thinking about making an offer on that cabin."

"Yes, he did. I'm working with Jeff Young at Bates and Young to get the legal issues resolved. He indicated that he thinks that can happen in a week or two. While it's an intriguing place up there, my intention is to sell it, so having you interested fits really well with my plans. My father bought the cabin a long time ago, and it would seem that he never used it very much. Not to divulge too many family secrets, but my mother and I weren't aware of the cabin until Mr. Owen tracked me down in Oklahoma City and asked if I would want to sell it. That prompted this visit, more out of curiosity than anything else, but I've never had any intention of keeping the cabin. So hopefully we'll be able to make a deal."

They wrapped up their conversation and exchanged contact info, agreeing that they should stay in touch.

Joe and Mike were back in the car. The only thing remaining on their "to do" list for the day was to contact Jim Emerson. Then, of course, they had the meeting at the bank. Mike said he wasn't very excited about getting in touch with Emerson—said he had a bad feeling about it.

"What are you, suddenly psychic? I think we ought to drop by his office—if he's in we see him, if not we leave a message. I don't know what the plan is either, but Bates seemed to think it was important that we make a connection with this Emerson guy, so we should do that."

"Joe, sometimes you're just a pain in the butt."

Joe had pulled into a What-a-Burger as they were talking, "How about a big juicy hamburger for lunch?"

"You know Joe, you still eat like a teenager. You're supposed to be the smart one, but you seem to have no sense at all when it comes to food and drink." Mike was right of course—but Joe didn't give a shit at the moment—he was going to have a green chili cheeseburger and fries.

After lunch, the smart thing to do would have been go back to the hotel and have a nap, but that would have made them lazy losers, so instead they headed toward downtown Las Cruces. Emerson's office was in the same small area of downtown where First National Bank and Citizens Bank were located, a freestanding building across the street from Citizens Bank. They parked in front and went in.

"Hi, my name is Mike Allen and I was wondering if Mr. Emerson was available?" The woman sitting at the front desk reacted with surprise—almost shock—when Joe and Mike entered the office. Her primary function was clear by the clutter on her desk: she was a bookkeeper. And by her reaction Mr. Emerson did not get many visitors.

"Yes. I mean no. No, what I mean is I will go check—please be seated." She left the front area and went down a long hallway toward the back of the building. She was gone for what seemed a long time considering her task. When she returned she seemed even more upset.

"Mr. Emerson is on the phone. He asked if you could wait a moment and he would see you."

"Thank you, we'll wait."

The wait had already stretched to more than fifteen minutes when Emerson finally emerged from the back office. It was hard to make out his age except he was obviously elderly. He walked with a slight stoop, which detracted from what was once probably a six-foot-plus frame. He appeared to be alert and totally in charge, and it was apparent that Mr. Emerson was used to being in charge.

"Mike Allen—it's a pleasure to meet you." They shook hands and Mike introduced Joe, who also shook hands with Emerson.

They followed Emerson, as directed, back into his office—which was the size of a small house. The appearance of the front office was dull and cheap, but Emerson's own space was large and expensive. He steered them to a large conference table that took up one corner. Plush leather chairs were abundant around the table. Emerson sat at the head of the table and Mike and Joe sat along one side.

"I don't know what you know about your father and my business dealings, but I'm not one to beat around the bush, so I'll just lay things out for you. I worked for your father for many years. I knew he was in the bootlegging business in Oklahoma, but all of my dealings with him were completely legal and mostly involved real estate. You father sold a bunch of his holdings in the 50s and he and I still communicated on occasion after that, but mostly I went my own way and so did he. I understand he and your mother passed away some years ago, so please accept my condolences."

"Thank you, Mr. Emerson. Yes, my mother and father have both died. I wasn't aware you and he had any business dealings. There was a small cabin that was apparently a part of my mother's estate that got lost in the confusion over the years. It came to my attention only a short while ago. I came to town with my friend Joe to resolve the legal issues regarding the property so I could sell it. I hired Jeff Young to assist with that and yesterday I had the opportunity to meet Mr. Bates and he suggested that it might be good if I dropped by and introduced myself to you. He was not real clear why I should do that, but maybe it was because he knew you knew my father."

"Mr. Bates has a big fuckin' mouth." This was said in a sinister tone. Joe wasn't sure Emerson was aware he had said it out loud.

"Well, it is true, I knew your father. He was a frequent visitor to Las Cruces and El Paso, and I was responsible for assisting him with some of his dealings with firms in Juarez. But, like I said, his bootlegging activities were something he kept separate from our dealings. I'm sorry I can't tell you more. Now, I don't want to rush you, but I wasn't expecting you to drop by today and I have another meeting I need to go to. Please leave your contact information with the lady out front and be sure to let me know the next time you are in Las Cruces." And now, get the hell out of my office.

Mike stopped at the front, gave the spooked lady his card, and said they were staying at the Holiday Inn, in case anything came up and Mr. Emerson wanted to see him.

Back in the car. Definitely should have rented a bigger car. "That guy was sure eager to get rid of us."

"No question. He didn't want to have anything to do with us. What do you think that was all about, leaving us sitting out there waiting on him?"

"Beats the hell out of me. I sure hope he's not a violent guy—I had the feeling he might like to kill Mr. Bates."

"Yeah. You know I don't think everybody is being real straight with us."

"Oh really, you think not?"

They were a little early for the bank meeting and didn't have enough time to go back to the hotel, so they moved the car to the bank parking lot and just sat for a few minutes, not saying anything.

As they got out of the car to head to the bank, they were joined by Jeff. "Hey, good timing. Were you able to see the sheriff?"

"We did. Seems like a nice man. He said the sheriff in the other county thought the shot was probably someone shooting rabbits—not sure anybody really believes that. He also said he had some ideas of his own he would explore. And he definitely seems interested in buying the cabin, although I think we may be still negotiating price."

"Well, that's good he is working on finding out about the shooting, but it could have been nothing. I understand the lake area attracts some pretty unique people, no doubt including some who don't like strangers. Could be they were just trying to scare you off and hit you by accident. And you're right, I think Sheriff Pacheco is a good man. He'll do his best to find out what it was about. How about Emerson, did you see him?"

"Yes, we did. He didn't seem pleased to see us, though. Ignored us for about half hour and then gave us the bum's rush and sent us on our way. Got a very uneasy feeling with him."

"Well, I'll pass that along to Bill. I'm fairly new to this area and don't have all of the history. I know Bill Bates and Jim Emerson are not buds. Anyway, sounds like you had a busy day. Now, let's go see what is in that lock box."

They entered the bank and waited to see Rick Lopez.

He walked out to where they were sitting. "I've got some bad news for you. I've been told that our legal counsel can't approve you opening the lock box today. I have to admit I'm a little surprised because when I talked to him earlier this afternoon there didn't appear to be an issue. But I just got off the phone and he said no. I'm really sorry you had to come back and go to all of this trouble, but I guess you'll have to contact the bank's lawyer."

Jeff was not happy. "What the fuck are you talking about? This man has the legal right to access his possessions—your lawyer has made one serious fuck up. I'll be in court tomorrow and we'll have access to that lock box." He was clearly pissed, probably because he had been embarrassed in front of his clients.

Rick Lopez seemed a little stunned by Jeff's outburst. He apologized, and once again said he didn't know what had happened but, without the bank lawyer saying it was okay, he didn't have the authority to do anything. He said that we should contact the lawyer and see if we could get things cleared up.

Jeff made it clear he didn't need Rick's advice.

Joe, Mike, and Jeff headed outside. "I can't believe this shit. I'm going back to the office right now. I will get hold of this asshole bank attorney and find out what the hell is going on."

Joe and Mike said they appreciated Jeff seeing what he could do. They were going back to the hotel to try to figure out what they should do next. They said their goodbyes.

Joe stated what they were both thinking. "No coincidence there. Jim Emerson owns the bank. He had something to do with what just happened with that lock box."

"Yeah, we may be trapped in small town hell."

When in doubt drink.

Back at the hotel, Mike went off to call Samantha. Joe went to his room to lie down for a while, then decided to call Liz—why the hell not? Of course, she wasn't home. He didn't leave a message, just headed to the bar.

Mike showed up a little later. "Talked to Jeff. He said he talked to Bates. Bates called the bank's attorney but couldn't get him to move off his position. He said they would file a civil complaint with the local court tomorrow to hear the matter as soon as possible. Jeff still sounded pretty pissed. But, bottom line, he said this could take a few weeks to get resolved."

"Sounding like we should head home tomorrow."

"Yep, I agree. I called the airlines and there's a flight out of El Paso tomorrow at 4:30 getting into OKC about 8:15—I went ahead and booked two seats."

"I think what I'm going to do in the morning is call Chuck and tell him I want to list the cabin. Even though it's not settled yet, I'll ask him to put the paperwork together. We can go by tomorrow morning and I'll sign it. Maybe if he goes ahead and lists it, someone else might be interested. The sheriff's deal is probably the best I'll get, but since there's going to be a delay anyway, I should advertise it and see what happens."

"Sure, why not? Of course, one point is that if the sheriff buys it you could cut Chuck out of a fee."

"Jeez, all of this stuff is giving me a headache. I think I'll just go ahead and sign the listing with Chuck and let him handle it once Jeff gets the legal okay."

"Okay by me." Joe was losing his enthusiasm. He was not real sure why he was even here.

"Joe, I know this trip hasn't been a lot of fun. Listening to all this crap about my father, having someone shoot at us—not exactly the most fun we ever had. But I want you to know something—if there is something out there from my dad, I want you to participate in the prize."

"What the hell does that mean?"

"Actually, I don't know exactly. But let's say there are millions, like he said—you can have half of it."

"That's just fucking stupid. First, there is no way there are millions. Your dad had some money and some of it may be in the lock box, but not millions—maybe hundreds or a few thousand. Second, no way I am taking money left to you by your dad. My god, Mike, you really are fucking stupid."

"Okay, I'm fucking stupid, and you're a fucking genius. If there's nothing but the cabin and a few thousand in the lock box I'll keep it and pay my accounting bill—okay, ass-hole? But let's say there really are millions. You've helped me my whole life, and if it was just me by myself I don't think I'd be have gotten this far in finding whatever there is to find—and I don't want millions unless we can share."

"I'm not going to argue with you. Just drop it. If this is something other than bullshit, it's your money, your cabin, your mother, your father—not mine—so forget it."

"Wow, what a fucking grouch."

They ordered drinks and let the conversation drift off into the distance. Neither was going to change his mind.

And neither believed there was anything real here anyway, except their friendship.

Several drinks later they had forgotten most of the day's events and were passionately discussing the likelihood that the OU Sooners would be national champs in football the next season. When things start to get personal, turn to sports.

CHAPTER 23

Las Cruces, New Mexico

The next day they quickly set up an appointment with Chuck and checked out of the hotel. After dropping by and listening to various reasons why Mike should go ahead and sign the listing agreement, which was why he had come in the first place, he allowed Chuck to convince him and signed it. Chuck said he would do his own quick appraisal of the cabin's value and let Mike know in a day or two what he thought it was worth. Then they could decide on the listing price.

What should have taken minutes had taken hours—but it was done, and they headed back to the El Paso airport with plenty of time. They agreed that they would check their bags and enjoy a late lunch at the airport before they boarded. Going home was the right decision, but there was a lingering feeling that they had not accomplished as much as they should have.

Joe reminded Mike that their biggest accomplishment was meeting the people who were going to be handling things for him in Las Cruces. Now it would be easier to deal with them over the phone. Mike agreed. They had a light lunch and a couple of fortifying drinks, then boarded the plane.

The flight was uneventful, though with a little more turbulence than the flight in. As they made their final approach to Oklahoma City, Joe realized that he hadn't told Liz he was returning. Probably didn't matter, but it felt rude. Something had to give in their relationship—it couldn't go on like this. He would have to talk to her. It was approaching nine o'clock—maybe he would run by Triples. No, that was just plain stupid. He would go home and face the music.

The landing was a little rough, but it was good to be home. They said their goodbyes and agreed to make contact in a day or two to discuss the trip and what was left hanging. Joe and Mike went to find their cars in the long-term lot, both of them feeling apprehensive.

Joe arrived home about thirty minutes after he had picked up his bags at the carousel, officially exhausted. As he approached the house, he could see there were no lights. More than likely, no one was home, and he felt a sense of relief—another sure sign that he really had to deal with Liz about their future. His guess was that Liz would be overjoyed to get a divorce as long as she ended up with every last fucking cent Joe had—which was exactly what was likely to happen.

Entering the house, it became clear that there was no one there. Joe turned on the lights and got the impression that there hadn't been anyone there for some time. He went into the kitchen and sitting on the kitchen table was a note.

Joe,

I have no idea when you will be home so that you can find this note. I thought about trying to track you down to tell you I wanted a divorce but decided

I just did not care that much.

Thanks a lot for keeping me and the kids informed about what you are doing. It's obvious you're doing something you shouldn't be—and I will not stand for it. The kids and I have gone to my mother's in Tulsa. We will stay there until you and I can get a divorce. That's the only solution to the way you treat me and your children.

You have become a boorish drunk who cares nothing about his family or their welfare. I have tried every way I know to make a good life for you, but you just keep spitting in my face—and that will not continue.

I have hired a lawyer who will contact you (if he can find out where the hell you are) and start the process of us ending this so-called marriage. I don't hate you, but you cannot treat me and your children like we are not even a part of your life. The kids and I will be fine. We have our faith and many good friends—we do not need you.

Liz

Joe started to cry. He wasn't sure why—after all, most of what she said was true. A little biased toward her viewpoint, but Joe had become an asshole. He felt alone and unloved, which he now was. He sat at the kitchen table and cried.

He went into his home office and collapsed on the sofa, almost immediately asleep—a very familiar pattern.

The next morning Joe awoke and wasn't really sure where he was. As it came back to him, he wasn't sure he wanted to be there at all. He fixed some coffee and re-read Liz's note. It made him feel bad. He got dressed and decided he would have to face the world whether he liked it or not. He drove to his office.

As he walked in, Lucille handed him a pile of mes-sages. It crossed Joe's mind that he hadn't called Lucille either, but she, without question, did not give a shit. His impression was that she was pissed he was back. If he had taken the time to have a shot of gin for breakfast, he might have just strangled Lucille first thing. Call the cops and confess. Start his new life as a convicted bitch killer. As it was, if he was going to divorce Liz and give up his kids, along with most of his money, he sure as hell was getting rid of Lucille.

Joe went to his cluttered desk and fell into his chair. The morning had just begun and he was already tired. Most of the messages were from clients wanting one thing or another—nothing critical. There were a couple of messages from Liz. He wasn't sure that he understood the sequence of the message at the Holiday Inn and these messages—he would think about that later.

He sorted through the client messages and returned some phone calls on the matters that seemed the most ur-gent—none of them were. After thirty minutes or so he was all caught up. Great. Go away for a few days and your wife divorces you but no one else really much notices. He wasn't sure what he wanted to do, so he simply sat there and waited for something to happen—maybe a sign from God.

The phone call from God didn't come, but one from the fucking devil sure did. Liz's attorney was a real piece of work. Within seconds he had claimed that Joe had had several extramarital affairs and had squandered most of the family's vast wealth—and, as a professional, had the skills to earn huge amounts in the future, which should all go to his grieving ex-wife and starving children. Someone else to add to the soon-to-be-killed list.

Surprisingly, Joe was almost calm. He told the man he would have his lawyer contact him and not to call him again, then hung up. Now, of course, he had to hire some goddamn lawyer to exaggerate his side of the deal. Or he could just call the asshole attorney back and say fine, everything was hers—of course he would never work again so any future earnings would be zero. He honestly wasn't sure which path to take.

It was early mid-morning, and Joe was basically done for the day. Working hard to support Liz, his kids, her attorney, Lucille, the IRS. Well fuck it—he was not going to do it anymore.

Joe, in his amateur way, realized that he was having some kind of crisis, and that a sane person would probably seek the help of a professional. A less-than-sane person would seek help of a bartender—Joe headed to Triples for an early lunch.

Mike took the seat next to Joe at the bar. It was about four in the afternoon.

"Hey, little early to be shitfaced isn't it?"

"What are you doing here?"

"Your buddy behind the bar gave me a call—said you might need a ride home."

"He's a wise man."

"Yep, he is." Mike helped Joe to his car. No question, Joe could not drive—but it was also obvious he needed a friend. Mike drove him home and started a pot of coffee—for himself. Joe fixed a drink. He talked for a while about Liz and the mess he had made of his life. There were no solutions, just a lot of misery. Joe fell asleep on his couch and Mike went home. He left Joe a note in case he needed a reminder in the morning of where his car was.

The next morning Joe was still not right, but he was no longer thinking about a kill list. Mike's note was much appreciated since Joe didn't have a clue where his car was. He called a cab and went to work.

The next few weeks blurred together for Joe. He worked hard and completed a lot of tasks he needed to get done to assist his clients. He had even been nicer to Lucille, who had not changed at all.

Joe hired an attorney—some guy he had met years ago at some alumni thing. The attorney listened to Joe's story and said Joe was screwed—as if he didn't already know that. Joe hadn't seen or heard from Mike since his friend had rescued him from Triples weeks ago.

Joe's life would never be the same—how exactly was that a bad thing? He kept trying to find a silver lining in his problems. What bugged him the most, he realized, was the change. He knew his old life was miserable, but he feared change. He didn't want Liz back, but he didn't know what was going to happen without her, and that made him worry. He called Mike.

"Mike, anything happening?"

"Joe—glad you called. I was going to call to see if you

wanted to meet for a drink later. Got a couple of things I need to go over with you."

"Sure. Say five at Triples?"

"See you then."

CHAPTER 24

Oklahoma City, Oklahoma

Joe's personal life was in the toilet, but it sounded like everything was going great with Mike. Joe suspected that Mike and Sam were getting along much better, and Joe was pleased. Joe didn't like Sam much, though he didn't know why, exactly. Maybe it was just that she obviously didn't like him—real mature.

Joe was sitting in a booth having a beer when Mike arrived. He was trying to cut back on the hard liquor.

"Beer? Really?"

"Yeah, everybody keeps saying I've turned into a drunk, so maybe I should listen."

"I take it things are still shitty with Liz."

"Hired a lawyer—he says I'm pretty much fucked. She will get most everything, and I'll need to work harder for the rest of my life to support her and the kids in the manner they deserve. Not so sure he isn't in league with her attorney. But I'm okay. It is, after all, my fault. Liz has always been the person she is now—I think I'm the one who changed. Anyway, I'm sick and tired of thinking about me—what's your news?"

"Let me know if I can help in any way with the divorce or whatever—okay?"

"Sure."

"Got a call from the sheriff in Las Cruces. He had a

strange story to tell me about the cabin. Some guy confessed to taking a shot at us. Turns out the guy was using the outbuilding by the cabin to store drugs. This guy was the son of the man who sold the cabin to my father. Some guy named Max was working with the other sheriff up there in T or C, moving drugs from the border up into Albuquerque and Denver. He said we should come by the next time we were in Las Cruces and he would tell us the whole story."

"Drug dealers in T or C, New Mexico—is there no place that's safe? What'd he say about buying the cabin?"

"Oh yeah. He said he had made an offer to Chuck and hoped we could close soon. Said he was sick and tired of the whole sheriff business—just wanted to have some peace and quiet. I really like the guy."

"Anything else?"

"Got another call from Jeff. He said they have all of the approvals in place now for me to access the lock box."

"Well, how about that? So when are we going to Las Cruces?"

"How about next Thursday? Flight number 321 leaves at 10:30 am and arrives about 2:30 pm. I've rented a car. A bigger one this time, and I'm on the rental as a driver whether you like it or not."

Mike had developed a new smugness that was both annoying and intriguing.

"Count me in. Can't wait to see what's inside the mystery lock box."

The trip to Las Cruces was a duplicate of the trip a few weeks ago except that Mike drove the rental, a full-size

Buick. Mike had been in an upbeat mood since they had met at the Continental check-in counter. Joe was subdued, which seemed to be his default mode lately.

Staying again at the Holiday Inn for both convenience and familiarity, they quickly checked in and got settled. There was nothing scheduled for the day, so they agreed to meet later for dinner. Joe took a nap and Mike talked to his wife.

"Well, what's on the agenda for tomorrow?" Joe asked Mike once they met up. Joe was having a beer and Mike was having an iced tea—change was in the winds.

"First, we'll go see Jeff. I was hoping that if everything was in place we could go to the bank and look in the lock box. Then the closing on the cabin is set for 2:00 pm at a title company in the same building as Jeff's office. Maybe squeeze in some time to spend with the sheriff and hear more about the cabin drug dealers—but that's not actually scheduled. So really, we could be done today and have tomorrow morning open. We're scheduled to fly back to OKC at 4:00 tomorrow afternoon and be back in Oklahoma late in the day."

"Sounds very efficient."

"Yeah, need to get back home so Sam and I can go to a special revival going on at the church."

"You guys seem to be more involved with the church lately."

"Yeah. Sam and I are really getting along great and a lot of it is the church and the people there. Kind of hard to describe, Joe, but I think all of this stuff with my dad, learning about his background and things, have made me

232

more aware of who I am and how I want people to think about me. You know it's still inevitable that I'll be closing the store and Sam and I are going to take a hit financially—something about all of that has made me closer to God."

Oops, there went their friendship.

"Sam told me about the money she got from her brother's estate. She wants it to go toward rebuilding our lives. We've just never been closer—and I've never been happier. I know this isn't the conversation we normally have, and I know everything in your world is all screwed up, but I tell you, Joe, I could not be any happier right now."

Joe ordered a gin and tonic. Screw the beer. "Mike, I couldn't be more pleased for you. You and Sam make a great team—maybe the financial hardship was what was needed to get you two pulling together." Jeez, did he just say that?

"Joe, I want you to know our deal is still on. If there are millions in the lock box, we're going to share. You'll always be my best friend."

Joe suspected that Mike really didn't believe what he was saying but felt that he should say it anyway. Joe knew that the friendship was over, and he also knew that there was no way in hell there were millions in the stupid lock box. Loneliness and depression, his old friends, had found Joe in Las Cruces.

"This may come as a shock to you, Joe, but Sam and I are looking into starting our own church. We're calling it Legacy Chapel. It'll be a non-denominational church based on the teachings of the Bible. I have a lot to learn, but I've never felt more alive. And I want you to become a member of our church."

Holy crap. Not only had he lost a friend, but now he would have to avoid Mike or put up with sermons and recruitment speeches.

"Wow, Mike—you, a preacher? This is quite a turnaround. I'm really impressed. I'm not sure what to say."

Of course, Joe was absolutely sure what to say. What the hell are you thinking? Have you lost your mind? But neither one seemed like an appropriate response. Joe suddenly realized that this was why Mike's driving had been so normal—he had found religion and given up speeding. Amazing.

They chatted for a while, but it wasn't the same. They were becoming different people. At least, Mike was. They had a sensible dinner and agreed to meet in the morning for coffee before they headed to the attorney's office. Mike left for his room. Joe lingered, but only for a short while. He was very tired.

The next morning, they met in the lobby of the hotel and had coffee, but there didn't seem to be much to talk about. They left for the attorney's office—they were going to be a little early, but they needed someone to talk to.

"Good morning, Joe, Mike. How was your flight?" Jeff seemed in a much better mood than the last time Joe had seen him.

"Just fine, Jeff."

"Well, why don't we head over to the bank? Rick'll be waiting for us. Once we got a judge involved everything was corrected real fast. Still don't know why they took the position they took, but I get the idea from Rick that it probably had something to do with Emerson—you know he owns the bank. I guess it doesn't matter, as long as you have access now. Ready to go?"

It was a quick walk over to Citizens Bank. Rick was literally waiting at the door when they arrived. He greeted Jeff and told Mike how sorry he was about the last time they had met. With a quick glance at Jeff, he said that sometimes lawyers just get in the way.

"Look, no problem. I know this was a little unusual, so it's understandable that there were some issues that needed clarification. But I guess we're ready to get the lock box now?"

"Absolutely. Right down these stairs." Rick pointed to a flight of stairs going into the basement.

At the bottom they found a large safe with its door standing open and a woman sitting at a table next to the safe door. "This is Ms. Sanchez, who'll get the lock box for you and show you into a private room. If you need anything more from me, please let her know. Thanks again, Mr. Allen."

Ms. Sanchez took the key Mike handed her and examined the number and the back. She returned the key to Mike and entered the safe. She came out with a bank box about the size of a large shoe box. She guided them into a small conference room and set the box on the table. She instructed Mike to insert his key into one of the two openings, then pulled a key from her pocket and inserted it into the other slot. They both turned their keys, and the box unlocked. She told Mike to let her know when he was finished, and she left.

"Do you want me to leave you alone, Mike?" Jeff was still in the conference room.

"No, I think maybe you should stay." Joe wasn't so sure but said nothing.

Mike lifted the lid of the box. Inside there was a wrapped package addressed to Sally Thompson, labeled private and confidential. Below that were certificates of some kind, bearing the name Blue Devils Development. Finally, there was a small slip of paper with a series of numbers written on it. That was it.

"Well, so much for millions." Mike looked a little disappointed.

Jeff looked at the certificates. "These are stock certificates for a company called Blue Devils Development made out to your dad. Kind of interesting—they're signed by your dad as president and Jim Emerson as vice president. There are two certificates for five-hundred shares each out of a total of a thousand shares in the company. So, this means that whatever Blue Devil is, your father owned all of it. Any idea what that means?"

"None. Strange Emerson didn't say anything about that company when we talked to him." Joe had already been pretty sure that Emerson wasn't trustworthy, and this seemed to confirm that he had been deliberately evasive.

"Well, I guess I'll take this stuff with me—no reason to leave it here." Mike stuffed everything into a briefcase he had brought for the purpose. They left the room, thanking Ms. Sanchez as they went.

Back in Jeff's office, they gathered around a small conference table in a private room. They were joined by Bill Bates.

"Maybe I should have told you this earlier, but before this I wasn't sure it was pertinent. I helped your father establish BDD, Blue Devils Development. These are the original stock certificates for the company. While you were at the bank, I called a friend of mine at the Secretary of State's Office and he looked the company up in their records. It still exists and it's still active. My guess is that Emerson has kept the company alive—no doubt, because it benefited him in some way."

"Mr. Bates, do you know who Sally Thompson is?" This was from Mike.

"I had limited dealings with your dad, Mike. So, I didn't know everything that went on in his life. Frankly, it was none of my business. But there were rumors, and some of them involved a very beautiful young woman who accompanied your dad on some of his trips to Las Cruces. I'm not sure I ever heard a name, but for some reason Sally rings a bell. My guess would be she was the girl who was with your dad."

Mike didn't look pleased with this morsel of news. It was one thing to have a father who was a bootlegger—it was something else to have a father who was "accompanied by a young woman." That just didn't fit into the image in Mike's head at all.

His father was his father, the husband of his mother. What did this all mean? No millions in cash—just some old stock certificates that were probably worth nothing, a slip of paper with numbers that likely meant nothing and had no obvious value, and a package addressed to his father's mistress. Not exactly what Mike had been hoping for.

Joe spoke up. "Seems like the first order of business is to go visit Mr. Emerson again and see what he has to say about this BDD company. Maybe there's a simple explanation as to why he didn't mention it before."

"That's probably the best approach. Emerson is ruthless, but I don't believe he's dangerous. He kept a pretty low profile over the years—except, of course, for purchasing Citizens Bank. He doesn't socialize with local people and he's not active in politics or local charities." Bates looked like he wanted to say something else but hesitated.

"Jim and I go back many years. We've had some major clashes and I would say we're far from friendly. For a while I was Citizens Bank's legal counsel, and I questioned some of the things the bank was doing. I'm not saying it was illegal, although there's no question that much of Emerson's real estate activity involved very favorable treatment by the bank. There are all sorts of rules about how owners and officers of a bank conduct business with that bank and I thought they crossed that line. Jim's solution to that problem was to fire me. You might say we've been enemies ever since. I've been concerned that some of that animus was rubbing off on you, Mike. More so than just something to do with your dad."

"Well, even if he doesn't like my choice of attorney, or my dad, or me—Joe's right. He's the next stop. I think Joe and I will go alone and see what happens. But stand by in case we need to be rescued."

It was amazing, anyone they wanted to see was somewhere within a two-block area. They walked to Emerson's office and once again startled the lady at the front. She probably needed to get a bell for the door or give up coffee—she was very jumpy. Mike introduced himself again and asked to see Mr. Emerson. She told them to have a seat and went down the hall. She returned and said Mr. Emerson would be right with us.

The wait was shorter than the previous time. Emerson looked like he had aged since they saw him last—and at his age that was a very bad thing. He didn't offer to shake hands but directed them back to his office and the conference table.

"Mr. Allen, I don't know why you're here today. As I told you the other day, I only knew your dad slightly and have no information for you, so you're wasting your time. And wasting my time. So, unless you have something specific to say, I need to get back to work." Not a warm and fuzzy kind of guy.

"Mr. Emerson, I believe there are some very specific things we need to discuss." Mike reached into his brief case and pulled out photocopies of the BDD stock certificates that he made at Jeff's office. "These appear to be stock certificates for a company my father owned outright, and you're listed as an officer. Why didn't you mention this to me the other day?"

"Mention what? I told you I was an employee of your father's back in the 50s. I'm not sure what you're trying to suggest, but I damn sure don't like the tone of your question. I think this conversation's over—if you need anything further you can contact my attorney, Frank Myers. Now, I'm going to get back to work." Emerson rose slowly, then waited for Mike and Joe to do the same.

"My attorney, Bill Bates, whom I guess you know, contacted the Secretary of State's Office—this company is still active. I bet we will find out that you're the one listed as the registered agent for Blue Devils. I'm also guessing that much of your holdings are tied up in this company—is that right Mr. Emerson? Believe me, I'm not going away, and I'll have Bates dig up every record there is until I find out what all of this means—got it?" Mike was pissed and it showed.

Emerson sat back down. He was quiet for a while, apparently deciding what he was going to do. He looked up and there was a new hardness to the old man. "Your father and I had a verbal agreement about the work I was doing for him. He promised me ownership if I would continue to operate the business. Then he dropped out of everything. I called him and wrote him, asking him what he wanted me to do. He just ignored me. I put everything into the business. I grew the business. It was all because your father had said it was going to be mine—I always did what I thought he would have wanted me to do."

Emerson went from being monstrous to forlorn. He wasn't the force they had thought he was—he was weak and seemed harmless, but there was evil there.

"I'm still confused, Mr. Emerson. What's Blue Devils Development?"

"It's your father's company, and it owns real estate assets in Las Cruces, El Paso, and Oklahoma City. Your father started it in the early 50s. But I was the one who ran it—I was an officer of the company and I bought and sold the property on that authority. At first, I would send your father reports and we would talk often, but then something happened, and he just stopped returning my calls. Eventually, I heard that he had died. I guess I thought someone would contact me and something would be worked out—but no one ever did—so I just continued running the business."

"Does that include the bank?"

"No, that was a different deal. I had some money already and then borrowed some more from First National Bank. I was able to purchase the bank with a partner. The partner later wanted out and I was able to get the money to buy the rest of the bank. That had nothing to do with Mr. Allen."

"Mr. Emerson, it sounds to me like you might have stolen from my dad, or maybe you just helped him—I just don't know what to believe."

"Look, Mike, maybe I've been an old fool. I've run this business as my own for so many years. When you showed up, I kind of panicked. I always trusted your father, but of course I don't know you, so I didn't know what to do. I thought I had an understanding with your father, but I don't have anything in writing so I'm sure Bates will say I'm shit out of luck. Of course, you know there's going to be one big legal mess straightening all of this out. Maybe, rather than having Bates spend the rest of his life in court, it would make sense to come to some kind of mutually beneficial deal."

"Like what kind of deal?"

"I don't know right now. Why don't you give me until the morning to think about this and come up with a proposal—could you do that?"

"Joe and I will be back tomorrow morning at ten. If we can't come up with something that makes sense, then I'll turn it over to Bates and Young."

"I will see you in the morning."

Joe and Mike left Emerson sitting at his conference table. They walked back across the street and got in the car. They decided not to go back into the attorney's office only to be told that they had made a bad decision in giving Emerson any kind of consideration at all. So, they decided to find a place to have lunch and then go to the closing on the cabin, which would be in the very same building.

Joe was driving this time and he headed north on Main Street—suspiciously, it was the way to What-a-Burger. "I can't decide what I think about Emerson. One minute I hated the guy and, then, the next I felt sorry for him." Joe wasn't going to mention What-a-Burger until they got closer.

"I know, Joe. I feel the same way. What he was saying about my dad just ignoring him for years—I can see that happening. When he started being a dad and husband again and not going on his trips, it was like he became a different person. I bet you he didn't want to talk to Emerson because it reminded him of his old life."

"Any ideas on what he might suggest tomorrow."

"None. I'm still not real sure I understand what we're talking about. Part of me says to just turn it over to the lawyers and see what happens. But you know, maybe I feel the same way as my dad—I want this done and then I want to put it behind me. What I want to do is go back to

Oklahoma City and get on with my new life."

"Yeah, I can understand that." Well, Joe could if he had a new life. Joe pulled into What-a-Burger.

"Joe you have all of the culinary skills of a country hog."

"Nice way to talk to your driver."

No matter what Mike said, lunch was great. The green chili cheeseburger with fries was at the top of Joe's list of the best stuff ever.

After lunch they drove around for a while and saw some of the sights. They thought about going down to Old Mesilla and walking around the Plaza but decided they didn't have time. So, they headed back to the First National Bank building to find the title company offices.

Based on information from Chuck, Mike had agreed to $16,500 for the cabin, after Chuck's fee. Agreeing to contribute $500 to the closing cost, Mike was going to net out $16,000 which would be transferred to his Oklahoma City account. The closing documents confirmed that the property taxes had been paid all these years by, apparently, the same Dallas law firm. Mike told himself that someday he would have to find out how that had been handled.

They waited in the title company reception area for the sheriff to arrive to sign the paperwork. Pacheco was only a few minutes late. He greeted Mike and Joe and seemed to be in a good mood.

"How soon is your retirement, sheriff?"

"Joe, I am looking at just six more weeks and I will no longer be the Dona Ana County sheriff. At one time I thought I didn't want to retire, just keep working. But as I've spent more time thinking about it, the more eager I am to stop chasing bad guys."

"Well, we sure wish you luck. Guess we'll have to take a rain check on the drug dealer story, but tell me, why do you think he shot me?"

"He said he thought you and Joe were feds. The DEA people had been monitoring Hector, the sheriff in Sierra County, for some time, and that was how they got onto Max. So the sheriff cut a deal with the feds and Max had heard about it—it was on the same day you drove up there—so he went into a panic when he saw you and decided to shoot and run. I really don't think Max was smart enough to be the person behind what was going on, and I also don't think it was the sheriff, but so far the DEA people can't determine who was running the show. This was a very elaborate scheme involving transporting drugs out of Mexico and flying them out of an old airstrip in T or C up to Albuquerque and Denver. Lots of moving parts, as they say, and it would appear none of the moving parts knew about the others—so, pretty damn sophisticated."

That set Joe to thinking. Who would know how to do all of that? Maybe an old bootlegger with connections in Mexico and experience transporting contraband. Could it be? *No way—he's too damn old.* "How much money do you think was involved?"

"Nobody told me an exact number, but the DEA agents indicated it was millions in annual sales. Big bucks—way beyond anything Max could have dreamed up."

The title clerk came out and said she was ready. They entered the conference room and took seats at the table with the sheriff on one side and Mike on the other, their pens at the ready. It took about ten minutes to get everything signed and notarized. Joe and Mike told the sheriff that they might be in Las Cruces again and that they would look him up, but they all knew they wouldn't. Everyone left.

"Why don't we go back to the hotel and rest a while?"

"Sure. Feels like we've put in a full day. I was wondering if you were listening to the sheriff when he was talking about the drug operation in T or C."

"Sort of—not sure I was real interested. Why?"

"Maybe this sounds farfetched, but when he was describing what was involved in moving that volume of drugs it sounded real similar to moving booze."

"Jeez, are you kidding? Old man Emerson is now a bigtime drug dealer? Joe, you need to find more productive things to dream up."

"Well, scoff if you want. But it's basically the same business. Let's suppose most of what Emerson was saying is true—but not all. He said he was only involved in the real estate business with your dad. Does that make any sense at all? Why would your dad hire somebody to run the real estate business—that's mostly about doing maintenance and collecting rents. There are plenty of property management companies you can hire to do that. No, what makes sense is that he needed someone to keep the supply lines open out of Mexico and get the booze shipped into Oklahoma. Now, there was a job he needed filled. I know you don't want to think about what your dad was doing—and fine, I understand—but I'm telling you that if there's anybody in Las Cruces who would know how to set up a drug smuggling business it's Emerson."

"Well, okay. If you assume that he was involved in the bootlegging business and transporting booze out of Mexico, I admit that's similar to drug smuggling. But he said he wasn't involved in the bootlegging part of my father's past and I'm going to believe him."

"Okay. Fine. Just bury your head in the sand."

Mike looked unhappy. "Joe, I'm not trying to deny that my father did some bad, maybe even horrible, things. I'm just trying to forget them. Whatever happened, he's dead. My mother's dead. I want to forget the past and live right now, from this point forward, and I'm just fine with not talking about my father and his wicked ways anymore."

Joe realized now how hurtful all of this information about his dad was to Mike. It hadn't touched Joe, but for Mike it destroyed all his memories of his father, and it hurt.

"All right. I'll shut up."

"Well, there's some good news." Mike smiled, although he didn't really look happy.

Back at the hotel they each went to their rooms to rest and regroup. Joe said he would probably be in the bar around five or so. Mike said he would see him later.

Mike didn't want to think about the past, but Joe did. He was convinced that there was a connection between Emerson and the drug operation in T or C. That was probably why Emerson was eager to put a stop to any investigation or court case around the development company before it even got started. He probably already had his hands full covering his tracks after two of his underlings had been arrested. But that didn't make sense. If those two knew about Emerson they would have already given him up to the DEA to get a better deal. And why was he even thinking about this? He knew nothing about drugs, the DEA, or anything else for that matter.

Joe had held onto the package addressed to Sally Thompson. If anyone was going to try to find Sally, it would have to be him. Mike was in his "if I don't think about it, maybe it didn't happen" mode. And Mike sure didn't want to be reminded about his father's less than virtuous past. But Joe wanted to know who Sally was. He would try to find her. He wasn't sure how, but it would give him something to think about other than Liz and the pending doom of their divorce.

Joe took a nap, then went to the bar, which turned out to be empty except for the bartender—the same guy who, on their previous trip, had suggested they leave. Maybe he wouldn't remember. "Hey, Joe, how about an El Grande?" Nothing worse than a wiseass bartender with a good memory.

"You know that El Grande may be more than a simple Okie can handle. How about a gin and tonic?"

"Good choice, sir." With a grin—wiseass bartender.

Joe nursed his drink for a while, expecting to see Mike. After a while he killed the drink and ordered another one. Probably Mike was practicing sermons on the phone with Sam.

The bar was starting to fill up and Joe no longer felt like he stuck out like a sore thumb. He ordered an appetizer plate with a selection of finger foods and another drink. By the time he had finished it was almost seven, so Joe paid his tab and went to his room. He called Mike, just to make sure he was okay, but got a busy signal. He was sure it had something to do with Samantha. He started watching a basketball game on TV between two teams he couldn't have cared less about, but after a short time he turned it off and went to sleep.

Joe woke up about four in the morning ready to start his day. Early to bed, early to rise may not actually contribute to wisdom or wealth but will have you up ready to go at a god-awful early hour in the morning. There was a small coffee pot in the room. He fixed some coffee and sat, just waiting for time to pass.

Around six Joe went down to the breakfast buffet area to see if they were open yet. They weren't, but they did have coffee ready. Joe got an El Paso paper and some coffee and took a seat.

Later Mike found his table. "Sorry about last night. I tell you we have so much to talk about with our new church. And Sam is so excited. She was talking to a graphic designer yesterday and the guy has come up with what she says is the neatest logo for the church. Man, I can't wait to get back and get that started. Anyway, time just got away from me, and I guess you went to bed early. I came down here about nine and the bartender said you had gone to your room some time before. I can sure understand that, I was tired too. Well, we can go see Emerson in a little while, find out what he's thinking and then head home."

Mike seemed a little wound up—it was irritating.

They chatted over coffee and some toast about nothing. They were losing the ability to talk to each other—no doubt this would be the last field trip for the boys.

By the time they got everything packed into the car and checked out, it was time to head to Emerson's office. Neither Mike nor Joe had any idea what might happen. Joe was starting to question whether it was wise to meet Emerson without an attorney present, but he kept his mouth shut.

Like all trips in Las Cruces, it didn't take long. They parked in front of Emerson's office. There was no one at the front desk. Joe hoped Emerson hadn't eliminated her as a witness or something.

"Hello." Joe called in a loud voice toward the back room.

In a while Emerson came out of his office and, without any mention of there being no one at the front desk, asked them to come on back. Once seated, Emerson began.

"Let me tell you what we're talking about. There are nine buildings in total, four of them here in Las Cruces, one in El Paso, and four in Oklahoma City. I estimate that the buildings in Las Cruces and El Paso are worth maybe $3.2 million with mortgages of about $2 million, or a net value of $1.2 million. The four buildings in Oklahoma City are worth just about $1.2 million with no mortgages. All of the buildings and the debt are in the name of the development company."

He paused to let the information sink in.

"As I said yesterday, your father told me that I would someday own half of this business if I would help him maintain it and watch over it for him. You can say there's nothing in writing and no way to prove that—and you'd be right—but I'm telling you that's what he said. We can fight forever over ownership in court. You'd probably win, but you don't know that for sure. I have lots of documentation supporting my claim that I own BDD. I've managed these properties for more than thirty-five years, I've filed all of the corporate papers, I've signed all of the tax returns, I've borrowed money as the owner of BDD—it goes on and on. What you have are some old stock certificates that may or may not be valid. I can say in court that your father assured me that he had destroyed those certificates years ago when he gave me the company—might be a lie, but I could say it."

Mike and Joe waited for the bottom line.

"I don't want to go to court. It would take forever and I'm old and tired. That goddamn Bates would make my remaining years pure hell, just for the pleasure of it. Here's what I propose. Obviously, the net value of the real estate in Oklahoma City and the net value of the real estate in Las Cruces and El Paso are about the same. You take Oklahoma City, and I keep Las Cruces and El Paso. You are immediately worth 1.2 million dollars—no lawsuit, no legal fees, and you avoid the possibility that you come away with nothing. Deal is done. You're not completely happy, I'm not completely happy, but we get on with our lives without dealing with a bunch of dickhead lawyers. What do you think?"

Mike stared at Jim Emerson as if he were some kind of strange creature. To say that this wasn't what Mike had been expecting would be a colossal understatement. My god, he would be a millionaire.

"Well, Mr. Emerson, I'm not sure what to think. Can you give Joe and me a little time so we can talk this over?" This was all about stalling. Mike was confused and needed to talk to Joe.

"Of course. There's an office just next door that's vacant. Why don't you and Joe step in there and I'll just wait here."

"Thanks." Joe and Mike went into the adjoining office.

"Okay financial guy, should I do that or not?" Perfect, now Joe was financial guy—soon he would be the fucking chauffeur.

"Mike, how the hell would I know? What he did was give us two figures that are equal to each other. It is meaningless until you know the properties and how much income they produce, where they are, and whether they could be sold quickly as-is. Not to mention if those values are even accurate. Also how do we know these are all of the properties? He's just telling us what he wants us to know—he could be lying. The only way we can know what's really involved is to do the research, hire the lawyers to do legal searches. You know, shit like that. Plus, do you want to cut a deal with this guy? You can't trust him. If you take it through the courts and you win, you know you have good title—here you won't know much of anything for sure."

"Okay, I hear you Joe. There's risk doing it this way, but there's risk going to court, too. I thought he made good points about his claim to ownership being about as valid as those old certificates. Even if I win it could take years to settle. I could waste a fortune in legal costs and lose! A fortune I do not have!"

"Yep. There's risk no matter what. If you want to consider this 'cut to the chase' approach, we need to decide the minimum of information you need to know about the properties and then, maybe, you can make a more informed decision. Keep in mind you're accepting just what he's showing us—we'll have no idea if there are other assets that should be included."

"I get it. Do you know what the information on these properties would be?"

"Yeah, I know."

"Okay."

They went back into Emerson's office. He was still sitting at the conference table.

"I think we can make a deal, Mr. Emerson. But there are things I'll need to see before I can agree. We'll keep it to a minimum and, if the data confirms what you've said, we can make this happen."

Emerson smiled for the first time since they had met. It wasn't pleasant. "Very good, what do you need?"

Joe took over and started writing out a list of what he would need to see on each property. Appraisal reports, tenant listings with terms of leases, income statements, tax statements, any environmental reports, copies of mortgages, and a few other items. Emerson took it all in stride. "I can have all of this gathered and available to you in a couple of hours—it's all information we already have."

They agreed to come back in two hours and once again use the office next door.

"I guess we don't go back to Oklahoma City tonight.

Let's head back to the hotel so I can change the flight and call Sam. Well, what do you think Joe?"

"Still not comfortable with Emerson, but I understand your reasoning about pursuing this kind of deal. Now I just need to see if those numbers he gave us hold up."

They drove back to the hotel a little slower than necessary. Joe and Mike were each lost in their private thoughts. Mike quickly checked them back into their old rooms, then went off to make phone calls. Joe went to his room and for some reason decided to take a shower. He needed to be on alert for anything that would indicate Mike should not do this deal—because if he didn't find something, he was sure Mike was going to agree to trade the properties for the stock certificates.

Before his shower he called Lucille. She didn't answer, but that didn't surprise him. He left a message that he wouldn't be back in the office tomorrow as he had thought, but probably would be a couple of days after that—although nothing was certain yet. She knew where he was staying and there hadn't been a message, so either she hadn't been in the office since he left or there was nothing he needed to know. Not very comforting either way.

They were back in Emerson's office in a couple of hours. The woman in the front office had returned. She showed them back to the spare office, where they found large stacks of newly arrived files. She said that if they needed anything at all to let her know. She seemed friendlier now.

Joe started through the files. He found some columnar pads in a desk drawer and began making a schedule of the properties and what files and information he had on each.

This was going to take a while. Mike stepped out of the office several times; then said he was going for a walk. Joe thought it was better than him hovering around, watching.

The information on each property was well organized and Joe quickly started compiling data. He worked through the afternoon and only took a couple of bathroom and water breaks. Mike was in and out, and mostly just in the way. At one-point Joe suggested that Mike should go find some place to get some sandwiches or something and bring them back. Mike checked with the woman in the front. She didn't want anything, but she suggested a small deli behind the building across the street and recommended the turkey on rye.

Somewhere around six Joe declared that he was done. "We need to go over this data and then talk to Emerson—have you seen him?"

Mike was exhausted from just hanging around all day. "Nope, I haven't seen him since we came back hours ago. Just a minute, let me check with Jane."

"Jane?"

"Yeah, that's the lady out front—she's really very nice." Mike left, then returned. "Well, she says he didn't come back after this morning, but he called and told her that he would like to meet with us in the morning. I told her okay, and to let Mr. Emerson know we're done with the files. Was that right?"

"Yeah, all I need are my spreadsheets and notes for us to discuss it, so if you want, we can go back to the hotel and talk about this stuff."

They left, saying good night to Jane, who no doubt had

been waiting for them to leave so she could lock up. They headed back to the hotel.

They went to Mike's room so he could check for messages, then decided they would stay there to go over the work Joe had done. Joe said he just had to have a drink first and that he would be back in just a minute, then returned with a gin and tonic.

Joe pulled out his stuff. "First, I would say what Emerson told us was basically true as far as the values of the properties. That's based on fairly current appraisals on some of them, and calculations of cash flow on others. Regarding the Oklahoma City properties, it's also based on my own knowledge, because I'm familiar with two of the buildings. One is a first-class office building on Classen Boulevard. I know about it because a few of my clients have offices there, and I estimated it to be worth about $950,000 or so. The other building that I know about is also on Classen—it's Triples."

"Are you kidding?"

"No. The building is owned by BDD and leased to Triples. That building is worth maybe $350,000—could be more depending on the land value and the cost of tearing down Triples. The value right now, leased to Triples, is in the $350,000 range."

Joe looked at another sheet of notes.

"So that's the $1.3 million value in those two buildings. The other buildings are on Second Street off of downtown. That's an area that used to be known as Deep Deuce and it was a mostly black part of downtown. That was mentioned in your dad's letter. Obviously, there must be some connection there with your father's past, but at this point the buildings are vacant and in poor condition. Plus, there may not be much value in the land. I said it basically had no value or could have a small negative value based on having to pay taxes and insurance on an abandoned building. So, the $1.2 million seems right."

Joe turned to his last set of notes.

"Regarding the buildings in Cruces and the one in El Paso, there were current appraisals on each of those buildings along with copies of the mortgages. And what Emerson said is true. The value is right at $3.2 million with debt of $2 million, for a net value of $1.2 million. I looked through every file and found nothing on any of the properties that would indicate there was anything materially wrong with the information. I ran an analysis of cash flow and it supported the assumptions of value contained in the appraisal reports. Bottom line, Mike, Emerson gave us accurate information."

Joe took a big chug from his drink. "Let me give you my advice before you ask. Take the deal."

"That's it, just take the deal?"

"Yeah."

"You can do better than that—*why* should I take the deal?"

"Well, mostly because you want to. But also, because it's probably the quickest and simplest way to resolve what could be an ugly, drawn out fight with someone I still don't think you want to get into a scrap with."

"I don't completely agree with your reasons, but I agree with your conclusion—that's what I'm going to do, take the deal. I want to figure out a way for you to get half, okay?"

"No, not okay. I've already told you, no. If it was going to be millions in cash, then fine, give me a pile, but this is real estate. You don't need it complicated with different owners. This is your legacy from your dad—just take it and get on with your life."

"We're not through talking about this."

"Yes, we are. Now, I'm going to leave you alone so you can call your wife. Also, I'm exhausted once again—this getting old crap is not fun—so I am going to go rest. See you tomorrow."

CHAPTER 25

Oklahoma City, Oklahoma

Samantha Rogers was the queen of the world with the promise of being someone important. She knew it was mostly because she was beautiful, but she couldn't have cared less if the reason was superficial—all she wanted was money and fame. She wasn't going to work for it, she just wanted it to happen because she looked good, and boy did she ever look good.

Sam would stand in front of her mirror for hours. Sometimes nude, often in an array of outfits. She loved to look at herself. She watched what she ate and exercised a little, but mostly she was a natural beauty. Thanks to her parents, she had been attractive her whole life with little effort. As thanks for that gift, she generally avoided her parents—they were tiresome.

During high school there had been no one who was more popular. She was the official best-looking girl in the school and was chased by every male who had the courage to approach her. She dated many and had sex with most. This was a violation of her beliefs—she was a devout Christian—but she was addicted to sex from a young age. She dealt with the moral conflict by denying it existed, at least for her. By some divine edict, she decided, she was so beautiful that she was entitled to this one privilege. Sam had sex and prayed for forgiveness, over and over, in a perfect logic that only she could understand.

One of her conquests was Mike Allen. Mike was handsome enough, but he wasn't as popular as most of the boys she allowed to be around her. She liked Mike because he was funny and appreciative of any attention she gave him.

In her senior year, Sam discovered she was pregnant. She contemplated suicide and she contemplated an abortion, but these options were closed to her because they violated her religious beliefs. She took her religion seriously and so far, there had only been one exception to her strict ethical code—the one regarding pre-marital sex— that she'd managed to justify, no others. She didn't even notice the logical contradiction. Realizing that she would have to do something, she decided she would marry one of her many admirers. After that it was only a question of selecting the lucky man.

Sam spent considerable time analyzing all the important qualities of the candidates: hair color, muscles, year of car, color of eyes, and other critical attributes. But the one thing that was going to determine Sam's decision more than any other was whether she could control her husband-to-be. She wasn't going to end up married to some creep who wanted to run the show—that was Sam's job. She needed a husband and a father for her kids who would do what Sam told him to do. Her winner: Mike Allen.

Samantha Rogers would become Samantha Allen. Mike was stunned. It was like winning the grand prize of all grand prizes. They had dated a little, but to have Sam as his wife was not something that he had even imagined happening—it was too farfetched to even fantasize about.

She asked him, he said yes. He had never told anyone, including his best friend Joe, that she had asked him. They wouldn't have believed it—*he* didn't believe it.

A week before the scheduled wedding, Sam miscarried. She was relieved because she hadn't really wanted to be a mother and she took this as a sign that she was destined for greater things. She spent a few hours debating with herself about the wedding. Her feelings for Mike were not love, though she liked him. On the other hand, it would be terribly embarrassing to call off the wedding and she really wanted to move out of her parents' house, so she decided to go ahead and get married. Mike never knew she was pregnant.

Being married to Mike was okay. Nothing special, but she did have the freedom she had wanted from her parents and she could buy things that her mother would never have approved of.

She developed her own friends and became very active in a new church that was just starting. Mike would attend sometimes, but mostly he seemed to drink a lot and hang out with his loser friend, Joe. She was not famous or rich, which made her unhappy, but she felt free, which made her happy.

After Mike's dad died, they had a little more money. Mike didn't seem all that upset when his dad died, but then they hadn't talked about it much. With Mike now running the hardware store, he was gone even more. She thought about getting a divorce, but she was reluctant to deal with the conflict it would require.

After Mike's mother died, he seemed to dig himself

deeper into the alcohol pit. He would stay out for days and not even let her know. Sam knew now that something had to change, but once again she focused on her church activities and shopping and time passed.

"Sam, I think I may be coming into some money. We talked about my dad and his crazy stories—well, it looks like some of them may be true. Or at least have some element of truth." Mike was talking to her from his hotel room in Las Cruces.

"How much money?"

"Right now, it looks like we could end up owning maybe a million dollars in real estate."

Sam was stunned.

"Did you say a million dollars?"

"That's what I said. Look, it is not a done deal yet, but this is about my father and some of his business dealings. It's not something I'm real comfortable with because of how he earned it, but I think we should take some of this money and put it into the church we've talked about. Turn bad money to a good purpose."

Mike really didn't know what he wanted, but he knew for sure he desperately didn't want to lose Sam and he knew she was getting close to leaving. The money problems and his drinking were about to drive her away. This money was a miracle.

"With more money we could really make this happen. Start our own church. Are you sure this is what you want to do?"

"Absolutely. I know this is what you want to do—and if you want to do it—so do I."

"Let's do it. We'll be good at this Mike; I just know it. You have a way with people that you don't even recognize. We'll be so good together. I can't wait. This will be our legacy."

They said their goodbyes and agreed that they would talk the next day. Sam was ecstatic. She had always dreamed of having her own church. There was so much she wanted to do—her real goal being to have a TV ministry. She desperately wanted to be on TV. If only that could happen, she knew her beauty would make her popular, just like in high school.

Sam knew at an instinctive level that if she and Mike could get in front of an audience, they could convince people to send money. She knew her role—she had been practicing it for years. Sam was wholesome and pure, the perfect woman to secretly desire but whom you couldn't have. She loved this image of herself.

Sam also knew all of the people to contact. She knew where she could hire the people with the skills they would need to make this church a success. Everything was about image and marketing and she was ready for success.

Sam also knew that Mike would do what she told him to. In an odd way she had transferred her sexual addiction to Mike—she had cured herself, but now used sex to completely control and humiliate him.

She needed to get Mike away from his useless buddy Joe. If there was money around, Mike would find an excuse to give some to Joe for no reason at all. Their long-term friendship had been kind of cute at first but had become annoying in the last few years. Mike had taken advice from this complete loser about his business, now he was bankrupt. She couldn't let Joe talk Mike into some stupid scheme involving her money. She needed to exercise even more control over Mike. She needed to do it right now.

CHAPTER 26

Las Cruces, New Mexico

The next morning, Mike called Jeff and told him what Emerson had offered, adding that he wanted to accept the deal.

"Mike, we can handle the legal transfer of the properties as payment for the shares in Blue Devils Development—that can be done in a few days. I guess I don't know if this is the thing to do, but it's a business decision so whatever you think is right is what you should do."

Mike thanked him and said that they should get started. He told Jeff that they were headed to Emerson's office, where Mike would agree to the deal. He would have Emerson contact Jeff to put all of the paperwork in place.

Joe and Mike followed the pattern of the day before: they packed up, loaded the car, and then checked out of the hotel. They made the quick drive to downtown Las Cruces and parked in front of Emerson's office.

Emerson was standing in the front area when they entered. He greeted them and showed them to his office.

"Mr. Emerson, we appreciate you sharing the information yesterday. Joe was able to determine that what you had told us regarding the values was correct. I've given this a lot of thought. I can't know for sure what you and my father agreed to, but I think there must have been some kind of understanding since he had left you alone for so many years before he died. If you had an understanding with him, I want to honor it. Of course, I could have convinced myself that none of that was true. My father may have ignored you because he just didn't care about any of that stuff anymore—he became a different man after he quit bootlegging. But it just doesn't matter. Bottom line, I want to complete the deal you outlined."

"I appreciate your candor, and I believe that is the best decision for everyone." Emerson hadn't been very expressive at any time since they had met him, but he seemed genuinely pleased that they had agreed. It was also clear that there would be no celebration party and that it was fine with Emerson for them to leave any time they were ready.

"I talked to Jeff Young this morning and instructed him to work with you or your attorney to complete the necessary paperwork. I'm sure I'll be able to sign in Oklahoma City, and you can do it here. Then we can exchange documents. I don't anticipate returning to Las Cruces. I wish you luck, Mr. Emerson."

With that Mike stood to leave. "I'll instruct my attorney to contact Mr. Young, and I'm sure we can get the documents in shape in a day or two. Thank you again, Mr. Allen, and I wish you a safe trip home."

Joe and Mike left. They had a 1:00 pm flight, so they needed to head to the airport. They were both quiet along the way. There was no doubt that this was going to change something. As they drove, they discussed how they should proceed in examining the properties. Mike wanted to make sure Joe knew to bill him for all of the time he took helping to make the deal happen. Joe kept his thoughts to himself—he had turned down $600,000 and now Mike was suggesting he write up a bill for a couple of thousand? Maybe Mike's newfound wealth was making him a complete asshole.

They arrived at the El Paso airport in plenty of time for their flight. They returned the car and went to the counter to check their luggage. The flight home was without incident and without much conversation. Joe thought he was sensing something from Mike, but he wasn't sure what it was, so he left it alone.

At the Oklahoma City airport, they went their separate ways, agreeing to touch base once the papers were signed so that they could inspect the properties and talk about how to handle the accounting and management. There was no mention of getting together and celebrating. It felt more like Mike had lost something rather than gained property worth over a million bucks.

The next week, Mike called and left a message for Joe that he had signed all of the documents and had received signed copies from Jeff, so the deal was done. He wanted to meet at Joe's office the next Friday to discuss accounting matters and maybe make a quick run by the Second Street properties to see what needed to be done with them. He said he should have all of the keys by then.

"Well, Mike, how does it feel to be a man of property?"

"Very funny. So far it's been nothing except a pain in the butt—but I guess someday the money will start to roll in."

Joe was starting to get a little annoyed at Mike's attitude. What the hell did he want, a big pile of cash to just fall in his lap? Jeez, what a fucking grouch this guy was—more assets than he had ever had and it sounded like he was having to clean the toilets in the damn buildings. What bullshit. Joe was getting pissed, tired of dealing with the "poor me" whining from Mike.

"Hey, why don't we run over to those Second Street properties and see how bad they are?" Maybe a field trip would help his mood—maybe Mike's mood, too.

"Yeah, I guess we don't exactly need to look at Triples." Mike was grinning, which was a little better.

"Something else Joe. I heard from the Dallas law firm. They confirmed my dad had hired them to perform certain duties including paying the lock box rental and the property taxes on the cabin. An escrow account had been established and funded to pay those things for approximately fifteen years or until the money ran out. Once they had been notified of the lock box being closed and the property being sold, they sent me a settlement letter. With the letter was a check for about $4,000 which was the remaining balance in the escrow account. So, I guess I'm wrong, some money has rolled in and I should cheer up. Sorry, guess I'm too busy or something to be cheerful. Let's go look at those old buildings."

The two properties were next door to one another, so they parked in front. Both had driven past since the purchase, so the condition of the outside wasn't a surprise. What the insides looked like; they had no idea. The outside was obviously in need of some attention, maybe a lot. Joe guessed it had been many years since much had been done on the buildings. Some windows were boarded up with plywood, while others had been painted over so you couldn't see inside. Layers of graffiti covered most of the walls. Joe thought Mike should probably just take a minimum offer on the old things and get rid of them and Mike thought that was probably right.

Mike unlocked the padlock on the front door of the first building, which had been a night club. Second Street had changed a lot from its heyday. Joe had been told that back in the 50s this had been a high traffic area, with lots of pedestrians. There had been numerous shops and small businesses that served the community—barber shops, shoe repair shops, and a couple of appliance stores that did a booming business. Now there was little automobile traffic and almost no pedestrians.

The door seemed to be jammed, but they were able to force it open. Once they were inside, they could see the remains of what had been a bar or restaurant. A huge bar counter wrapped around one side of the building, while off to one side there was what appeared to be a bandstand with a dance floor in front. Everything was filthy, but it didn't appear to have suffered a great deal of damage.

"Some of this old stuff, like that monster of a big bar, could be worth some money." Joe was amazed that everything was in relatively good shape. They looked into what must have been the kitchen area. All of the equipment had been removed, and there appeared to be some damage to one wall, maybe where something had been taken out.

"This is a huge kitchen. Must have done a hell of a business at one time. Kind of strange to grow up in a town and not be aware that places like this even existed. I mean, we were just kids, but it still seems like it should be better known than it is—don't you think? I bet it was an interesting place back then." Joe was much more interested than Mike, who said nothing.

They poked around for a while without finding much. "Looks like the building is in better shape than I would have guessed but still, in this part of town right now I'm not sure you could rent it for much of anything. And it would take a bunch of money just to clean it up. Maybe you could find someone opening a bar with a 50s theme who would pay to have some of this stuff, but that would be a long shot."

Mike agreed with Joe. It was an old building full of a bunch of interesting junk. "Look over here." Joe was standing in front of a door. "Stairs going down to the basement—shall we complete the tour?"

Mike was not real sure they should, but Joe had his flashlight on and was headed down. "Watch your step! Coming down I found a couple of places where there are some loose boards." Great—inherit a million bucks and kill yourself inspecting this old death trap.

Joe was at the bottom. He poked around for a while, but mostly just found junk. "No need to bother coming down Mike—all I see is more junk and dirt." Joe cautiously went back up stairs. "Just one big goddamn mess down there."

Mike said, "Joe please watch your language."

Joe wished he had the old Mike with him, because this new one was a pain in the ass.

"Guess we should look inside the building next door. Do you know what it used to be?"

"No, all I could find out was that it's been vacant longer

than the night club building, so more than likely the inside is in even worse shape. Keep in mind, Mike, you basically paid nothing for these buildings and someday the land might be worth something."

Mike grunted something Joe couldn't make out and they headed next door. Surprisingly, the door to this building opened more easily than the one in the first building. They entered what obviously had been a small lobby area in a hotel. While incredibly dirty, the overall condition of the inside was amazingly good.

"Never would have guessed that this had been a hotel. Must be about fifteen or so rooms. Man, I bet there are some stories about this old place."

Once again Mike hung back, standing close to the front door, as Joe ventured off to explore. The building had only two stories. On the first floor was a small dining room and kitchen, the lobby, an office, and five guest rooms. Joe started opening doors and looking into the rooms.

"Hey, Mike. Don't just stand there, help me out. Why don't you go upstairs and look in the rooms there?"

"Look, Joe, I know you still think we're going to stumble across millions, but I don't. I've seen enough of these old broken-down buildings. Let's go before we hurt ourselves."

Joe couldn't believe this was the same Mike who used to be the adventuresome one of the pair. Joe poked around the front desk area as he listened to his one-time best friend whine. Suddenly Joe stopped.

"Son of a bitch—look at that." Joe was pointing above the key area behind the front desk.

Mike walked up and looked where Joe was pointing. "Son of a bitch!"

Faded but still visible were the words *St Francis Hotel.*

They both recalled the letter from Mike's dad. *And remember, your path to financial independence goes through Deep Deuce at the St. Francis.*

"I'm not sure I'm believing this."

The boredom had left Mike's face and there was something close to the old gleam in Mike's eyes. They quickly looked around the front desk, as if there might be stacks of money just lying around. They looked at each other and began laughing—it felt like old times.

Joe began organizing their search. He had Mike go upstairs and check each guest room, looking for anything out of place. Joe searched the main floor—guest rooms, lobby, offices, and kitchen.

After several hours they stopped and sat down on the floor, dirt be damned, in the lobby.

"I don't know, Joe. Maybe my dad really was crazy, and this is just some kind of old man's sick joke."

Joe started to laugh. Soon they were both laughing. Sweaty, dirty, and tired, now everything was funny. No matter what happened today, at least they had enjoyed a few good laughs, just like they used to.

"Well we're not done, yet. There's an area in the kitchen I was going to explore some more. Come on, let's finish this and go have a drink."

"Not sure about a drink, but let's finish." The new Mike was back.

Joe showed Mike what he was talking about. There

was a large cabinet that looked out of place. Joe said he wanted to move it to see if there was anything behind it. The cabinet was empty, so with both of them they were able to move it aside. Behind the cabinet was an unusual door—it looked almost like a small elevator door.

"I think that's some kind of dumbwaiter or freight elevator. Jeez, I think there must be a basement."

There was no visible way of opening the door. Joe went off looking for some kind of tool to pry it open. He came back with a fire hatchet.

"I guess if I can't pry the damn thing open, I can always just chop it up." Mike looked sullen again. The time for joking had passed.

Joe managed to pry the door open. It was a small freight elevator, about five feet high inside, so a man could get in but would have to stoop. It appeared to be a mechanical operation, with a pulley in place. Joe grabbed the pulley chain and pulled—the elevator started to move down. He reversed the action and the elevator moved back up. Neither Joe nor Mike were anxious to test the thing. They decided the better course of action was to look for stair access to the basement, but after another lengthy search they decided it didn't exist, as odd as that seemed. Joe got his flashlight.

"I'm going down. If I'm not back up in about thirty minutes, call the fire department." Cautious Joe had become Indiana Jones.

He climbed into the elevator, testing each step. Once inside, he worked the pulley and the elevator crept slowly down. The basement had a low ceiling, so the distance he descended wasn't great, but to Joe it felt like it took forever. There was no door on the basement level, so Joe could immediately see into the room with his flashlight. The area was large, with a huge, room-like structure in one corner. It was surprisingly uncluttered. He got out of the elevator and yelled up to Mike that he was down. Looking around, he found a set of stairs going up to a door. He couldn't believe that they hadn't found the stairs from above. He went up the stairs and opened the door—and there was another door. The second door slid sideways, and he found himself in the office area behind the front desk. Joe stepped out and saw that the door had been carefully hidden. It matched the wall perfectly—no wonder they hadn't found it. He went to find Mike.

They went back down the stairs. Joe went over to the boxy structure and cleared away the accumulated junk from the front.

"This thing looks like a safe."

"Did you say a safe?" That seemed to get Mike's attention.

"I guess—at least that's a safe door." Joe pushed some more stuff out of the way. "My god, this thing is huge. It's a fucking room." Mike made a face. "Look at this. It must be thirty feet long by about fifteen feet across and eight feet high."

"Probably used it to store food or something."

"Why would you have a safe to store food?" Joe was not enjoying new Mike's attitude. "Wait a minute, look at this—this is a combination lock. Son of a bitch! Do you have that piece of paper from the lock box?" Joe was excited—could that be the combination to this gigantic safe? He knew it sounded farfetched, but Mike's dad was connected to all of this—the safe in the basement of his old building, a combination code in a lock box owned by his dad—why the hell not?

"I think it's in my briefcase in the car. You really think that could be the combination? And even if it is, no doubt the thing will be empty, or full of old rotten food."

"Just go get the paper, Mike, and let's see. If it's full of rotten food, we'll shut the door and leave. Okay?" Joe almost hoped it *was* full of old food—just what sourpuss deserved.

Mike was getting pretty good at making holier-than-thou faces, and he made one now, but he went back up the stairs to get the briefcase.

It took Mike what seemed like a long time to get the briefcase and get back down the stairs. Of course, standing in the middle of an old creepy building next to an old spooky safe might have had something to do with time moving slowly. Joe began to imagine all sorts of things that could be in a safe that large—things that might jump out and grab him when they opened the door. Blimey, he was going to have a drink after this was over.

Mike handed the slip of paper to him. Joe began turning the dial, which was surprisingly smooth. Don't build them like that anymore. Joe completed the combination and looked up at Mike, "Ready?"

"Yeah, open it." It worked! That old slip of paper had the right combination after all.

Joe moved some more stuff out of the way to clear a

path for the door, then turned the handle and opened it. Joe shined the light inside: there were hundreds of boxes, wooden crates that all looked alike. They were heavy duty, and most were marked as restaurant supplies.

"What do you think they are?" Even Mike sounded a little excited.

"No idea. Let me get something and let's see if we can open one." Joe went off looking for something to use as a lever, something less dangerous than the hatchet. He searched for a while without any luck, then went up to the kitchen and came back with a mallet and knife. "Probably not the safest tools, but it was all I could find—still better than the hatchet."

Joe stepped into the safe and began working on the closest crate. It had been put together very well. He had some trouble, but eventually got the knife under what he thought was the right board and hit it with the mallet and it came off. Inside the crate was money, lots and lots of money. "What the fuck?" The old Mike seemed to come back for a moment.

"Jeez, look at this. These are twenties and hundreds. This crate is full of money." They stared at the mountain of crates. Mike sat down on the floor.

"What the hell have we found?"

"I think we've found my dad's millions."

"I can't believe it. He was telling the truth about everything—I thought he was out of his fucking mind, and he was telling the truth."

Mike didn't look well. Something was going on in his head. "My God, Joe, this is money from bootlegging—this is money from selling booze illegally. How—how did he accumulate this much money?"

"Don't know Mike. But this is a bunch of money. There are hundreds of crates in here. If they're all like this one, it's millions for sure."

"What the hell are we going to do now?"

Good question. Joe hadn't expected this to actually happen. Mike's father had buried millions in an old safe in the basement of an old building in Deep Deuce—fucking amazing!

The first thing they did was seal the crate back up and lock the safe. Joe even pushed some of the junk back up against the door. They went upstairs and re-locked the building, making damn sure it was secure. Suddenly the neighborhood didn't feel very safe. Back in the car they just sat there for a minute.

"What the hell are we going to do?" Mike seemed dazed.

"Well, Mike, I think we should revert to our old selves and go to Triples and have a drink."

"Maybe you're right."

They went to Triples and found that the new bartender didn't know them. The world had moved on while they weren't looking. Joe got a gin and tonic, but Mike pulled himself together and had a diet Coke.

On the drive over, Joe started giving this thought. While on the surface it was obviously a good thing, there was also a lot of risk. This much money could cause serious problems. First do you keep it? Obvious answer, yes! Now what do you do with it? Where do you keep it? How can you spend it? Lots of issues. But the biggest problem was Mike.

"First, Mike, you can't tell anyone about this. I know the new you doesn't lie, but you mustn't tell anyone—and yes, that means Sam. We've got something going on here that, if we handle right it will be great, and if not could be really bad. So, number one, you can't tell anyone, okay?"

"I don't know, Joe. This is so confusing to me." Mike was looking like his thinking had stalled. Joe was very concerned that events were overloading some critical function in Mike's brain. He knew that Mike was changing and that he was trying to get everything sorted out about his dad, plus Sam seemed to be exerting more and more control over him. He was being pulled in too many directions.

"Mike, just promise me you won't tell anyone until we can put together the right plan to deal with this. And no, I don't know what that is. So, we're going to have to think and then decide what to do, but you cannot tell anyone."

"Okay, already. I won't tell Sam or anyone. But we have to decide what to do quickly or I'll go nuts. How much money do you think it is?"

"I'm not sure. That one crate had to have $50,000 or more in it. I'd guess there are sixty or maybe eighty crates. So, that would be $3 million, maybe $4 million. Millions anyway. And the next crate could be different, with even more money. We just won't know until we look at each one, but you can be damn sure it's millions—millions!"

Joe thought: *man, that is a lot of booze.* Was that all Patrick Allen was selling? Because it sure seemed like a lot of money. But maybe over a number of years it was possible.

And Mike said they had always lived a simple life. He needed to think and come up with a plan about how to handle the money and keep Mike from confessing to his father's sins.

"Mike, meet me in the morning for breakfast. I'm beginning to think of a way to handle this, but I need to think it through and make sure it'll work."

Mike agreed. He wasn't looking very happy for someone who had just found millions. Some guys are never satisfied.

Joe knew there were big potential problems with this much money. It could cause Mike some real grief if he didn't keep quiet and figure out a way to use the money without anyone suspecting he'd suddenly struck it rich. Joe also knew it was up to him to prevent Mike from doing something real stupid—he needed to come up with the plan, and quick.

CHAPTER 27

Oklahoma City, Oklahoma

Joe and Mike met the next morning at a Village Inn, just off of Broadway. They settled into a back booth that offered some privacy. Joe ordered coffee and his usual breakfast of eggs, hash browns, and wheat toast with sausage patties. Mike had coffee and toast.

"I gave this a lot of thought last night. This money is a gift from your father—he wanted you to have it, wanted you to be happier. He went to a lot of trouble to make sure you were the only one who could put all of this together and discover his secret. Think about everything he did, from arranging for the money to be in that old safe in the first place, to making sure that the lock box payments were made, and the tax payments on the cabin. Having the letter and key delivered to you, having the stock certificates in the lock box. I mean, my god, he went to a lot of trouble. All of it to benefit you. Well, right there is a lot of responsibility—you can't let your father down."

"Well, that's true, but it's ill-gotten gains. How can I keep it? I know you think this stuff about my new beginning is just crap, but it's not. I want to be someone else, a better person, and that someone doesn't have a bootlegger for a father and sure does not have millions of dollars hidden in a basement under an old hotel. It almost drove me insane not to tell Sam. I can't live a life based on a lie—I am not my dad!"

Joe could see this was going to be a challenge. While he didn't like it, maybe he should just let Mike give the money to charity or to the IRS and forget about it. Joe thought Mike was wrong about his dad. He didn't understand why Mike had become so angry with his dad for not being perfect—as if any dad was perfect. But Joe wasn't going to let Mike make such a stupid mistake if he could help it.

"First off, your father made this money selling something people wanted—which by the way is perfectly legal today. He sold a lot because he was good at selling. I think you know that your father never hurt anybody. This wasn't a gangster selling booze and killing people. This was your father providing a service to his neighbors." Okay, maybe laying it on just a little thick here. "I knew your father and he was a kind, gentle man who lived a simple life—but he wanted you to have this money so you could do something good with it, make your life better." Talk about salesmanship.

"Okay, I see your point."

"You could just take the cash and go deposit it in the bank and every alarm in the whole country would go off. There would be more feds and cops and bank people than you could count. They would want to know where it came from, where it had been, how you found it, and on and on. They might decide that it wasn't just from bootlegging, that your father must have been a member of organized crime. They would confiscate the money, might even try to put you in prison because you had hidden it for all of these years, or maybe say you must have been selling drugs to have made this much money and that this stuff about your dad was a smokescreen."

"Could that really happen?"

"This much money involved, people go nuts. What started off as a good thing could become a nightmare."

Joe paused to let Mike absorb the risks he would be running by being Mr. Goody Two-Shoes. He could see some of it was sinking in—good.

Their breakfasts arrived and the waitress refilled their coffees and left the check. This was why Joe had breakfast at a Village Inn—all of the waitresses were the same person, doing the same thing, over and over. It was comforting to know there was one place in the world that was always the same. He picked things up with Mike.

"I have some ideas on how to handle the actual cash. Some of this will feel like cheating to you but trust me, you'll be paying taxes on this money over time, just not exposing it to the world in one big chunk. First, we need a cash business that can be used to channel some of the cash on a regular basis into the system."

"Money laundering—I'm not stupid Joe."

"Yes, it's money laundering, and the government says we shouldn't do it, but under these circumstances it's the least of several evils."

"Okay, I'll shut up and let you finish. Sorry if I'm being difficult—I know you're just trying to help."

"Mike, there's no way around this. If you tell the authorities about this money there's a chance they take it all and you come under suspicion for committing a crime.

I know you can say well, that's just wrong, but trust me, wrong or not that could happen. If you want to use this money to do some good and honor your father, you have to work with me here on skirting a few things."

They each took some bites of their breakfasts. Joe was having trouble reading Mike, something that seemed to happen a lot lately. There was a distance between them that had never been there before. But Mike seemed calm and ready to hear more, so Joe continued.

"I happen to know that Triples is for sale. You already own the building, so it might make sense to buy Triples and start to funnel some of the money into that business and then to you. Restaurants and bars are good for this because they operate with so much cash. That's the first thing I recommend. Also, I think there's an area in the basement at Triples that could secure the crates after a little work. Obviously, that's a big issue, getting those crates to a more secure location."

"I know I said I'd shut up, but let me butt in. I like the plan so far. I don't want to hand the money over to some arm of the government and have it wasted on what they consider important. But before we go any further there's something we have to get resolved—half of this money is yours. Don't give me any bullshit about my father's legacy or whatever. That was our deal and you said our deal was only valid if there was a big pile of cash—well, there's a big pile of cash. If you don't agree to that then I'll just give it to the government and let them do whatever they want with it." Some of this sounded like the old Mike.

"Well I guess I can't talk you out of this foolish idea of

giving me a bunch of money, so you've got a deal, Mike."
Joe was smiling.

CHAPTER 28

Dallas, Texas—October 1987

Michelle Lewis was thirty-four today and it was her tenth anniversary at Duncan's Department Stores. This afternoon there was going to be a little celebration in the basement cafeteria for everyone who had an anniversary this month. No one knew it was her birthday—she didn't want them to know. Michelle had been Michelle Thompson until she was married. She divorced some years ago after a difficult two years of marriage. She still used her married name mostly because of the hassle of getting everything changed over again, but she also had limited attachment to the name Thompson.

The previous month Michelle had been promoted to assistant buyer in women's fashions. It had been an important step for her. Most of the assistant buyers and buyers all had bachelors or master's degrees, generally from well-known colleges. Michelle had an associate's degree from a little known graphics school. Nonetheless, she was proud of her degree because of the effort it had taken to get it without any help from anyone. Well, actually she had some help.

Life hadn't been easy for Michelle. She had been raised by her mother's brother and his wife, although Michelle did not know that until she was sixteen. The man she thought was her father had been dying and had told her that everything she thought was true was really a lie. A short time after he died, his wife asked Michelle to leave. She now knew she had a mother, Sally, who had died because of complications when giving birth to her. The dying man whom she had thought for so long was her father had told her that she was a sinner just like her mother. These memories haunted Michelle for years. She believed she was a sinner, even though as far as she knew she had never sinned.

Michelle was attractive, so she had many opportunities. But she was shy and withdrawn. Most men just went away. During the time after she left her so-called home, she stayed with one of her high school friends. The friend's parents were wonderful to her and she slowly developed some self-esteem. She worked at several restaurants waiting tables, and soon became a little bit more outgoing. It was the encouragement of that family that had prompted her to go to graphics school. She had always been able to draw and seemed to have a keen eye when it came to color and form. She fell in love with the school, and it provided her with loans for tuition. She still had to work, though, so she could only go to school part-time. It was the best time she had ever had.

Michelle imagined there was a family curse of sin that would follow her all her life. She was frightened of any relationship with boys, and mostly tried to stay by herself at school, seldom making eye contact in public. But her work was outstanding, and several teachers had said that she had talent. Every day she became more secure in who she was and what she was doing.

As she had approached completion of the requirements for her associate's degree, she had gone into one of the teacher's offices, a particularly nice woman who had often complimented her, and asked if she knew of any place Michelle might get a job. The teacher said her brother was in the personnel department at Duncans and she was sure he could find her something.

He did. It wasn't much, but it was a start. She began in the mail room, delivering mail to the various departments in the headquarters building. That had been years ago today. To Michelle it had felt like an accomplishment. She fought her shyness every day just to do her job and then, knowing that the only way someone would hire her in one of the creative departments was if she asked. She asked. She asked again, and kept asking, until finally she was moved into the display department as a junior clerk.

Nobody there had worked as hard as Michelle. She had no social life and only felt alive when she was at work. She had volunteered for every bad job, every late night, every weekend assignment. She had not only been eager, she had been good, and people had started to notice.

One of the people who had noticed was Michael Lewis. He had been an assistant buyer in men's shoes and had become very attentive to Michelle. She had shunned him, but he hadn't given up, keeping it up for months until she'd finally agreed to go out with him. He was handsome and he was a buyer—well assistant buyer—and Michelle had been intimidated. As a result of the family curse of sin, she had still been a virgin, though it hadn't made her feel special, just odd.

Michael had been relentless. He seemed to relish the challenge Michelle presented. She had been about to tell him that she did not want to see him anymore when he asked her to marry him. Michelle had thought that it was absurd—they had been on maybe six dates; they had only kissed once. What the hell was he thinking?

Once again, he hadn't taken no for an answer, and before Michelle really knew what was going on she was married. It was like she woke up one day and thought, *what the hell just happened?* Married and having sex. Michelle had discovered that she liked sex, and that she was a warm and loving person. The joy of sex had made the first six months of marriage a wonderful, fulfilling experience. If he hadn't already been dead, she would have found a two-by-four and attacked her self-righteous ex-father. The baggage she had carried for so many years seemed to lift. She was smiling and laughing a lot.

But their first anniversary had been a sign of things to come—Michael was nowhere to be found. It had only gotten worse from there. Some of her co-workers told her Michael had been seen with other women at clubs around town. She tried to ignore it but it got worse. The topper had come when two female employees at Duncans filed sexual harassment charges. Michelle had told him she wanted a divorce and he hadn't even seemed to care.

It had taken a while, but eventually Michelle divorced Michael and shortly thereafter he was fired from Duncans. She had been upset, but maybe she had needed a hustler like Michael to break through the barrier she had set up—maybe he had done her a favor without meaning to.

Michelle had rededicated herself to work. She had a couple of flings, but they hadn't meant anything to her. With her life focused again on work, she experienced more and more success.

Michelle had never shared her dream with anyone: to one day run a business like Duncans. She knew it wasn't going to happen, but it was still her dream. She wasn't really sure where it came from—it seemed she had dreamed it for so long that it had no beginning she could identify.

One day one of her co-workers, who regularly read the personal classifieds, asked Michelle if she was related to Sally Thompson. The woman worked in the human resources department, so she knew Michelle's maiden name. Michelle was so stunned she almost couldn't answer. She eventually told the woman that she didn't know of any relative named Sally. The woman said she was just curious because over the years there had been several ads for information about a Sally Thompson—she just thought it was weird.

Weird it was. Michelle had no idea who would be looking for her long-dead mother and it unnerved her. So much about her mother was a mystery to Michelle, and there was no one to ask. She often felt completely alone.

Michelle went to the basement for the group anniversary party. She liked many of her co-workers and enjoyed their company. Many of them had known her through her shy days and her horrible marriage and were the closest thing she had to a family.

"Hey, Michelle congratulations on your new promotion." This came from Betty, one of her best friends at work.

"Thanks Betty."

"Pretty soon you'll be the big boss, and everybody will work for you. I hear all kinds of people say there is nobody who works any harder than Michelle."

"Well, thanks again Betty. Not sure they are going to put me in charge anytime soon."

"Why don't you go with us a little later and get a drink?"

"I wish I could, but I have to get home and make sure my cat is fed—but thanks anyway."

Ugh. How pitiful was that? Plus, Michelle had made it up, she didn't have a cat. It had been many years since her stupid marriage ended and she was increasingly lonely, but she still didn't feel comfortable in many social situations.

Michelle did not know what the future held for her—she did know that there was someone out there who was right for her—and that when she met him, she would know. Might not happen next week, but it would happen.

CHAPTER 29

Oklahoma City, Oklahoma—December 1987

Even with everything in his life changing—some good, some bad—Joe loved Christmas. He liked the cool weather, the hectic atmosphere, the lights, the Christmas trees—everything about it gave him pleasure. But mostly he just loved the feeling of joy that replaced gloom at this time of year. It was magical. Suddenly almost everything seemed to be better.

Almost everything, but of course not everything. He had signed what he believed were the final divorce papers last month. He hadn't heard if Liz had signed or not. None of that surprised him. His lawyer treated him with the same disdain as Liz's lawyer. Liz had been very successful at convincing everyone that he was a loser who drank too much and was a lousy husband and a thoughtless father. She had a flair for the dramatic and took every chance to damn him for his evil ways. Some of this was extremely hurtful, and definitely uncalled for. He had agreed to everything she had asked for. Now Joe was very done with Liz.

He had closed down his accounting practice the previous month. As much as he had hated accounting, it still made him sad. He had been an accountant for many years—it was who he was, it was his title. Losing that identity was troubling. Even some of his clients seemed sad. That surprised Joe—he thought they couldn't care less. He had never formed friendships with his clients, except for Mike, even though he did try to give them the best service he could.

Of course, Lucille wasn't happy. She actually became quite livid and called him names he had no idea she knew. Every day she had worked for Joe seemed like misery to her, yet Joe firing her was apparently cruel beyond belief. She claimed to have worked thankless hours to help build this business and now he was throwing her out into the street. She linked him numerous times, in her parting tirade, to the devil. Joe was mostly shocked by the passion—he had never even seen her smile. He briefly thought she might be dangerous—then he forgot about her.

Everything was ready to close on the purchase transaction and Joe would officially take possession of Triples on January 1, 1988. He was excited and nervous. Just because you spent way too much time in a bar didn't mean you knew anything about running one. In the last two months he had visited a lot of restaurants in several cities, observing and asking questions. He was struck by how open the restaurant people were, and how ready they were to offer advice and assistance. They all seemed like nicer people than he was used to dealing with, or maybe it was he who had changed. He knew he was feeling better about himself and, other than his children, he wasn't worrying about much.

Joe was headed to Will Rogers World Airport for the third time this year to make a trip to El Paso and then Las Cruces. His earlier trips with Mike had been hectic and always about Mike—this trip was just for Joe. He was going alone and looking forward to having time to reflect a little and maybe decide if he really was the bad guy Liz had so passionately described.

Joe and Mike had taken a small cash withdrawal the month before from the Second Street vault, so Joe was feeling flush. He had booked a first-class seat for his trip to El Paso. By his standards this was a lavish expenditure and it ran counter to his puritan ways, so he was a little nervous about paying for such luxury as he checked in. His worries disappeared when he was seated immediately, and the hostess brought him a drink and some nuts before anyone else had even boarded the plane. *Shit,* he thought, *this is the only way to fly!*

The flight was smooth and entirely enjoyable, and pampered as he was, Joe felt almost important. As they approached the El Paso airport, though, he grew melancholy. He knew that his relationship with Mike would never be the same, and he missed his friend. They had so many good memories.

Joe had decided to stay at the Mason de Mesilla instead of the Holiday Inn for the variety and also because it was closer to the restaurants he had wanted to visit. He had rented a full-size car and he drove from El Paso to Las Cruces in great comfort.

The hotel was decorated for Christmas, with luminarias along its walls and colorful lights strung in the trees. Joe couldn't wait for nighttime so he could see the lights. After he checked in, he went to his suite, and he was impressed with the old-world charm of the room.

Joe spent several days enjoying the ambiance of the

area and visiting local restaurants, especially La Posta and Double Eagle. He knew that La Posta had the charm he wanted to capture at Triples if he could figure out how to accomplish it with his limited knowledge of running a restaurant.

On his last evening he took a stroll around the Plaza to enjoy the Christmas atmosphere. The night air was cool, but without any wind it was very pleasant. There was a band playing mariachi music in the gazebo and several couples were dancing. His melancholy was turning to depression. He felt great about what he was learning and how he could apply that to Triples, but he was lonely.

As he sat on a bench listening to the music he thought about Pat and Sally. He wondered what they had really been like. And could the old man he knew as Mike's dad really have had a love affair with a beautiful young mistress? It almost didn't seem possible.

Joe walked back to the hotel intending to go to his room—he ended up in the bar. He had a gin and tonic, but only one, and then went to bed. He dreamed that night about an angel named Sally. She was the most beautiful and exciting person he had ever seen. He wanted to be with her. He didn't want to be alone.

PART FOUR: 2004

CHAPTER 30

Oklahoma City, Oklahoma

Joe was sitting at the bar in Triples. Some years before he had the bar redone, incorporating some of the materials from the old Deep Deuce bar. He loved the irony of it, plus the bar looked great. Customers often commented on its massive size and the craftsmanship of the bar, which made it feel like it was from another era. Even when not drinking, Joe's favorite spot was the bar.

It was morning and Joe was having coffee while reading the paper. Damn paper sure seemed to be getting smaller lately. He turned to the metro section, where he knew there was going to be an article about Joe Meadows—one of OKC's top restaurateurs. Restaurateur—Joe liked the sound of that.

After Joe and Mike made their deal, things moved along pretty quickly. Joe made a low down payment deal to purchase Triples, borrowing a little cash from the Second Street vault. From that day on, Joe had given up accounting—he had always hated it. He fired Lucille—oh happy day! —and began his new life, sans Liz, as a restaurant owner.

The divorce from Liz had started out very messy, but Joe quickly acquiesced completely, giving her everything. She got the house, furniture, cars, bank account, the kids—Joe got nothing; although his attorney was able to get Joe off the hook for any alimony or child support—the kids were almost adults anyway. This was possible because Joe declared that he was closing his accounting practice and was going to run a bar. From Liz's point of view this was a sign that Joe was falling deeper into his alcoholism and she wanted to get as much as she could right now—she didn't figure Joe would be able to pay in the future anyway, given the direction he was headed. What she got was substantial and it seemed to make her happy.

Joe was sorry for the kids. But, after so many years under their mother's control they weren't very fond of Joe. Maybe someday when they were thirty or forty, they could all reconcile, but Joe doubted it.

Triples became his passion. He spent months researching every aspect of the food business. He already had a pretty good feel for the bar business. During the research phase, Joe went to several cities and observed some of the best restaurant operations. One trip, based a little bit on nostalgia, had been to Las Cruces. He had introduced himself to some of the staff at La Posta and collected their contact information.

Joe spent several days at the Mason de Mesilla hotel, an old adobe building with great character. During that time, he ate at La Posta several times, as well as enjoying the ambiance at the Double Eagle on the Old Mesilla Plaza. The Double Eagle bar area was worth the visit—not to mention the room with the ghost. He loved the elegance of the place, took numerous notes, and enjoyed every minute of his trip.

Step one was convincing Mike that they needed to do

some major remodeling on Triples as a smoke screen for building a secure room in the basement for their newly found fortune. Within months of purchasing the restaurant, they began expansion. Along with the upgrades, Joe offered jobs to two of the kitchen staff he had met at La Posta. They brought with them all of the food expertise he had experienced at La Posta, along with a complete dedication to him for the opportunity he was giving to them and their families.

Joe changed everything about the menu. The flavors of New Mexico blended in with Oklahoma traditions to create unique, delicious offerings in the restaurant and the bar—haute cuisine for the restaurant, with a unique Nuevo Mexican menu, and "truck stop specials" for the bar. Joe's perfect place. Business doubled overnight.

Joe was energized and enjoyed the daily activity of running a successful restaurant. He still drank a little too much, and on his bad days he still fought loneliness, along with his old friend depression. His new apartment was close to Triples, so on the worst days he just went home and took a long nap. Generally, though, Joe was more content with himself.

The years were also very good to Mike. He and Sam started their church, The Legacy Chapel. Mike was in his element. He had a slow beginning, but word soon spread. Before long they were expanding into a much larger building. Joe had never attended, but there were constant stories in the paper and on the television news about the rapid success of Oklahoma City's newest megachurch. The chapel now had TV broadcasts featuring Mike and

Samantha. Joe had watched one and could see why they were so appealing. Mike was a natural on television, and the couple's interaction was obviously based on a deep love they felt for each other. Sam was still one of the beautiful people. Joe didn't watch again.

Joe read somewhere that Legacy Chapel had taken in over thirty million dollars in the previous year. How ironic that Mike had no need for the money hidden in the basement at Triples—although, of course, up until a few years ago Joe sent him a check every month anyway.

Mike would call Joe every once in a while, and catch up on the business and on how Joe was doing, but the last call had been almost two years before. Joe understood—in some ways Joe represented Mike's past, something that Mike was no doubt trying to put behind him.

The real estate holdings that came through Emerson had changed. Besides the remodeling of Triples, the office building on Classen had gone through an extensive remodel and was filled with first class tenants on long-term leases. Joe had been surprised that Mike hadn't sold it, but the last time they had discussed it Mike had said he wanted to keep it. The buildings on Second Street had become part of an urban renewal project and were sold to the city at a substantial profit. Joe had often wondered about those buildings and their history. He was sad when they were torn down.

Joe handled all communications with the property management company that took care of the office building and the CPA firm that completed the tax returns. Everything had been put under a corporation called BDD II, though Mike's name wasn't on any of the publicly available documentation. Joe sent Mike quarterly reports regarding the buildings, but it had been years since Mike had asked any questions.

The one area where Joe felt he had failed was in finding Sally Thompson. Mike had made it very clear from the beginning that he wanted nothing to do with Sally or the package that they'd found in the lock box. Since that day Mike hadn't asked Joe about the package or ever mentioned Sally. Mike had uncovered a lot about his father and had managed to rationalize most of it to fit his image of his dad, but Sally couldn't be explained away so Mike just pretended that that part of his dad's life never happened.

It was only a few months after they had found the package addressed to Sally that Joe started his search for her. Finding her and delivering the package was the one thing he could do for Pat Allen that his son could not. He did not know Sally's age when she was involved with Pat, but his guess was she was in her middle to late twenties, so he calculated that she would be about fifty when he started looking for her.

For the first few years, Joe mostly placed ads in newspapers, and he covered as much territory as he could since he didn't really know where Sally might have gone. He would occasionally get a response, but none of them ever checked out. Then, in 1990, Joe hired a local private investigation company, someone recommended by one of his bartenders—bartenders seemed to know everything.

Price and Pope Investigations turned out to be Bob

Jones—Joe never did get an explanation of the company name. Bob had quoted Joe a fair price to try to track Sally down and Joe had given him all the information he had, though he didn't share anything about the package or Mike's dad. Bob was mostly a researcher and he seldom ventured out into the world—not exactly your movie PI.

It took Bob almost three months to find out anything about Sally. He asked Joe to meet him at his office. "Joe, I want you to know that I still have a lot to learn but there is something I thought you needed to know right now."

Joe waited. "Okay, Bob, what is it?"

"She's dead."

Joe hadn't been expecting that, and he felt a great sense of loss. He had never met her, knew almost nothing about her, but she had become more important to him than he had admitted. At a very deep level she had become Joe's Sally.

"Dead? How do you know? Do you know how or when or where?"

"The where and when, yes. She died in Chicago in 1954. I know because there's a death certificate and the timing is right for when she most likely would have been in the city. The how, I'm not sure. Based on other information I have; my guess is that it could have been complications during childbirth."

Joe felt like he just wanted to flee—he was having a panic attack about a woman he didn't even know. He took a few deep breaths while Bob waited.

"There's a child?" This wasn't what Joe had expected either. He had dreamed about meeting Sally, giving her a great gift from her past, and witnessing her joy. Now it turned out that she was dead and there was a child.

"Well, I don't know if there really is a child. What I know is that she gave birth to a girl at St. Joseph's Hospital in 1953. The baby was named Michelle, Sally Thompson was the mother, and the father was listed as unknown. At this point I haven't been able to determine what happened to the baby."

Dead end. Literally a dead end. Maybe Joe should just give up. Somehow the sadness of knowing that Sally was dead was overpowering. Why was it so important to Joe? Mike didn't give a shit, why should he? But it *was* important. The package was a loose end and Joe hated loose ends. He had wanted Sally to know what was in the package from Pat and now she never would.

"Bob, I'm not real sure where to go from here. I hired you to find Sally Thompson and I guess in a way you did. Now I'm thinking that I need to know about the daughter. For me to be able to close this connection I had with Sally, I need to talk to the daughter. So, let's continue with your current hourly rate and see what you can find out about the daughter, okay?"

"It's okay with me, Joe—this is what I do. But let me caution you. The child would have been a newborn when her mother died. She might have gone to relatives, or she could have been taken by the state and eventually put up for adoption. If she was adopted, my chances of finding her are almost zero. Those records are sealed for the protection of the child and the adopting parents, so it would be another dead end. But if you want me to try, that's fine—it's my job."

Bob didn't seem to lack self-esteem. "Yep. Continue on and see what you can find out. Any information at all will be appreciated. Thanks, Bob."

Joe went back to Triples, and in an unusual act had a gin and tonic at the bar—it was only 11:00 am.

Joe felt bad about Sally, and it had stayed on his mind for a few days—but life goes on. He got busy with the restaurant and soon the pain lessened. Maybe part of the sadness was that there was no one to talk to about it. He was the only one who seemed to care, and that made it especially poignant.

As time wore on, Joe heard from Bob once in a while, but never with any real news. Bob told him he had narrowed down the list of likely towns where he might find her to two, Dallas and Chicago. He now knew that Sally once had a brother in Dallas and had a sister in Chicago. He hadn't been able to locate the sister and had determined that the brother had died in a construction accident. None of this seemed of use to Joe. He decided that Bob's reports were just depressing him, so he asked him to stop searching and to send his final bill.

Joe didn't want to completely give up, though, so he continued to run ads over the years in the Dallas and Chicago papers for any information about a Michelle Thompson. As the internet came into his world, he placed some ads in various locations there as well. No responses.

By now Joe hadn't thought about the ads in months. The last ones he had placed had probably been over a year before. He thought that someday he would open the package and just see what was inside, but he was still reluctant to do it, as if it might break some sort of spell. Gosh, he was getting more mystical every day.

Joe spent most of his time at the restaurant. It was his business, of course, and he wanted it to be well run, but he was also most comfortable there. People would often comment that they had never been in the restaurant when Joe wasn't there. He knew this was a little obsessive—or maybe a lot—but it didn't matter. It was where he wanted to be.

CHAPTER 31

Oklahoma City, Oklahoma

Mike was not sure why he sometimes still felt depressed. Everything he had ever wanted had come true in the last few years. He was successful, respected, and wealthy—there was nothing missing.

For the first time in his life he felt like he deserved Samantha. His beautiful Sam was not stuck with a loser anymore. He loved her so much but was still uncomfortable around her. They shared intimacy and said sweet things, and that should have been enough, but Mike always felt like it was part of an act in which they played the perfect couple. It didn't make sense that two people could look so perfect and be so messed up.

The Legacy Chapel was a success beyond anything Mike could ever have imagined. His goal when they had started had been to be able to make a modest living doing something he and his wife loved. They were most alive when they were in front of people. Telling stories, giving a sermon, or just talking in front of an audience had become Mike's addiction. It replaced booze and made him a happy man. He realized that he needed to be loved by many people—one just wasn't enough. Legacy Chapel filled that need.

The adulation of his followers was what Mike now craved and he couldn't get enough of the thrill of having people praise him. He could no longer stand solitude—he had to have an audience. Somehow this love of the crowd was felt by his followers, but rather than sensing that Mike was filling a void in his own life, they perceived his need for love as a great warmth and affection coming from him to them. He was mesmerizing and seemed to connect at a very deep level with almost everyone. This connection turned into a huge financial success for his church.

As the church grew more successful, Mike and Sam grew closer in their public roles, but in private they grew apart. Their love was played out on the stage for everyone to see, but when they were alone, they were uncomfortable with each other. They adapted to these roles and seemed to find a routine that avoided conflict. They were still sexually active, but it took on the routine quality of a task that had to be done, like taking out the trash. They didn't discuss their feelings but settled into a pattern that seemed to fit the couple they had become.

Mike hadn't had any contact with Joe in some time. He thought about him a lot, wondering what was happening and how things were going. Mike still felt the old urge to call Joe and meet at Triples for a drink—their friendship and companionship over the years was something he wouldn't forget—but that just wasn't who he was anymore. He had given up Joe the way you would a smoking habit—it had been enjoyable once upon a time, but it was harmful, so you stopped. Joe knew too many secrets. Mike had to wash those secrets from his mind, as if they had never existed, and Joe was washed away along with the dreaded past. Mike wasn't going to think about his father's past—it hurt too much.

Mike had lumped Joe into the mess with his father. He didn't want to spend time trying to discover why his father's misbehavior troubled him so much—he just wanted it to disappear. He had worshiped his dad when he was growing up. Pat had been distant, but his mother had always talked about him as a warm and caring man, only ever saying good things about him, so that was how Mike saw him. His mother had told Mike how wonderful Pat was, how hard he worked so that they could have all the nice things they had and said that his dad loved them both very much. His picture of his dad was of a larger-than-life person who could do no wrong.

All the revelations about his father had been shocking to Mike. He had heard some stories growing up, but it wasn't the same as knowing they were true. So, he was a bootlegger—maybe Mike could have adjusted to that reality. But Pat's infidelity with Sally was something he couldn't handle. It made a joke of everything his mother had ever told him about his dad. It was like there were two dads now—the good one and the evil one—and Mike hated the evil one.

The money from his dad was a source of anguish. Mike had never fully explained the money to Sam—he was afraid she would reject him if she knew how weak he was. He had told her that he had gone into business with Joe and bought Triples. She had thrown a fit, saying Joe was an asshole who would steal money from Mike. Mike assured her that he had everything covered and that it was a good investment. Of course, when the money from the crates started rolling in, supposedly from that investment, Sam changed her tune. She still thought Joe was a bad person, but apparently, he knew how to run a bar—not a huge shock given his history.

The Triples money allowed them to grow the church much faster than donations would have allowed. It was this premature appearance of success that seemed to create the real success they eventually had from their ministry. People were attracted to the church because it was the place to be—the next megachurch. Mike knew that without his dad's money they would never have gotten to where they were now. And this became another reason to stay away from Joe. He was the only one who knew Mike's secret, and Mike didn't want anyone to know the importance of the bootlegger's legacy.

The person Mike missed the most was his mother. She was the one who had made him feel special. She had been the one who was there when he needed something—she had always cared. Mike had worshiped his father based on the image his mother had created, but his mother had always been genuinely perfect. He knew now his mother had been the backbone of his family, not his dad. She was the one who had made every day something special for Mike and had never been disappointed in him. She was Mike's ideal for what a mother should be, and he missed her greatly.

The church was Mike's family now. He wanted to help people. Where this impulse came from, Mike wasn't sure, but it was there, and it was real. He was energized to help people to a better life—he believed it with all of his being.

The fact that it made him feel so alive and loved was an important aspect of his driving desire to help others, and it didn't make his service to those people any less real.

CHAPTER 32

Oklahoma City, Oklahoma

One quiet afternoon around three, Joe's assistant manager came into his office and said there was someone outside who had asked to see the manager about a private matter. Joe wasn't sure what that meant, but he said he would be right out.

Joe walked toward the front desk area. Waiting there was an extremely attractive woman.

"Hello. My name's Joe Meadows, I'm the manager. Can I help you?"

"Hi. My name's Michelle Lewis. I'm looking for the person who placed an ad in the Dallas paper last year. Was that you?"

Joe felt suddenly disoriented. Michelle Lewis. Looking for the person who placed the ad. Was this Michelle Thompson? After all these years, was this really happening? He had waited years for something to happen, and now, out of the blue, someone walks in and says *I'm here.* Joe became aware that he was just standing, staring.

Michelle Lewis was a very striking woman. Probably in her mid-forties, with a very professional demeanor. She was about five feet five and had a very youthful, shapely figure. Her hair was a sandy brown color and she wore it short. She was a beautiful woman, but she also seemed a little wary, as if she was anticipating trouble.

"Yes, that'd be me, at least if you're talking about the ads for information about Michelle Thompson?"

"Yes, that was my maiden name."

"Oh my goodness." Joe felt like an idiot. He was at a loss for words for a moment. "Sorry, I'm just so taken aback. I've run those ads for years—I don't know. Just to have you show up—I guess I'm a little flustered." Flustered? What was he, some schoolgirl? *Oh, I am so flustered!* Jeez, shut up.

"Well, I'm sorry. Maybe I should have called, but I was in town and I don't know—I guess I thought I wanted to meet the person before I talked to them. Wow—that did not make much sense did it?" Okay, having her act like a schoolgirl too was making Joe feel a little better.

"Please, let's go into the bar and I'll get us some coffee or iced tea." Joe led her to a booth at the back, then went to the bar and came back with coffee for himself and iced tea for her. He probably should have asked her what she wanted, but he was flying on autopilot at the moment and not thinking straight. He slid into the booth and started staring again. She looked up into his eyes and then smiled. Joe thought he might faint—what a wonderful smile.

Joe was struck by the odd feeling he had met Michelle before, like she was someone he knew, but of course that wasn't the case. He had just met her, but maybe he had thought about her so much that it seemed like she was already a friend. He blinked a few times, trying to clear his head—his own thoughts seemed crazy to him. *My imaginary friend just walked in.* He was having trouble deciding what to say.

"I need to tell you what this is all about but give me just

a minute to kind of get used to you being here."

"Sure, just relax. I'm very curious as to why you were looking for me, obviously—but I can tell that it's nothing sinister. You wouldn't believe the things I imagined about why someone might be looking for me."

Joe realized he wasn't being very thoughtful. This must be incredibly stressful for her. And what courage to just walk in here, not knowing what was going on. Brave, smart, and beautiful. Joe blushed.

"Of course. I'm so sorry. I'm not sure how to say this other than to just say it—this is about your mother, Sally."

Michelle's expression changed from curiosity to dread. "I'm not sure what you're saying. My birth mother's name was Sally, but she died years ago. What's this about?" This was a much more forceful response and Joe could see she was starting to get angry.

"This is a long story. Let me give you some information before I try to relate everything. This starts with a friend of mine receiving a letter from his father after his father had died. The letter was sent by a lawyer and had been arranged by the father. The letter said that there was something this son might want to find, and the letter came with a key. The man's name was Patrick Allen—he was a bootlegger in Oklahoma in the 40s and 50s. His family didn't know anything about that side of his life."

Michelle looked intrigued but also confused. "What does this have to do with me or my mother?"

Joe took a deep breath. "Michelle, some of this is guess work—it all happened a long time ago—but it seems likely that your mother, Sally Thompson, was Patrick Allen's girlfriend for a period of time in the early 1950s." Joe stopped.

Michelle looked thoughtful, troubled and sad—all at the same time. Joe realized that he hadn't thought this through well enough. He hadn't really considered how the daughter might react—this could be devastating to her and he was beginning to regret the whole thing. He wanted to comfort Michelle, but she was giving him a look that suggested she wouldn't accept his comfort.

"Mr. Meadows, I still don't understand why you were trying to get in touch with me. I'm sure it couldn't be to just discuss some ancient, slanderous rumors about my mother. My mother died right after I was born, so of course I didn't know her. She died in Chicago and what that has to do with some guy in Oklahoma City, I have no idea. Something about this whole thing strikes me as a little unseemly and I think I've heard enough, so unless there's something more useful to discuss, I'll be leaving."

My God. She was leaving. She was pissed. Joe had always envisioned this as a joyous occasion. What an idiot he had been. What should he do now?

Michelle stood to leave.

"Wait, look, I've handled this poorly. I'm sorry if I've offended you in any way. I can't tell you how much I didn't intend to upset you. Please, let me tell you why I was looking for you—give me just another minute or two."

Michelle continued standing, staring at Joe, then slowly sat back down. "Mr. Meadows, there's something going on here, and if you want to talk to me any further, you'd better get to the point damn quick." God now she hated him.

"Patrick Allen left a package addressed to Sally Thompson in a lock box in a bank in Las Cruces, New Mexico, almost fifty years ago. We discovered it about twelve years ago and have been looking for her ever since to give her the package." There—when in doubt just spit it out. Joe was still unsure how she was going to react.

"Do you know what's in the package?"

"No, it hasn't been opened."

"Why did you try to find me?"

"I hired a PI who found out that your mother had died. He also discovered that she had given birth to a child— you. I guess I thought that if I couldn't give the package to the mother, I should give it to her daughter. I'm sorry if I shouldn't have done that."

Michelle's expression softened. "Mr. Meadows . . ."

"Please call me Joe."

"Joe, I'm the one who should apologize. As you can imagine, I'm a little sensitive when it comes to my mother. There's so much about her I don't know. But I overreacted. It sounds like you've been trying to do what you thought was the right thing for many years, and I had no right to jump down your throat—forgive me."

"I'm just happy you're not mad at me. If you like, I can get the package. Don't let this make you angry at me all over again, but if you have some identification you could show me so I can be sure you're Sally's daughter, I'll give you the package."

Michelle laughed. It was contagious and soon had Joe laughing as well. A few heads turned their way. "Touché, Joe. I won't be angry with you again—well, I hope I won't.

Not knowing what this was all about, I brought all kinds of documentation about who I am, including my birth information. And I do understand that you would want to verify who I am."

She got her purse and pulled out a file. Inside was ample documentation proving her identity.

"I'm a buyer for Duncan's Department Stores and I was in town to attend a conference at one of the stores here in Oklahoma City. Our last meeting starts in about thirty minutes. I was wondering if we could meet this evening for dinner and, if you're satisfied with the information I just provided, you could give me the package then."

"That's perfect, Michelle. I'd like it very much if you would join me here at Triples for dinner. Would that work?"

"It does—say about 7:30?"

"I'll see you then."

She left. Joe, still being part teenage boy, watched her walk out, enjoying the view. He realized immediately that he was attracted to her when he first met her, which was strange for Joe these days. He had given up on women after a couple of disastrous relationships with waitresses at Triples and had settled into a chaste existence over the last few years, figuring that that's how things would stay. He had definitely sworn off dating anyone who worked for him.

Now this wonderful woman drops in unannounced and Joe is suddenly in love. No, no—slow down. She's just here to find out about the package. She'll open it find whatever and be gone forever. Now he felt nervous. Did she like him? Would she go out with him if he asked?

Joe made arrangements with his staff for his favorite table to be available at 7:30. He also cleaned out his office some, in case she wanted to be somewhere private to open the package. He felt a little silly, but he also ran home and changed his shirt. He was nervous.

Michelle was very punctual, something Joe liked. He met her at the front desk and escorted her to the table. Joe had opened a bottle of white wine earlier, a dry Riesling that he had become fond of over the last couple of years. He offered, and Michelle accepted a glass. He watched her while he poured—he found it hard to look away.

"You have a beautiful restaurant, Joe. And I've also heard great things about the food here."

"Thank you very much. I'm very proud of the restaurant. I came into this industry late in life, but I've developed a real passion for it. Every day is a new challenge. I've heard people say that running a restaurant must be fun, and on good days it is. But there are employee problems every day, which can sometimes be overwhelming. We have a small army of wait staff, kitchen staff, managers, and people handling the books and paychecks—it's an amazing operation. It's brought a lot of joy into my life that I'd never experienced before. I love it."

He gestured in the direction of the kitchen.

"As far as the food goes, that credit goes to two of my good friends, Carlos and Jesus. They've helped me learn to appreciate the talent it takes to prepare an outstanding meal. But the amazing thing is they do it for hundreds of customers every day. What they do in the kitchen is magic."

"Carlos and Jesus—must be a story there?"

"Yeah. The simple story is that I stole them from a restaurant in Las Cruces, New Mexico. When I bought this business, I quite literally knew next to nothing about running a restaurant. I knew a little bit about the bar, but that was mostly as a patron. I started looking around at places that I thought were doing it right—I went to Dallas, Denver, Kansas City, and some other places, and just paid attention—then stole everything I could. I'm not sure, but maybe I just confessed to a crime."

Michelle grinned. A beautiful grin. "Probably not a crime if you just stole ideas. Actually, I think that's a proven business model."

"Whew, that's good to know. I have been to Las Cruces and enjoyed the most wonderful food at a restaurant called La Posta. While I was there, I met some of the kitchen staff. Later, as I was trying to develop ideas about how to change the menu for Triples, I thought of those people. Strictly on a lark, I called and offered Carlos and his cousin, Jesus, a job. They showed up about two weeks later. I introduced them to the head chef, and he told me I was an idiot and he wouldn't work for me. He left. I promoted Carlos to head chef on the spot. Most everyone else quit, and Jesus became second in command."

Now she was laughing. Joe really liked to make her laugh.

"This was no doubt the dumbest thing that I have done since I bought the place, but then a miracle happened. It turned out that Carlos had been head chef at some fancy big bucks place in Mexico City and had gone to Cruces to help his mother, who was sick. She had died, and he stayed working at La Posta just until he could find something better. He designed a whole new menu of absolutely wonderful dishes. They were delicious, and something different for Oklahoma City. Within weeks, Triples was the talk of the town—and I was a restaurateur."

"That's a great story, Joe."

"Plus, Carlos and Jesus and their whole families love me. They think I helped them, while the truth is that they saved me from disaster. Like they say, better lucky than good."

The mood was pleasant, with Michelle laughing and smiling, he realized just how attracted to her he was. Everything about her was wonderful. Even the fact that she was Sally's daughter was special to him.

"Michelle, I don't want to change the mood—but there's something I was wondering."

She looked a little worried.

"You know I stopped running those ads years ago—how is it you walked in here today?"

"Great question. I guess it was kind of like you, doing something on a lark. But there's some history. I have seen your ads over the years and I've been told about earlier ads looking for Sally Thompson. A co-worker asked me about them. At that time, I just ignored the whole thing, thinking it had nothing to do with me. Then I found out about the ads with my name. I don't remember how or why I saw the first one, but after that I would look for them. I have one of them in my purse right now. They haunted me in a way. I wanted to know what they were about, but I was scared. You know some of my story, but not much. When my mother died her sister took me. She was single and living in a tough neighborhood in Chicago. She had a lot of problems herself and decided after a short time that she couldn't keep me. Apparently, neither she nor my mother got along very well with their brother, who lived in Dallas, but even so he was about her only option. She pleaded with him to take me into his family. He was married and they had one child and his wife was expecting. He was probably not eager to do it—I don't know the details about that part—but he did take me, and I was raised as one of his kids."

"Excuse me sir, are you ready to order?"

"Sorry, Michelle. Would it be okay if I ordered for you?"

"That would be wonderful." Her eyes sparkled.

"Do you like Mexican food?"

"I love it!"

Joe ordered and had the waiter pour more wine.

"Please, go on with your story."

"Well, for a bunch of those years there isn't much to tell. I had no memory of my real mother or anything to do with Chicago—my memory started with the home in Dallas. My mother's brother became my father and his wife became my mother. They eventually had four children of their own and as far as I knew I was just another one of their kids. He was a strict and very religious man, so most everything was very stern. But he took care of me and his family the best he could. I wouldn't say it was a happy home, but we always had food and a roof over our heads. He was in construction, and one day, when I was about sixteen, he had an accident—something to do with pumping concrete. He was knocked off a roof and fell three stories. He didn't die but was busted up real bad and the doctors said he wouldn't live long. He asked to see me.

"I didn't understand why he wanted to see me in particular. I was very nervous when I went into his room and he was obviously in a lot of pain. He said there was something he had to tell me. I wasn't his child—I was his sister's child. He said his sister had been a sinner, and had sinned with men, and I was the result. He said he had tried his best with me, but that I was too beautiful. If I wasn't careful, I would end up a sinner like his sister. I think I just stood there and looked at him. I had no idea what to say. The nurse came in and showed me out of the room. He died within an hour or so."

Joe was mesmerized. "I can't believe someone would say those things to you—or say them to anyone."

"I know it sounds harsh and believe me it crushed me at the time. But, in his defense, he was doing what he thought was right. He thought that if he wasn't going to be around, I would fall into a life of sin. In some ways maybe his harsh words worked, at least for some years. I was so afraid of being a sinner I stayed away from all boys and was generally terrified of every encounter with males."

"And even though I was a cute little thing." She gave a perky smile. "Most boys stayed away. I think they could sense that I wasn't a willing participant in the boy-girl thing. Well, after high school, my Dallas mother suggested that I move out. That's another thing I worked on for years—why did she ask me to leave? I decided after a lot of self-reflection and observation that she just couldn't handle everything that had happened to her and wanted a new and different life. She didn't seem all that sad when her husband died. I learned later, after I left, that she was quickly married to another man. So, in just a short while, I'd learned that my real mother had died years ago, that I was not really part of the family I thought I belonged to, my fill-in dad died while telling me that I was from a long line of sinners, and my fill-in mom kicked me out so she could go live with her boyfriend."

Joe refilled her wine glass. "Michelle, I'm sorry your life has been so hard."

Michelle laughed. "Joe, you're a sweet man. That was the bad part I just told you. The good part is that I borrowed some money, put myself through a graphics school in Dallas, graduated, and got a big bucks job with Duncans—well, the first job wasn't big bucks, but I'm doing well now. Oh yeah, got married for about two years and found out he was a jerk—got divorced. But all in all, considering what could have happened, I think I did okay."

Their food arrived. The waiter seemed a little nervous serving his boss—Joe usually ate in the bar—but the food and the presentation were wonderful. Michelle commented several times on how amazing it was. Joe had ordered for each of them something he called a fancy remake of classic enchiladas: lobster enchiladas with cream sauce—it was Joe's favorite, one of the special menu items created by Carlos that had been recently featured in a national magazine. Joe asked the waiter to tell Carlos that Joe's guest was impressed. Michelle gave Joe a genuine I'm-having-a-wonderful-time smile.

They dropped the heavy conversation about personal history and talked about her job at Duncans, and it was quickly obvious that this was the area where she felt most comfortable. Her life at work was under control and she was proud of what she had accomplished—outside of work, not so much.

After their table had been cleared, Joe suggested they go to his office and he would retrieve the package. She seemed subdued at the prospect but said that was a good idea.

Joe brought their wine glasses and a new bottle to his office. "I cleaned up a little in here earlier, though you probably can't tell. At least, I cleared off the table." Joe had a small round table in one corner of the office with four chairs, and she sat down. He brought the package over, joined her, and handed it to Michelle.

Michelle seemed reluctant to open it. She handed it back to Joe. "Why don't you open it?"

Joe took the package back and very carefully unwrapped it. He slid the lid off and looked inside. Michelle leaned across the table a little to get a better look. On top was an envelope, addressed in the same handwriting as on the outside, to Sally Thompson. Below that was some packing material with a smaller box buried in it. Joe removed the envelope and used a letter opener to slit the top. He removed several pages of a handwritten letter and handed the pages to Michelle.

"Why don't you read the letter, and I'll step outside."

"No way—you stay right there."

Joe liked the sound of that.

Michelle began to read. After a while she began to cry. In another minute she stood up and came around, Joe stood up and she gave him a hug. He held her for some time while she cried.

Joe was very comfortable holding Michelle and in no hurry to let her go. She pulled away a little and said she wanted him to read the letter, which she handed to him.

Dearest Sally,

What a mess I've made. This letter will reach you sometime in the future—I don't know when. I could have said these things to you tonight, or I could have given you this letter—but I didn't. I do not know if I am being brave or if I am a coward. I have fallen in love with you and if I could I would live the rest of my life with you. But if I did, I would hurt you and many other people. I cannot do that.

I'm an old man and I have no business talking this way to a beautiful young girl. You have your whole life ahead of you—I'm almost done. I never intended our fun time together to become so important to me. You knew I was married, and I thought we were just having some fun—but it became so much more. Before our trip I had purchased a ring. I was going to tell you that I was getting a divorce and once it was done, I wanted to marry you. Instead, I told you we were done and sent you away. It broke my heart.

I knew you cared about me and thought that maybe you would even have said yes. But it wouldn't have stayed that way. I was going to get older and weaker and sicker—it would have been a huge mistake.

I have come to realize what a special person you are. Everybody can see how beautiful you are, but I have been able to see how smart, how kind, and what a completely wonderful person you are. You are worth a hundred old bootleggers like me. You must find your way and become something special—I know you will.

My hope is that you find someone soon who will make you happy. Maybe even have a family. I will not follow you or try and find you, even though I will worry that you are alright.

I am sorry if I caused you pain. I love you very much. You are the treasure that I was always looking for—and now I must give you up so you can find your own treasure.

With all of my love,

Pat

"Funny, after all of these years I always thought it was going to be something happy—maybe a happy message or a map to some treasure. I don't know, I just never thought it would be this sad."

"She must have died within a year or so after he wrote the letter." Michelle was obviously controlling her emotions. She looked thoughtful and sad, but strangely calm.

"Yes. And Pat lived many years after that. Ironic isn't it?" Joe wasn't sure what to say to Michelle, but he decided he would answer any questions she had as honestly as he could.

Michelle picked up the box and unwrapped it. It was a jewelry box from John A. Brown and Company. "Small world isn't it—Duncans eventually acquired Browns."

Inside was the biggest diamond either one of them had ever seen. "Wow, that is one big diamond." Stupid comment, but Joe didn't know what else to say.

Michelle examined the ring and seemed pleased. Joe could tell she had something on her mind.

"Joe, you said your friend was Pat's son. What's his name?"

"Mike Allen. You may have even heard of him. He is a preacher now and has a huge church here called Legacy Chapel. He's on TV and has radio shows. He's become quite famous and successful."

"Yes, I've heard of him. Why isn't he here?"

Joe couldn't be sure, but he sensed that Michelle was thinking very hard about everything she had learned. He couldn't imagine all the thoughts she must be having about her mother and Pat, how their encounter had affected her and made her who she was. It was amazing she was handling it so well.

"This is part of the long story I mentioned. But in a nutshell, he had trouble dealing with some aspects of his father's past—and especially your mother's part. I think he's kind of blocked it out and just doesn't acknowledge it at all. He also hasn't talked to me in a long time. I think I became part of the story he didn't want to deal with, so he forgot about me like he forgot about Sally."

Joe realized this made Mike sound worse than he was. He had been Joe's friend for a long time and he wasn't a bad person, just someone who couldn't deal with his family's past and had to handle it in the way that worked for him.

"I don't think I want to meet Mike. I've had my fill of the righteous religious people."

Joe thought, well, that should work out fine—he was pretty sure Mike didn't want to meet Michelle, either.

"One more question and then I'll shut up. Do you think that Pat was my father?"

"I don't know, Michelle. I guess the timing is right, but she could have met someone in Chicago. I just don't know."

"I know you don't know, I just wondered what you thought." She was giving him that look that said *cut the bullshit and tell what you think.*

"Michelle, I have no way of proving this, but based on everything I've seen there's no question—your father was Patrick Allen, world-famous bootlegger."

Michelle gave him a smile that just had to be the best smile anyone had ever seen.

"You know, Joe, it surprises me a little, but I think I like the fact that my father was a bootlegger and that he loved my mother so much he was willing to let her go."

"I think you're a very wise woman."

Michelle looked like she needed another hug—or was it simply that Joe needed one? He hesitated. It had only been a few hours since he had met her, but at a deep level he felt like he had known her forever. Michelle looked at Joe—they stood and embraced tenderly.

Michelle went home with Joe that night. They both felt that they had found their treasure and would never let it go—never.

They became the best of lovers and the best of friends.

Joe said it was like they each found a missing part of themselves.

Their romance was whirlwind by most standards. Joe asked Michelle to marry him within a week of meeting her, and they planned the wedding for the following month in Dallas. Joe's list of invitees was going to be small, so it made sense to accommodate Michelle's friends and co-workers. Joe thought that once it was in the papers he would hear from Mike, but he didn't. Maybe Mike didn't even know who Michelle was. Or maybe he did—it really didn't matter.

Joe missed his old friend Mike; in the odd way you can miss a toothache. They had spent a lot of time together, and it had seemed that they would be friends forever. Joe spent time thinking about what had happened with Mike and decided that he had never really liked his father but growing up he had wanted to be like his dad. Then finding out his dad had cheated on his mother, Mike decided somehow, he was at fault, and therefore he didn't like himself. He decided that the old Mike was still his friend, locked away in the new Mike's body—maybe someday the old Mike would escape and meet him at Triples.

After the wedding, he was going to spend a week in Las Cruces getting to know his new best friend, Michelle Meadows. He had planned their trip—where they would stay, where they would eat—and smiled a lot, thinking about the fun they were going to have together.

Michelle was excited about visiting some of the places she had heard Joe talk about in Old Mesilla, and even though a Paris honeymoon might have sounded more romantic to her friends, she couldn't think of a better place for her and Joe to be together.

It occurred to Joe that his depression might be cured.

EPILOGUE

Mike and Samantha Allen. Everything continued to go well for Mike Allen. The Legacy Chapel grew into a national broadcasting powerhouse and Mike expanded into all kinds of activities, with books, several syndicated television programs, a radio talk show, and more. He was quite literally everywhere. He and Sam had become worldwide celebrities. The stream of money from his various enterprises had made them one of the wealthiest families in Oklahoma. They lived in a 20,000-square-foot mansion, with a household staff of ten. Mike had found his calling in life and was being richly rewarded. He took himself very seriously, had lost his sense of humor, and was considering a run for the U.S. senate.

Then trouble came knocking. One of his youth ministers, a very attractive twenty-three-year-old blonde woman, came forward and accused Mike of sexual harassment. She claimed that she and Mike had been having an affair for the past two years. In the midst of the media firestorm over these revelations, three more women, coincidentally all blonde, attractive, and young, came forward and accused the reverend of less-than-reverend-like deeds. Mike's empire was looking shaky.

In an Oscar-worthy performance, Mike went on one of his TV shows with his lovely wife, Samantha, and confessed to his sins. He asked for forgiveness. He told his audience of the pain he had experienced when he had learned that his father had been a bootlegger. He had suffered greatly learning that the man he had worshiped had led a double life of sin. He begged for a second chance. Samantha tearfully joined in the appeal. She asked everyone to pray for her and Mike, and to give her husband a second chance—she had forgiven him, and they had rededicated themselves to each other. Their ratings went through the roof.

Not only was Mike given a second chance, donations doubled the following week. Whether Mike noticed a pattern in any of this, no one knows. He was his father's son, giving the customers what they wanted.

In an effort to expand its national and international audience, Legacy Chapel moved its headquarters to Colorado Springs, Colorado. They opened one of the largest private broadcasting studios in the country. Mike gave up his political ambitions and concentrated on his role as a church leader. He never saw or talked to Joe again. He never knew about Sally's daughter or found out that she and Joe had married. He was entirely focused on his vital role as the moral leader of his devoted flock.

Liz Meadows. Liz moved back to Tulsa where she reconnected with an old high school classmate, now a well-known Tulsa surgeon who was recently divorced from his third wife. She pursued him with a vengeance. Observers thought she chased him shamelessly, but Liz didn't care and felt no shame. She wanted status, she wanted to be someone—and Mrs. Doctor, living in a million-dollar mansion, fit the bill exactly.

They were married in one of the major social events of the year. For a short while everything was fine—Liz kept busy with a very full social calendar, and the doctor kept busy doing whatever he did—she hardly noticed that he wasn't around much. But the doctor had an ugly secret, he was a drug addict—prescription drugs, self-prescribed. When regulations and disclosure requirements for prescription drugs were tightened, the doctor found himself in trouble with the law and the Medical Board. As the scandal became known, Liz began to berate her new husband, much as she used to dress Joe down. The doctor had a different reaction and beat Liz on several occasions. After a beating that resulted in a hospital stay, she moved to her mother's and filed for divorce.

Liz and Joe's children grew tired of their mother's ways, and after she married the doctor, they broke off contact. As they grew older, they thought that they might not have given their father a proper chance. As they approached their thirties, they both decided to make contact with Joe. They visited Joe and Michelle and found that they liked them both. They also discovered that their father was one of the funniest guys they had ever known. They started having family gatherings and seemed to enjoy each other's company. Not much was said about Liz.

Jim Emerson. Jim Emerson's downfall started soon after his deal with Mike was completed. Jane, his browbeaten bookkeeper, contacted the DEA and made a deal for immunity. Emerson had applied the booze-smuggling skills he had developed working with Pat to building a drug smuggling operation. As the state and DEA investigated, a mystery developed as to where all the money had gone. By most accounts there should have been many millions of dollars somewhere, and while Emerson was a wealthy man, the wealth they could track down all appeared to be based on legitimate business dealings. He had lived simply and had always had frugal ways. His assets were larger than they should have been, but only because he had lied to Mike. There were a lot more properties, mostly in Las Cruces, than he admitted. He had always been a good liar. The authorities never did uncover the missing money, which weakened the case against him since it relied almost entirely on Jane's evidence. During the investigation she disappeared, and the prosecutors were forced to drop the case against him.

But Emerson's victory was brief. His health had deteriorated rapidly during the investigation. Several weeks after the case was dismissed, he died. At his funeral, several people commented that they could not remember ever seeing him smile.

Jane was never found, but someone who looked a whole lot like Jane was living in grand luxury in Baja California with a very attractive young Mexican man.

Ray Pacheco. Sheriff Ray Pacheco moved into the T or C cabin and took up fishing. With the aid of an eccentric local fishing guide, Ray became very skilled at his new pastime, even winning some pro fishing tournaments. While his new love of fishing filled a special need for Ray, his true love remained law enforcement, and his passion for it didn't stay dormant long. In a move to stay active in his retirement years, Ray started a private investigation company. Pacheco and Chino, Private Investigators, was a partnership between Ray, his Apache fishing guide, and the aptly named owner of the fishing bait shop on the Elephant Butte Lake, Big Jack. Accompanying this somewhat odd group of misfits was Ray's new, much younger wife. With an unexpected windfall from reward money, Ray fixed up the cabin and outbuildings, creating an impressive corporate headquarters.

Ray often said, "You just never know where life might take you." Private investigator and philosopher—Ray had come far.

Molly Thompson. Molly was emotionally spent after giving up Sally's baby to her brother. She didn't return to Chicago but stayed in Dallas and became involved with a Catholic orphanage—she was considered one of its kindest and most thoughtful employees. Due to her efforts and dedication over many years, she was recommended to head up a new orphanage that was being established in Los Angeles.

Molly had become a strong leader despite still speaking with a soft voice, and her caring ways made her a hero in the eyes of many people who needed her help. Today she is seen as a spiritual inspiration in the movement to make adoption a viable alternative for unwanted and abandoned babies. Molly never married. She thinks of Sally constantly and wishes their lives could have been different.

Molly never made any effort to contact Michelle because she was embarrassed that she had abandoned the little girl in her time of greatest need. She never spoke to anyone about the great shame of her life and she asks God for forgiveness every day.

Carlos and Jesus. Carlos and Jesus bought Triples from Joe. Carlos's uncle from Mexico City backed them with ample financing. They kept the restaurant very much as it was when Joe owned it but added some additional outdoor seating and an open-pit fire for roasting all sorts of wonderful things. They also changed the name to C and J's. C and J opened new restaurants in Dallas, Denver, and Kansas City, and will soon open in Las Vegas, and they are considered some of the finest restaurants in each market. Carlos and Jesus were always thankful that Joe had trusted them and had risked turning over his kitchen to two men he barely knew, conveniently forgetting that it was mostly based on a fiasco that had worked out for everyone except the old chef.

Joe and Michelle Meadows. Joe and Michelle lived the dream. After they were married, they moved into a new house in Dallas. It was a little too grand for Joe, but he got used to it. Once he moved, he made the deal to sell Triples to Carlos and Jesus. He knew he would miss it, but he wanted to be with Michelle, and she didn't want to quit her job. She said it was a big part of her identity and that she loved the work—so Joe agreed.

Joe was very surprised when his children made contact. They both visited Dallas, and Joe was amazed that they had turned out so well. He was expecting younger versions of Liz, but instead they seemed to be thoughtful, funny, happy people—go figure. He decided maybe it was because he had essentially left them alone in their formative years. They all knew the story of Liz's marriage, but no one talked about it. They spent some time planning future family events and, to Joe's amazement, he looked forward to them.

Shortly after finding the money in the safe on Second Street, Joe had made a better estimate of the amount. He counted several crates at random and then counted the number of crates and estimated that there was $3,860,000 hidden in that old safe in Deep Deuce. Over the years almost $2.8 million was distributed to Joe and Mike, mostly by laundering the money through Triples. With everything that was going on—the success of Triples and the huge success of Mike's Chapel—Joe had stopped distributing money to either of them in the last few years. He expected to hear from Mike about it, but never did. Before he sold the restaurant to C and J, he moved the remaining money into a shipping crate—very well sealed—and had it transferred to his new house in Dallas. There he stored it in the basement—the money was used to being underground.

Joe gave the money a lot of thought. He didn't regret what he and Mike had decided. He still thought they had done the right thing and, of course, it didn't hurt that both he and Mike were now wealthy, Mike much more so than Joe. He realized that Mike's financial success and his chosen career path had a lot to do with him shunning Joe, and he didn't begrudge Mike his selective memory issues.

The one thing that troubled him was what had happened with Sally and her daughter. He just knew that if Pat had known that Sally died giving birth to their daughter—there was no question in his mind that Michelle was

Pat's daughter—he would have wanted some of the money to go to Michelle. Maybe this was all just a rationalization to excuse taking the remaining money, but he thought he was doing the right thing for everyone.

On their first anniversary Joe gave Michelle a little note:

> *Dearest Michelle,*
>
> *Joe has helped me accumulate a little over $1 million, which is yours—the inheritance your mother never received. This is for you and only you, because you are the most wonderful daughter an old bootlegger could ever have.*
>
> *Love, Pat*

She turned and looked at Joe. "A million dollars—is this some kind of joke?"

"I hope you don't mind that I took the liberty of writing Pat's note, but I think I've gotten to know Pat over the years and I know this is what he would want to happen. He loved your mother and he would have loved you—and I know I love you. So, congratulations on being a millionaire."

Joe said he would explain all the details later.

She gave him one of those most wonderful smiles.

Happiness was the greatest treasure of all.

AUTHOR'S NOTE

The Bootlegger's Legacy was my first book. As my oldest book you might think the later ones would be my favorite—nope, the book I like the most is TBL. I like the others for different reasons, but this one was special.

Many of the characters, and some of the story, were loosely based on my own experiences; of course, much of it was just made up. I think fiction with some kind of connection to reality often become some of the most interesting stories.

You may not know this, but the character of Ray Pacheco returns for his own series, *Pacheco & Chino Mysteries*. That series begins with *Dog Gone Lies*, which tells the story of Ray becoming a private investigator and teaming up with his partners, Tyee Chino, often-drunk Apache fishing guide, and Big Jack, bait shop owner and philosopher. If you haven't yet, you might enjoy reading *Dog Gone Lies* to see where Ray finds himself next.

If you have time, a quick Amazon reader review of *The Bootlegger's Legacy* would be most appreciated. Reader reviews are a great way to communicate directly with the author. It may come as a surprise to you that I read every review, and while some are more appreciated than others—each one has value.

To leave a review, just go to Amazon.com, make sure you're signed in, and click "Your Orders" to look at your past orders. Find *The Bootlegger's Legacy* in the list and click the button that says "Leave a Product Review". That's it!

I look forward to reading your review and hope you will read some of my other books. For a list of my books, please visit my website at **www.tedclifton.com**.

KEEP IN TOUCH

Once a month, I send my readers a newsletter with a little of everything in it: southwest US culture, be it art, recipes, or local sights; my thoughts on writing and reading; book recommendations; updates on my current writing project; and from time-to-time a short story.

To sign up, visit www.tedclifton.com and either wait for the pop-up window, or scroll to the bottom of the page. Everybody who signs up receives a mystery gift, with my compliments.

You can also learn more about me and my latest books by visiting www.tedclifton.com or emailing me at ask@tedclifton.com.

Thanks for being a reader!

ABOUT THE AUTHOR

Ted Clifton has been a CPA, investment banker, artist, financial writer, business entrepreneur and a sometimes philosopher. After many years in the New Mexico desert, he now lives in Denver, Colorado, with his wife and grandson.

BOOKS BY TED CLIFTON

*All books are available from Amazon.com,
or by request at your local bookstore.*

Pacheco & Chino Mysteries

#1: Dog Gone Lies
Sheriff Ray Pacheco returns from his introduction in The Bootegger's Legacy to start a new chapter as a private investigator, along with his partners: Tyee Chino, often-drunk apache fishing guide, and Big Jack, bait shop owner and philosopher.

#2: Sky High Stakes
Lincoln County, New Mexico was best known as the site of The Lincoln County Wars, featuring the likes of Billy the Kid. Martin Marino, the acting sheriff, is also short in stature, just like The Kid—and no doubt also like The Kid, Marino is crazy. Lincoln County survived Billy the Kid, but Martin Marino might be a different matter.

Ray Pacheco and Tyee Chino have been asked by the state Attorney General to find out what the hell is going on in the Lincoln County Sheriff's department. Ray is sure there's some big trouble waiting for them and his gut is right: murder, lust, madness and greed are visiting the high country.

#3: Four Corners War

Navajos, Apaches, militias, good sheriffs, and bad sheriffs are all drawn to a small town by millions in stolen money and a small army's worth of stolen military equipment. Is this the start of a Four Corners War? Nothing is as it should be as Ray Pacheco and Tyee Chino try to untangle the mix of greedy businessmen, corrupt politicians and a slightly unhinged sheriff—along with the usual dead bodies.

Farmington, New Mexico's unique mix of cultures is the backdrop for Ray and Tyee's most dangerous assignment to date from the bombastic Governor of New Mexico.

Vincent Malone Mysteries

#1: Santa Fe Mojo

Vincent Malone, a classical private investigator at the end of his career, finds himself in the middle of a murder mystery in Santa Fe, New Mexico with a dead big time sports agent and his professional athlete clients as suspects.

#2: Blue Flower Red Thorns

One dead body; many suspects. Sex, money, hate, love, artistic egos explode in Santa Fe high-end art community; Vincent Malone, down-and-out legal investigator, wants to know whodunit!

#3: *Fiction No More*

A mystery author staying at the Blue Door Inn claims she is being followed. Vincent Malone volunteers to find out what is going on, and things quickly get complicated. The author's first book details a murder that took place forty years in the past, but is suspiciously specific. The victim's adult son would like to know how the author came by this information. Soon, a bullying sheriff and a wayward priest are involved, along with a priceless—and stolen—collection of Pueblo Indian artifacts. When the situation turns deadly, Malone must find out who committed the murder, and why. Past misdeeds long buried will come to light, and fiction will be separated from fact, as Malone pursues the truth.

Muckraker Mysteries

#1: *Murder So Wrong*

Follow Tommy Jacks, a recent journalism grad, as he becomes involved in his first newspaper job in middle America during the tumultuous 1960s. Within days of Tommy being on the job, a reporter from the competing newspaper is found dead at the state capitol. Tommy's beat is politics but he cannot ignore the murder of a fellow reporter right under his nose. His quest begins. Tommy's dad had been a leader in politics until he was framed and went to prison. The connection with his dad had led him to the OK Journal, a fledgling newspaper competing with a well-established media giant. It was the owner of that powerful newspaper who had his dad framed and tossed into prison.

As the story develops we are introduced to an amazing cast of characters: Ray Jacks, Tommy's dad, Taylor Albright, mentor and tormentor; the Gilmores, father and son, who run the entire state, Joe Louongo, Attorney and oddball—and many more; including Judy Jackson, Tommy's soon to be girlfriend and a co-worker at the capitol. Mystery, adventure, and some romance come together in this story of personal growth and great tragedy. This is the first book in the Muckraker Trilogy which leads Tommy into the complicated world of state politics and the newspaper business.

#2: *Murder So Strange*

Tommy Jacks has taken on a new role as a political columnist and he is making enemies, very powerful enemies. Tommy's recent tragedy involving sudden and violent death has left him shaken and emotionally damaged. Spending most of his adult life on his own he is discovering a whole new family life with his new "mother" and recently out-of-prison father. Also entering his world is the most beautiful person he has ever seen. Tommy can't stop staring.

This story begins with the sudden and unexplained death of the state's U.S. Senator. Tommy Jacks and his fellow journalists don't believe the police chief's story blaming it on natural causes. It has the smell of a crime.

Many strange things are happening in the city. New crime bosses seem to be causing lots of mayhem. Tommy has a lot to write about in his "My View" political column, including some not so subtle references to the police chief. Lurking in the shadows is the powerful and corrupt chief, who seems to think it might be best if Mister Jacks, even if he is very young, was dead.

#3: Murder So Final

Tommy Jacks, reporter, encounters new love and old threats while covering one of the most brutal U.S. Senate races in history. With a massive oil fire threatening the city of Tulsa, three candidates face off: a ruthless oil baron, an idealist college professor, and a reverend running under the God Party. When the race suddenly turns deadly, the winner may be the last man standing.

The final book in the Muckraker trilogy, Murder So Final brings to a close the stories of Louongo, Albright, Robbie Gilmore, Tracy and Ray Jacks, and Tommy himself.

The Bootlegger's Legacy

Meet Ray Pacheco, pre-retirement, in this prequel to the Pacheco & Chino Mysteries.

When an old-time bootlegger dies and leaves his son Mike a cryptic letter hinting at millions in hidden cash, Mike and his friend Joe embark on a journey that takes them through three states and 50 years of history. What they find goes beyond money and transforms them both.

An action-packed adventure story taking place in the early 1950s and late 1980s. It all starts with a key, embossed with the letters CB, and a cryptic reference to Deep Deuce, a neighborhood once filled with hot jazz and gangs of bootleggers. Out of those threads is woven a tapestry of history, romance, drama, and mystery; connecting two generations and two families in the adventure of a lifetime.

> *"Superb character development ... vivid backdrops, brisk pacing, and meticulously researched ..."*
> *—Kirkus Reviews*

> *"A rollicking good time." —Self-Publishing Review*

> *"... interesting characters, true-to-life situations, and intriguing twists ..." —Stanley Nelson, Senior Staff Writer, Chickasaw Press*